GLOBALIZATION, WAR, AND PEACE IN THE TWENTY-FIRST CENTURY

Also by William R. Nester

Globalization: A Short History of the Modern World (Palgrave Macmillan, 2010)

Globalization, Wealth, and Power in the Twenty-First Century (Palgrave Macmillan, 2010)

GLOBALIZATION, WAR, AND PEACE IN THE TWENTY-FIRST CENTURY

William R. Nester

First published in 2010 by
PALGRAVE MACMILLAN®
in the United States—a division of St. Martin's Press LLC,
175 Fifth Avenue, New York, NY 10010.

Where this book is distributed in the UK, Europe and the rest of the world,
this is by Palgrave Macmillan, a division of Macmillan Publishers Limited,
registered in England, company number 785998, of Houndmills,
Basingstoke, Hampshire RG21 6XS.

Palgrave Macmillan is the global academic imprint of the above companies
and has companies and representatives throughout the world.

Palgrave® and Macmillan® are registered trademarks in the United States,
the United Kingdom, Europe and other countries.

ISBN: 978–0–230–10699–4

Library of Congress Cataloging-in-Publication Data

Nester, William R., 1956–
    Globalization, war, and peace in the twenty-first century / William R.
    Nester.
        p. cm.
    ISBN 978–0–230–10699–4
    1. War. 2. Politics and war. 3. World politics—21st century.
    4. Globalization—Political aspects. I. Title.

JZ6385.N47 2010
303.6′6—dc22   2010014446

A catalogue record of the book is available from the British Library.

Design by Newgen Imaging Systems (P) Ltd., Chennai, India.

First edition: December 2010

10 9 8 7 6 5 4 3 2 1

Printed in the United States of America.

CONTENTS

TABLES

ACKNOWLEDGMENTS

I want to express my deepest appreciation to Farideh Koohi-Kamali, the Editorial Director, Erin Ivy, the Production Manager, and Rohini Krishnan, the proofreader for all their wonderful support in producing my book. They are all as nice as they are true professionals.

Introduction

There is nothing so likely to produce peace as to be well prepared to meet our enemies.

George Washington

A country cannot simultaneously prepare and prevent war.

Albert Einstein

Violence is as old as humanity. Organized violence or war is as old as the first organized societies. Throughout history most states were preparing for, engaging in, or recovering from war. Yet recently the threat or use of violence in international relations, known as geopolitics, has sharply diminished as nearly all states are at peace all or most of the time. The reason is globalization.

Globalization is just another word for the ever more complex economic, technological, psychological, social, legal, cultural, environmental, and, thus, political interdependence embracing, in varying ways and degrees, all nations and individuals on the planet.[1] Thomas Friedman explains the paradoxes at globalization's heart: "globalization is everything and its opposite. It can be incredibly empowering and incredibly coercive. It can democratize opportunity and it can democratize panic...While it is homogenizing cultures, it is also enabling people to share their unique individuality farther and wider...It enables us to reach into world as never before and it enables the world to reach into each of us as never before."[2]

That entangling web of ever denser interdependence does pose risks. For many the images of Osama bin Laden cradling a Kalashnikov and airliners exploding into skyscrapers define the times in which we live. Yet, for many others, that image obscures rather than illuminates the nature of today's world. Their worry is not that some terrorist will take their lives, but that poor but bright, skilled people in China, India, or elsewhere will take their jobs. They contend that globalization is accelerating the pace of a race to the bottom in wages, work conditions, and pollution. While people in rich countries might enjoy the cheaper prices for products that corporations have outsourced to cheaper labor markets overseas, over the long term, the First World's economies will be locked into a vicious cycle in which national wealth, worker wages, and government revenues drop, while joblessness, crime, and despair rise. Also, there are those whose primary fear is that the world as we today know it may die with the proverbial whimper rather than a bang. Global warming has a deadly boomerang effect. We are contributing to it and it will inflict ever worse economic and human disasters upon us, its creator.

Nonetheless geopolitical conflicts and violence instigated by rogue states, militant ideologies, transnational terrorist groups, revolutionary movements, voracious, ruthless economic interests, and environmental collapse continue to plague countries and regions around the world. Although each geopolitical conflict has unique causes, underlying them all is some volatile mix of the best and worst of human nature. Many a war has been fought under the lofty banner of justice, freedom, and equality, whether those goals were sincere or not. Regardless, nearly all are provoked by the far darker motives of greed, aggression, fear, vengeance, hatred, and ignorance.

Globalization, War, and Peace in the Twenty-first Century explores humanity's most persistent and tragic problem by answering five crucial questions: How is power in general and military power in particular best created and asserted? Why do nations go to war or stay at peace? What continuities and changes characterize recent warfare? What are the sources, methods, and results of terrorism and counterterrorism? What are weapons of mass destruction and what is the likelihood of them being used? What constraints, if any, do international laws and organizations have on war? All along, this book reveals why war persists even though the ever thickening web of interdependent relations among nation-states and peoples, known as globalization, sharply raises its costs and reduces its benefits.[3]

CHAPTER 1

The Nature, Creation, and Asserrtion of Power

You see what power is—holding someone else's fear in your hand and showing it to him.

Abraham Lincoln

THE NATURE OF POLITICS AND POWER

The modern world dawned with the Renaissance more than half a millennium ago, born of a dynamic of interrelated intellectual, technological, economic, psychological, sociological, and aesthetic revolutions. Since then history has unfolded through a series of distinct stages in which the pace of change is ever swifter and the duration ever shorter. As the modern world advanced, the ways to wage war metamorphosed dramatically. What, for instance, could that ever more distant past when men battled with swords, muskets, and sailing ships possibly share with today's nuclear-powered aircraft carriers, satellites, cybertage, and drones armed with Hellfire missiles?

The answer, of course, is power. Though manifestations of power change, the essence of power is eternal. Power is inseparable from but is not synonymous with politics. Politics exists wherever the interests of two or more people or groups clash, and is about how the participants assert their respective interests. Power, its distribution and the skill with which each side wields it, determines the results of politics. Political systems, whether on a local, national, or international level, are devised to manage political conflicts and assertions of power. Politics and power thus decide "who gets what, why, when, and how."[1]

Power can span everything from rational or emotional persuasion to the most brutal forms of coercion and violence. Yet power is not just about talking or hurting. States can offer others incentives—alliances, open markets, economic aid, technology, and so on—to change their behavior. Or they can simply give to others what they need or want without asking anything in return. Not all assertions of power are intentional. When they fall, the more powerful can drag down the less powerful who are dependent upon them. It is often said that when the United States catches an economic cold (recession), its weaker neighbor Mexico can suffer from economic pneumonia (depression). And, conversely, when the powerful rise, they can pull up others with them. Economic expansion in the United States invariably stimulates Mexico's economy.

At times power is not wielded for any justifiable end, but is simply to destroy. For instance, in 1991, Iraqi President Saddam Hussein did not gracefully accept the American-led defeat of his attempt to conquer Kuwait. Instead, the dictator ordered his retreating troops to ignite Kuwait's oil fields, destroying billions of dollars of that country's wealth and creating an environmental disaster in the weeks before fire fighters could extinguish all the flames.

So power, essentially, can be the ability of an individual or group to 1) to try to get others to do things they would rather not do; (2) to try to get others not to do things they would rather do; (3) to take from others things that they would rather keep while giving little or nothing in return; (4) to intentionally help or hurt others for whatever ends; (5) to unintentionally help or hurt others.

Power is often described as a type of currency. States want something and they use power to "buy" it, which can simply be more power. Some countries spend their power wisely, investing it in ways that enhance their abilities and goals; others fritter it away in wasteful wars, consumption, or projects; and yet others miserly accumulate power while rarely using it.

Power is relative. The power of one individual, group, nation, or alliance is measured against that of others with which it has conflicting interests. Vietnam is economically and militarily weak when compared to China, and economically and militarily strong when compared to Kampuchea. National power varies widely from one issue to the next. Each state faces a different distribution of power and interests for each issue with which it is involved. One might be relatively powerful in one issue but weak in the next. Finally, power is relative to the perception of and ability to achieve one's interests. If a government is too ambitious and wants, say, to conquer another country or put a man on the moon and cannot do so, then it is relatively powerless. States with far less ambitious but easily obtainable goals can be considered relatively powerful. Even the smallest of states in territory, population, wealth, natural resources, or military forces can be considered powerful if it protects and enhances its national interests.

So how is power most often asserted? To many, power's bottom line is simply the ability to hurt others worse than they can be hurt. Yet the most blatant assertion of power—holding a gun to another's head and demanding money or marching an army to another's frontier and demanding territory—are the least common. Power is manifested in many ways of which military force in an ever more interdependent world is the least cost-effective for advancing national interests. Most power is wielded much more subtlety.

Logic, bribes, and threats are three ways in which power can be asserted.[2] Logic involves persuading the other side to concede through reasoned arguments. Bribes are given to the other side to change their behavior. Threats are made and sometimes acted upon to force the opponent to yield. The more of these means a state employs in a conflict, the more likely it will prevail. For example, Washington's efforts to integrate Europe into a liberal global political economy after World War II involved all three methods. Washington used the logic of liberal economic theory to convince the West Europeans that it was in everyone's interest for them to open and integrate their economies, and sweetened that logic with the bribe of the Marshall Plan that dispensed over $14 billion in economic aid to help develop the region. Finally, the United States used military threats to deter the Soviet Union from disrupting or possibly invading West Europe.

States can use threats to compel, deter, or defend against others. Compellence is an attempt to force someone to give up something he or she values. Deterrence is designed to convince someone not even to try to engage in compellence owing to the adverse consequences that such an effort would provoke. "Defense is an action taken to protect oneself when an opponent ignores or fails to understand one's deterrent efforts and initiates the act of compellence. Under such circumstances, defense usually centers on the ability to defeat the opponent in a trial of strength."[3] Thus, in a conflict in which threats are made, one side attempts to compel and the other side attempts to deter, and if that fails, defend against that compellence.

It is relatively easy to tell when defense or compellence succeeds. Not so deterrence that demands that the status quo be maintained. It is tough to prove why something did not happen. For example, the United States created the North Atlantic Treaty Organization (NATO) in 1949 and built up its conventional and nuclear forces to deter a possible Soviet attack on West Europe. Did that deterrent strategy against the Soviet Union succeed? Certainly, the Soviets never attacked West Europe. But maybe Moscow would not have attacked even if NATO never existed. In that case, the United States and NATO deterred nothing.

Power is not always what it seems. For instance, in 1979, Iranians captured the American embassy in Tehran and held 52 personnel hostage for 444 days. In addition to diplomacy, President Jimmy Carter used economic sanctions and a military raid to free them but those means failed. He did not consider an all out war against Iran, reasoning that the costs would far surpass any conceivable benefits, and the hostages would most likely be killed by their captors. The Iranians released the Americans only after the Carter administration left office. The United States was powerless to gain the release of its hostages.

Every assertion of power must include several ingredients to bolster the chance of success. A state must clearly communicate what it wants in a conflict and the means by which it intends to get what it wants, whether that be logic, bribes, and/or threats. A state has a greater chance of success if its demands require its opponent to make relatively minor rather than major changes. In order to be taken seriously, a state must demonstrate both the capacity and credibility to employ the power it claims to possess. Obviously, the greater a state's relative capacity to punish another state and the more determined it seems to use that capacity, the more credible its potential power. Finally, the credibility of a state's capacity and will must be communicated in a way that weakens rather than strengthens the opponent's resolve on the issue.

For example, in July 1990, Iraqis dictator Saddam Hussein threatened to invade Kuwait. President George H.W. Bush and his officials warned him not to do so. On August 2, Iraqi armies invaded and quickly conquered Kuwait. Why did Saddam disregard the Bush administration's warnings? Although the reasons are complex, essentially Baghdad understood Washington's military capacity eventually to defeat Iraq, but judged that the Bush administration lacked the will to back up his warning. The American ambassador to Iraq, April Glaspie, made a vague, ambiguous last-minute statement to Saddam that he and his advisor interpreted as the United States valued its relationship with Iraq over anything Iraq did to Kuwait. Thus the White House's attempts to deter an Iraqi attack were undermined by poor communication, which, in turn damaged the credibility of America's threat. After deterrence failed, the Bush White House then had to attempt to compel Iraq to withdraw from Kuwait. Even then, after a six-month buildup of American-led coalition forces, which eventually numbered over half a million troops, Saddam believed that Bush was bluffing. He refused to give in until after the coalition destroyed, captured, or routed most of his army in Kuwait. Power is both a means and an end. Ideally, each side in a conflict marshals all the means at its disposal to protect or augment its interests. The winners often have their power enhanced so that they have a better chance of realizing their interests in future conflicts. Thus does a state at once use power to win a struggle and try to bolster its power by its victory? The increased power might include a legal precedent, territorial gain, monetary compensation, open market, and/or reduction of the other side's power resources.

The Foundations of National Power

How is power measured? Power is rarely absolute; it is almost always offset by the power of others. There is often a wide gap between a state's human and material resources and its ability to achieve its goals. States rarely mobilize all the resources at their disposal in any one conflict. Thus a state's potential power may differ greatly from what it actually wields in a conflict. Power cannot be truly measured until it is used.

Despite these analytical challenges, many experts have tried to measure power with the assumption that relative economic and military size are its most important measures.[4] One study combined total population, urban population, steel production, energy consumption, military personnel, and military budget to rank the eight leading countries every five years from 1900 to 1985.[5] Another measured 236 variables among 82 countries to determine whether a country was developed or developing, had an open or closed political economy, and was a large or small country, all of which were said to measure that country's power.[6]

The significance of such number crunching is questionable. At best all those statistics only measure a state's potential power; they tell nothing about how governments muster and assert their resources to protect or enhance national interests. The most vital components of power are often the most difficult to weigh.

A state's ability to get what it wants from others in the international system is based on a range of tangible or "hard power" economic, military, political, or technological resources, and intangible or "soft power" resources like leadership, national cohesion, cultural appeal, critical information, and political will. "Smart power" is the mobilization and assertion of enough appropriate "hard" and "soft" power resources to prevail in a conflict.[7]

It is soft power that usually decides the winner in a contest whereas hard power is relatively evenly matched. Yet when many people think of power, they often picture tangible sources and believe bigger or more is better. Take, for instance, population. If all other power factors are equal (which, of course, they never are), one could argue that the most populous state is the most potentially powerful. A population's quality or soft power, however, counts more than its quantity or hard power. China and India have the world's first and second largest populations, respectively, but with most of their populations poor and all of them fighting for and steadily degrading the available land and resources, both countries would undoubtedly be better off with far fewer but better educated and enterprising people.

While one of every five people on earth is either Chinese or Indians, Americans are only one in twenty. Yet which country more consistently and decisively shapes the world's fate? Indeed, the great powers have not necessarily been the most populous states. Portugal, Holland, and Britain became leading European powers despite having populations well below those of their rivals France or Spain. However, for those nation-states with educated, enterprising, skilled populations, the more people the better. With 300 million and 130 million prosperous people, respectively, the United States and Japan enjoy huge markets within which their industries can achieve large-scale production, profits, and wealth.

One might also think that the more natural resources a nation has, the better. But, as with anything else, it depends. Fertile land bountiful enough to support one's population is always an important pillar of power. Throughout the pre- and early modern era, nations with more natural resources usually had at least that advantage over those with less. Imperialism has often been motivated by the attempt of one state to seize the resources of another.

But globalization diminishes the importance of directly owning vast realms of natural resources. Wolfram Hanrieder captured very concisely the shift in how states view territory and resources: "access rather than acquisition, presence rather than rule, penetration rather than possession have become the important issues."[8]

Many richly endowed countries concentrate on extracting rather than refining their resources. Iran, for instance, has the world's second largest oil reserves yet has to import gasoline because it lacks refineries. And that is an enormous vulnerability and thus weakness. Often, as in Zaire, Indonesia, or Nigeria, to name a few, the result is a capital intensive mining sector that brings great wealth to a few while much of the population remains mired in poverty. Finally, the prices for natural resources are notoriously volatile. Oil prices, for instance, soared to nearly $150 a barrel in 2008 before plummeting to $40 a barrel a mere half year later. Such wild price swings crimp the power of "petro-states" to realize their ambitions.

In the short run, the wealth extracted from mining, logging, or drilling natural resources can be used to prop up the rest of the economy. But over the long term those resources will inevitably run out. And then the country is mired in mass poverty because its economy has failed to diversify. As a resource dwindles, it too can be an economic liability rather than an asset. For instance, in Germany and Belgium, coal or iron ore mining corporations have used their political clout to suck in huge government subsidies long after their mines' viability has ended. The nation's competitiveness weakens because its industries are required to buy that more expensive domestic resource rather than find the cheapest international source.

So a dearth of natural resources can actually be a blessing rather than a curse. The Japanese, for instance, lament their country's lack of natural resources. Yet Japanese industries actually benefit because they can search the world for the cheapest possible sources, which helps bring down their products' final costs. Armed with that enormous comparative advantage, Japanese firms can undercut their foreign rivals and reap enormous wealth for their country.

A nation-state's location, topography, and climate can all enhance or diminish its power. Geopolitically, size is important. A small state like Kuwait or Lebanon is easily overrun by enemies while the vast lands of Russia and China have swallowed up most foreign invaders. Size, however, does not matter geoeconomically. Singapore is a small city-state with 3 million people, yet its per capita income in 2009 was five times higher than that of China, and ranked number twenty-one in the world while China was number ninety. A country's terrain can affect a nation's power as well. Vast deserts or mountains, or extremes of heat and cold or humidity or dryness can at once impede potential invaders and national development. Simple accidents of topography can help seal the fate of nations. The shallow bays on the Netherlands's coast prevented the Dutch navy from adopting the huge warships that might have enabled it to win its naval wars against Britain in the mid-seventh century.

A state's location is clearly important but just what location is the most advantageous is debatable. Sir Halford Mackinder asserted that "he who rules Eastern Europe commands the Heartland of

Eurasia; who commands the Heartland rules the World Island of Europe, Asia, and Africa; and who rules World Island commands the World."[9] The naval historian Alfred Mahan argued the opposite, that naval supremacy was the key to global power: "if a nation be so situated that it is neither forced to defend itself by land nor induced to seek extension of its territory by way of land, it has, by the very unity of its aim directed upon the sea, an advantage as compared with a people whose boundaries are continental."[10] Nicholas Spykman agreed with Mahan and argued that the industrialized "rim land" of Europe, the Middle East, and South and East Asia were the world's most important regions.[11] Spykman's theory, in turn, greatly influenced George Kennan's containment policy. History supports the Mahan rather than Mackinder thesis.

Geography has often protected the most powerful states. The power of England, Japan, the United States, Portugal, Spain, and Russia has clearly been enhanced by their existence on the fringe of power systems, either outright protected by an ocean or enjoying mountain ranges or vast steppes upon which to defend themselves or launch an attack. As island nations, Britain and Japan have natural moats protecting them from foreign invaders. With oceans east and west, and weak neighbors north and south of a continental-wide territory, the United States has been blessed geopolitically and geoeconomically. In order to even contemplate invading the United States, an aggressor would need complete naval and air superiority; to march inland and occupy the United States would require millions of troops. Geoeconomically the United States benefits greatly from being the centerpiece of both the Atlantic and Pacific basin trade systems.

If hard or tangible power is about things people can count, soft or intangible power is about things that people believe. A nation's cohesion, culture, institutions, information, prestige, world view, and, above all, determination can trump economic or military numbers for achieving goals.

While population, resources, and geography are power's raw materials, it is leadership and organization that give them shape and purpose, and it is strategy and will that deploys and unleashes them. History is filled with examples of states disadvantaged in population, resources, or geography besting much larger states. Israel, for instance, with only a fraction of the land, people, and resources of its neighbors, has defeated alliances of surrounding Arab states in five wars.

Power begins in the mind; its essence is psychological rather than physical. Thus power is best wielded through psychological (soft) rather than physical (hard) means. The most effective use of power is the ability to get others to obey one's dictates unquestioningly. In national crises, people tend to set aside their internal conflicts and "rally around the flag" against the external threat. Governments have been known to provoke international conflicts just to divert internal conflicts. Why do most people tend to march off to war without wondering whether their government was right or wrong? Through such institutions as schools and the mass media, governments can socialize a deep and unquestioning loyalty in the people toward the country and leadership.

The loyalty of populations, however, to their government and country varies considerably. During World War II, when faced with imminent defeat Japanese soldiers charged in vast human wave attacks and were often wiped out by the defenders, while at home Japanese women, old men, and children were armed with bamboo spears and grenades and trained to charge any American invaders. Only the atomic bomb forced the Japanese to surrender rather than fight to the death. During the Persian Gulf War (1990–1991), although faced with imminent defeat, the Iraqi army deserted or surrendered by the tens of thousands while large segments of the population rose in revolt against Saddam Hussein's regime. In retrospect, however, the willingness of Japanese soldiers and civilians to toss away their lives without any chance of victory did not prevent Japan's defeat any more than Iraq's disloyal soldiers and civilians caused Iraq's defeat. Other power factors in both wars were much more important.

Followers need leaders. Leadership clearly is a crucial element of soft power. When many people think about politics, the faces, words, and actions of famous leaders come to mind first. What would have been the world's fate if the decisive Winston Churchill rather than the timid Neville Chamberlain were prime minister when Hitler marched into the demilitarized Rhineland in 1936 or demanded Czechoslovakia's Sudetenland in 1938?

Yet do leaders make history or does history make leaders? Even the greatest leaders are prisoners of their time and place, shaped and limited by historic forces far beyond their control and at times understanding. All other things being equal, the side which has more to lose and thus is more willing to sacrifice to prevent that loss will usually win.

An essential element of power is the ability to assess one's own compared to that of one's enemies, allies, and fence-sitters. Thus every government must have some means of gathering and analyzing information vital to understanding the capabilities and intentions of other states.[12] Ideally, the better the "intelligence" or understanding of what one's foes and friends alike are up to, the better a government is able to devise policies to deal with existing or potential friends and foes.

Intelligence gathering and assessment is a difficult and expensive business. Even the best funded and trained intelligence organizations equipped with the latest satellites and supercomputers have trouble gathering and assessing all important information. And it is much easier to count weapons and military units than assess motivations and plans.

Poor intelligence can be costly. December 7, 1941, and September 11, 2001, are days that will live in infamy because America's intelligence community failed to detect those devastating attacks before they occurred. Overestimating an enemy's power can be as self-defeating as underestimating it. In 2003, the Central Intelligence Agency (CIA) admitted that it had grossly exaggerated Soviet military and economic power every year from 1974 to 1986. As a result, American taxpayers paid tens of billions of dollars more to the Pentagon each year than was needed to maintain a stable power balance with the Soviet Union. In 2003, President George W. Bush used false intelligence that Iraq had weapons of mass destruction and collaborated with Al Qaeda as an excuse to war against that country.

While popular films and novels tend to focus on the real and imagined paramilitary activities of spy agencies, the key role of any intelligence organization is gathering, assessing, and presenting intelligence to policymakers. Information can be gathered by human and technical sources. The ability of supercomputers linked to listening devices on earth and in space gather most information. Yet human sources are crucial. Those sources must often be obtained by illegal or unethical means such as the "three Bs"—bribery, burglary, and blackmail. The most common technique is for a "case officer," usually under diplomatic cover, but at times under "nonofficial cover," to try to persuade foreigners to betray their respective countries.

The "intelligence cycle" includes planning what countries, groups, individuals, or issues to investigate. Then comes the other steps of collecting, processing, and analyzing the intelligence. The final product is then disseminated to appropriate government officials. But intelligence is only as good as several interrelated criteria. First of all, the intelligence must be relevant and timely to challenges facing the nation. It must be accurate not just factually but untainted by partisan and/or ideological imperatives. Finally, the intelligence must reveal a context or its relative importance to the larger foreign policy picture.

Diplomacy is an essential element of international power.[13] The key elements of diplomacy are communicating what one wants and the consequences if one's wants are not satisfied. That message can be conveyed through a myriad of potential channels of which diplomats haggling across a table is only one.

In diplomacy, setting the agenda and terms of the debate can be as important in winning one's goals as any other "power" one brings to the table. Ideally that would affect how others see and act in the world.[14] For instance, America's creation and management of a liberal global economy has been both an asset and burden to the United States. Yet that system of international organizations, laws, and ethics straitjackets the power of most countries with different agendas to conform.

What is variously known as public relations, public diplomacy, or propaganda is a vital part of global politics. Virtually all governments try to promote a favorable image of themselves and unfavorable image of their foes. There is a clear distinction between education, which presents all sides of an issue, and propaganda, which presents only one side. The most effective propaganda should not seem like propaganda. Propaganda based on facts is obviously more effective than that based on falsehood since outright lies can be exposed. To be effective, a message must appeal to an individual's identity, beliefs, and conscience.

Effective public diplomacy does not just try to influence hearts and minds in those countries directly involved in the conflict but also targets the wider international audience who might be induced to take sides, as well as one's own public. It often involves a government's leader and ministers making televised speeches, attending press conferences, or even addressing the United Nations. For instance, President Barack Obama's conciliatory speech at Cairo University in 2009 was designed to bolster America's image in the minds of Arabs and Muslims whose hatred of the United States soared after the Bush administration invaded Iraq in 2003. Surveys indicated that Obama's public diplomacy worked by inspiring a slight but distinct decrease in anti-Americanism.[15]

Much of the Cold War was a propaganda war. The United States Information Agency (USIA) was created in 1953 to help Washington win the Cold War's public relations front. Washington spent billions of dollars transmitting news and commentaries to communist and other countries through the Voice of America, Radio Liberty, and

Radio Free Europe. To promote its own views and undermine those of the United States, the Soviet Union had Radio Moscow. In addition, both the Americans and Soviets bankrolled numerous conferences, demonstrations, publications, advertisements, labor unions, student groups, and peace movements, to name the more prominent. Mass media include not only the obvious like newspapers, television, radio, journals, magazines, and Web sites, but also posters, films, flyers, billboards, murals, monuments, museums, postage stamps, street names, and even rumors. More recently as part of its war against Islamism, the United States created the Al Hurra broadcasting station to send its message to the Arab world.

But public diplomacy can also be expressed through more belligerent acts. A state might make "saber-rattling" gestures to intimidate the other side into giving in. In geopolitical conflicts, forces may be put on alert, naval flotillas, air squadrons, or ground units may be redeployed across the regional or global chessboard, or the military budget may be increased. In geoeconomics conflicts, threats might be made to raise tariffs or lower quotas on imports, cut off exports or aid, or freeze the other side's financial accounts.

When it comes to direct diplomacy, there is an art to knowing whether, when, and how to negotiate. Going to the table too soon might be seen as a sign of weakness to be exploited by one's opponent. Going too late might not prevent a military or economic war that neither side may have wanted. There is a similar golden mean with deciding what concessions to make and when to make them. Too little too late might kill any chance of a deal. Too much too soon might mean giving up a lot in return for little or nothing. Negotiations are complex and challenging enough when they are just bilateral or between two parties, but become far more so in multilateral talks with three or more parties.

Negotiations usually involve two stages. The first involves negotiating where, what, and how to negotiate. Each side tries to frame the talks in a way that gives it an initial advantage. One key decision is whether they will talk directly or via a third neutral party. Regardless, will they be in person, teleconferenced, or over the telephone? "Virtual diplomacy" can save time and money at the cost of missing valuable hints of body language and the pressures of time to make decisions.

Where the talks are held and who will conduct them can also be vital. Will they take place in one of the country's capitals, alternate between them, or be held in a third country? As in sports there may be a home court advantage to diplomacy. Another is what level of diplomats will negotiate. Will they be the most minor of emissaries, a "summit" between the actual heads of government, or so some other rank in between?

Yet another essential item is what kind of deal will be cut, a legally binding treaty or just a mutual understanding sealed with a handshake rather than signature. American presidents prefer so-called executive agreements to treaties, which must be ratified by the approval of two-thirds of the Senate.

Even the most minute details of talks can themselves be subject to negotiation. For instance, the United States and North Vietnam spent months bickering over the shape of the table at which they would sit to negotiate the end of the war between them! Why was that important? It would determine the relative status of their respective junior partners, the South Vietnamese government and South Vietnamese communists. In the end they agreed on a diamond shape that appeared to give each pair of partners equal status.

Once those preliminaries are resolved the parties can roll up their sleeves and address the central issues. This stage also involves tough decisions over strategy. "Step-by-step diplomacy" involves resolving relatively minor problems that can build trust and momentum for tackling tougher differences. "Linkage diplomacy" involves tradeoffs for issues that might not be immediately related to the central problem.

What happens when negotiations deadlock? The parties may agree to a deadline to pressure themselves for an agreement. That can be a risky strategy if one side has a weaker position and feels compelled to make concessions rather than end the talks. The parties may agree to bypass formal and often semipublic negotiations with informal secret talks.

Heads of government rarely sit down together to hash out a problem. They prefer to leave diplomacy to professionals because they usually lack the expertise and risk losing prestige should the talks fail. Usually a summit is held only to sign a treaty already painstakingly negotiated by diplomats. Then those national leaders can bask in the applause for a diplomatic coup that might well promote international peace and prosperity.

The technical ability to send one's message to others has expanded enormously. During the 1950s, Egyptian President Nasser achieved ascendancy in the Arab world partly by skilful use of the "transistor revolution" to beam the message of Arab nationalism and unity under his leadership to surrounding states. Today's leaders can beam their messages all around the planet via such technological marvels as satellite television and the Internet.

Those same technologies have affected the settings of direct diplomacy. Traditionally, diplomats and government leaders met and negotiated only with their counterparts. Today and into the future, they can use the electronic and print media to directly address not only their foreign counterparts but the populations as well.

Prestige is having something few or no others have but want or for doing things most others cannot do but wish they could. Prestige involves both symbols and concrete accomplishments, and is both a sign and source of power. Prestige can be gained by countries when they win wars, negotiate peace, build nuclear bombs, put men on the moon, enjoy high economic growth, productivity, literacy, and longevity, and low crime, inflation, and unemployment, or develop new technologies and products or great works of art, literature, architecture, or music, to name a few.

While prestige is clearly a sign of power, how is it a source? States with less prestige are more likely to give in or not challenge states with more. The power to deter is also the power of prestige. The perception by some states that another is powerful can become a self-fulfilling prophecy. The more powerful a state is believed to be, the less likely others will challenge it and the more likely they will yield to it. It is often said that military power does not have to be used to be useful. Threatening a country with war can be enough to force concessions.

Yet prestige can also be a constraint on power. The more prestige a state has to lose, the more carefully a government will try to avoid sticky situations where it can be easily lost. The United States lost enormous prestige as well as 58,000 lives and $200 billion in Vietnam. Resolved to avoid any further loss of prestige, the Pentagon has since usually pressured presidents to avoid any wars in which the United States might be defeated militarily or politically. That did not deter the Bush administration from invading and trying to convert Iraq from a dictatorship into a democracy. But America's initial failure to crush a worsening insurgency and Civil War clearly cost the United States enormous prestige and power to assert its other vital interests elsewhere, especially in pressuring North Korea and Iran to give up their nuclear weapons programs or defeating the worsening insurgency by the Taliban and Al Qaeda in Afghanistan and Pakistan. The Bush administration's crusade in Iraq caused anti-Americanism to swell not just among traditional foes, but traditional friends as well all around the world. And that loss of prestige and moral authority can weaken the United States in countless other issues.[16]

Culture is yet another potential source of soft power. For instance, although many around the world do so, the French are especially fond of condemning what they call "American cultural imperialism." Although there is no evidence of a secret Washington agency that forces peoples around the world to listen to Madonna or Hip-Hop, drink Coca-Cola, eat at McDonalds, watch *Raiders of the Lost Ark*, or ingest other icons of American pop culture, the fact that countless people do so can subtly aid Washington's pursuit of its overseas interests. Theodore Von Laue argues that

> cultural understanding is a matter of raw power; who has the power to make his own understanding prevail? Similarly, in all cross-cultural comparisons, the question is: who compares himself to whom on whose terms? Who has the power to impose their own terms in the comparison? Who provides the premises of comparison?[17]

"How Many [Army] Divisions Does the Pope Have?": Religious Power and Global Politics

When Joseph Stalin, the Soviet Union's dictator from 1928 to 1953, scornfully asked that question, he revealed a misunderstanding that he and countless others share that power ultimately flows from gun barrels. In reality, nothing could be further from the truth.

Stalin's question, however, would not have been ironic during the Middle Ages when the pope was the sovereign ruler not only of all Catholics, but also vast territories and armies (Julius II actually led his army into battle!), at times ordered kings and other princes to launch crusades against Muslims and peoples of other faiths, and divvied up the territorial spoils among Christian conquerors.

The power of the papacy has changed enormously since then. Today Vatican City where the pope resides is a microstate with only 1,000 residents and 15,000 employees squeezed into about 107 acres in Rome, Italy. Yet the pope has power far beyond the confines of his tiny realm. One of six people on the planet are Catholic. The Vatican's position on many issues, most notably its condemnation of birth control including condoms, can have an enormous impact on the health and wealth of hundreds of millions of people around the world. The charisma of John Paul II, who was pope from 1979 to 2005, inspired countless Catholics and non-Catholics around the world, and his efforts to undermine communist rule in his native Poland and elsewhere in Eastern Europe may have hastened the Cold War's end.

Catholicism is hardly the only religion with international power. One of modernity's many paradoxes involves religion. The scientific revolution in critical thinking, experimentation, and invention is central to modernization. Scientific research and methods have exposed many traditional religious beliefs as myths. Yet paradoxically, for billions of people around the world that has provoked not skepticism but a backlash against science itself. Religion can be a comforting refuge from an alienating, dangerous world of diverse secular beliefs and temptations. The morality of modern societies demands that each individual think critically about him- or herself and the world, and then act accordingly. Countless people find that profoundly disturbing. Much more appealing is the morality of fundamentalist religions that simply demand that adherents believe blindly in the creed. Religious belief thus can be an enormous source of power. Those who insist that God is on their side tend to have a psychological edge over those who do not.

The fundamentalist Christian beliefs of President George W. Bush and most of his fellow conservatives powerfully shaped how they interpreted and acted in the world, with the rejection of the global warming treaty, cutoff of American money to international family planning programs, and invasion of Iraq perhaps the most prominent policies partially justified in religious terms.

Today Islam appears to be an even more powerful religious force in global politics than Catholicism. For instance, in 1979, fundamentalist Muslims dramatically shifted the power balance in the Persian Gulf when they overthrew Iran's pro-American Shah and erected an anti-American Islamic theocracy. To varying extents, Islamic fundamentalism threatens every state in the Middle East and southwest and central Asia. The Islamists are fiercely anti-Western, and their possession of oil rich Persian Gulf states might dramatically affect the global economy. Waving the banner of Islamism, Osama bin Laden and his terrorist group Al Qaeda has launched a series of deadly attacks against the United States and other enemies culminating with September 11, 2001.

In other words, when one state accepts willingly, unwittingly, or by force another state's cultural values and symbols, it makes itself vulnerable to the culturally more powerful state. For over 500 years, international relations have been shaped by Western culture and power. The West has imposed its values and institutions on the rest of humanity largely by military or economic force, but often by sheer example.

Since 1945, American mass culture has penetrated virtually every society around the world. America's most potent source of cultural power, however, has not been its pop culture let alone its rich culture of literature, painting, architecture, sculpture, music, theater, or dance, but its political philosophy. "Liberty," Paul Nitze wrote, "is the most contagious idea in history."[18] No country has more deeply explored or attempted to fulfill the concept of liberty than the United States. It was Washington that was largely responsible for ensuring that the Western conception of human rights was enshrined in the 1945 UN Charter and 1948 Declaration of Human Rights, which every UN member is pledged to uphold.

Traditionally, however, despite the United Nations' clear human rights standard, most countries scorned it. Recently, the elite and mass acceptance of human rights is growing and serves as an increasingly powerful check on state behavior. In response to international moral pressure, countries as diverse as Nicaragua, the Philippines, and Kampuchea have held United Nations-sponsored elections. The power balance between liberal democratic and authoritarian states is tipping decisively in favor of the former and with it will come increased international cooperation, peace, prosperity, and more subtle ways of wielding power.

GEOPOLITICAL POWER

Geopolitical power is the ability to threaten or use military force to defend or enhance one's interests. Does military spending equal geopolitical power? Hardly. Spending merely reveals a state's potential military power. Military power, like all power, can only be ultimately measured according to whether or not it is successfully used. Forces other than military budget and personnel size are often decisive.

For all its military might, the United States has suffered since 1945 a series of humiliations by countries with much smaller forces. American and other allied forces were fought to a standstill in Korea. The United States lost the Vietnam War. A communist government seized and continued to maintain power in Cuba despite enormous American efforts to overthrow it. In 1968, the North Koreans seized an American spy ship and held it for nearly a year. In 1979, Iranians overran the American embassy and held its 52 employees hostage for 444 days. Although the violence is lower in Iraq today than in previous years, the war's only victors there are appear to be anti-Americanism, Islamism, and Iran. Why did the United States lose these geopolitical conflicts? The reasons, as always, are complex and unique to each case. But essentially America lacked the full spectrum of both "hard" and "soft" power to prevail.

Other countries thought to be more powerful have also been humbled by countries believed to be less powerful. Soviet military superpower failed to subject Afghanistan; after nearly a decade of bitter guerrilla fighting, Moscow was forced into a humiliating retreat in 1989. The Chinese army invaded northern Vietnam in 1979 to retaliate for Vietnam's invasion of Cambodia; China's supposedly crack divisions were repulsed by supposedly second rate Vietnamese units. In 1982, Britain had difficulty mustering enough troops and ships to fight Argentina after it invaded Britain's Falkland Islands, and might have lost had not Washington shared important intelligence of Argentina's fleet movements with London, along with essential logistical support. Thus raw power—the number of troops, tanks, and bombs a state holds—tells nothing about how skilled a government is in brandishing that power.

Given all this, can we identify a decisive factor in a military struggle? Scholars differ over whether the side with the larger military usually prevails or not. One study found that the side with the larger force won twenty-one of thirty-two wars between 1816 and 1965, or two-thirds of the total. In contrast, a much more comprehensive study of 164 conflicts between 1816 to 1976, most of which were resolved peacefully, found no correlation between military size and victory.[19]

Other factors are often much more decisive. History is filled with examples of armies with smaller numbers defeating far larger forces. With an army that never exceeded 40,000 troops, Alexander the Great conquered a vast empire from the eastern Mediterranean across the Middle East to Central Asia and Pakistan. In the nineteenth century, the great powers could humble large but technologically backward states by dispatching a few gunboats to bombard or blockade coastal cities, and well-trained, armed, and equipped infantry to defeat native armies many times larger.

Those days of "gunboat diplomacy" are long past. The transfer of advanced weapons to the Third World has undermined the ability of the superpowers and other great powers to win militarily, and has even led to their defeat, such as North Vietnam over the United States or the Afghan rebels over the Soviet Union. During the Falkland Islands War, French Exocet anti–ship missiles supplied to Argentina made Britain's victory much more costly. The Argentineans used Exocets to sink two British warships. American shoulder-fired Stinger anti–aircraft missiles supplied to Afghan guerrillas broke the Soviet command of the air and were probably the most important reason that Moscow eventually chose to withdraw from that country.

Some weapons in Third World hands are overrated. The SCUD missiles that Iraq lobbed in the Persian Gulf War against Saudi Arabia and Israel did minor damage and may have actually been inferior to the German V-2 bombs launched fifty years earlier. However, the mere Iraqi threat to place chemical weapons on their SCUD missiles caused the Coalition enormous political problems. Israel threatened to retaliate if Iraq launched chemical SCUDs, and Israeli retaliation might have caused the Coalition's Arab members to withdraw or even change sides. To prevent that possibility, the Coalition diverted tens of thousands of air force sorties in a largely unsuccessful effort to search and destroy the SCUDs rather than other far more dangerous targets.

What about the most destructive weapons of all? How does nuclear power enhance or detract from a nation's total power? Theoretically nuclear weapons deter foreign attack, although we can never know if potential enemies would have attacked had they not faced those nuclear weapons. The knowledge that they would destroy each other in a nuclear war, known as Mutually Assured Destruction (MAD), may well have deterred a war between the United States and Soviet Union. Washington's rattling of its nuclear saber during the Korean War (1953) and Quemoy and Matsu crises (1958) may have enhanced its bargaining power with its opponents during those conflicts. Certainly nuclear power confers a dark prestige on those countries that possess it.

Weighed against these factors, however, are the enormous financial, human, and technological resources that must be diverted to build up and maintain a nuclear force, resources that could be invested much more profitably elsewhere. Like other forms of military power, nuclear weapons mostly drain a nation's economy. Unlike other military weapons, nuclear bombs that are accidentally or purposely exploded can kill millions and render land uninhabitable wasteland. According to the Brookings Institute, Washington's nuclear weapons programs cost American taxpayers a mind-boggling $5.8212 trillion from 1940 through 1996 alone!

The constraints on the use of nuclear power largely eliminate its military function. International morality and an absence of vital interests at stake may well have prevented the two superpowers and other nuclear powers like China, France, Britain, or Israel from using their weapons in wars with smaller states. America's tens of thousands of nuclear weapons did not prevent OPEC from nationalizing its oil fields and quadrupling oil prices in 1973, North Vietnam from conquering South Vietnam in 1975, the Soviets from invading Afghanistan in 1979, Al Qaeda from attacking America on September 11, 2001, or an insurgency against American forces in Iraq after the invasion in 2003. More than other forms of destruction, nuclear weapons are a double-edged sword.

In addition to advanced weapons, the effective use of nationalism, modern arms, the mass media, and international organizations
like the United Nations has empowered Third World countries to
successfully resist Great Power intervention. The diffusion of military technology to the Third World and the ability to mobilize entire
populations behind "people's liberation wars" makes the costs of
Great Power intervention excruciatingly painful and often ultimately
fruitless.[20]

Militaries must not only be paid for, they need a purpose.
Governments often divert enormous financial and human resources
preparing for threats, which do not exist or overspend for those that
do, and thus undermine their total power. For example, what is the
United States going to do with 8,000 battle tanks in its arsenal?
Military budgets are often shaped by political rather than strategic
demands. Politicians lobby for a military base or armaments factory
because it brings jobs and money to their district, even though those
resources might have been better invested elsewhere. The result is
that a nation's potential power sources are squandered rather than
invested.

And then there is the "security dilemma." Ironically, the military
buildup that one state undertakes to feel more secure often makes
other states feel more insecure, so they in turn build up their own
forces. The original state then feels even more threatened so it accel-
erates its buildup. The other state reciprocates. The result is an arms
race, which may lead to a war that all sides would have preferred to
avoid. Washington and Moscow were caught in just such an arms
race from 1945 to 1991, a race that ultimately ate away the economic
power and thus the total power of both countries, leading ultimately
to the Soviet Union's implosion and America's grave weakening.

The greater a nation's military spending, the greater the sacrifices
made in foregone investments and opportunities in more economically and socially productive pursuits. Alliances would seem to be a
way to share defense burdens, but not always. Whether alliances help
or hurt their members varies considerably from one to the next. There
can be weakness as well as strength in numbers.

There are many kinds of alliances. States balance or counter threats,
not power. What is important is not how powerful another state or
group of states is, but whether it is threatening. Some alliances are
between states of a similar ideology facing a common ideological
threat, such as the American-led North Atlantic Treaty Organization
(NATO), which helped contain the Soviet Union and its Warsaw
Pact alliance for over four decades. Most are based on the principle

that "the enemy of my enemy is my friend," which are "marriages of convenience" between countries of quite different ideologies facing the same threat, such as when the democratic powers, America, and Britain teamed up with the communist Soviet Union to defeat the fascist powers Germany, Japan, and Italy during World War II. Since its creation in 1948, Israel has maintained its security in part by playing off the various intra-Arab, Sunni-Shiite Muslim, and Arab-Iranian rivalries through secret diplomacy in which it would favor one side against the other. During the Cold War, India formed an alliance with the Soviet Union and Pakistan with China to strengthen themselves against each other.

How do governments decide whether or not to join an alliance? An imminent or actual attack is an obvious reason. But what happens when those conditions are not present? By one theory, alliance "participants create coalitions just as large as they believe will ensure winning and no larger." The reason is that while the chance for victory grows with the coalition's size, the share of the spoils diminishes accordingly. This may have been true of coalitions before the mid-twentieth century when the victors often took territory and wealth from the losers. The benefits of contemporary alliances are more intangible than in the past—security, community, and prestige rather than the spoils of war.

When faced with a threat, it sometimes pays not to join an alliance if it is clear the alliance will defeat or deter that threat. France dropped out of NATO in 1964, thus regaining its independence and shedding its duties while continuing to shelter under that alliance's conventional and nuclear umbrella. The United States sat on the sidelines of both world wars until it was directly attacked. It can be argued, however, that the United States would have gained more by joining an alliance with Britain and France in the late 1930s, since it possibly could have led to a negotiated settlement or bolstered allied forces in France, which would have made a German victory there in 1940 much less likely and perhaps deterred an attack altogether. The human and material costs of waiting may have been greater for the United States in the long run. The trouble with this scenario is that, given America's deep isolationist sentiment before Pearl Harbor, it would have been politically impossible for President Roosevelt to formally ally with Britain and France unless the United States was directly attacked.

The benefits of being in an alliance seem obvious. A nation's security tends to strengthen with the alliances' troops, weapons, geographical expanse, coordination, and will. Alliances can deter aggression. States with smaller populations, economies, and militaries can especially benefit by joining an alliance. A study of alliances between 1815 and 1965 found that, if attacked, states with allies received help 76 percent of the times; without allies only 17 percent of the time.[21]

The balance of power theory holds that weakness invites aggression while there is strength and a greater chance for peace in numbers. In a world of sovereign states, each struggles to enhance its interests, often at the expense of others. When one state grows too powerful and aggressive, other states tend to ally to offset that power and potential threat. Being in an alliance, however, does not guarantee victory. More often than not, the key to victory in war from 1816 to 1976 was who initiated it rather than whether or not there was an alliance.[22]

At times an alliance's costs exceed its benefits. For very sound reasons, George Washington in his farewell address warned his fellow Americans against entanglements in foreign alliances: "it must be unwise...to implicate ourselves by artificial ties in the ordinary vicissitudes of her [Europe's] politics, or the ordinary combinations and collisions of her friendships or enmities."[23] Or, as Thomas Jefferson put it even more succinctly: "Commerce with all nations, alliance with none, should be our motto."[24] George Kennan eloquently explored the reason for the caution with which most states approach alliances: "The relations among nations...constitute a fluid substance...This is why "wise and experienced statesmen usually shy away from commitments likely to constitute limitations on a government's behavior at unknown dates in the future in the face of unpredictable situations."[25]

Great powers sometimes force minor powers into alliances in order to more easily dominate and extract benefits from them. The primary reason that the Soviet Union created the Warsaw Pact was to justify subjugating and exploiting East Europe.[26] Far less convincingly, some have made the same claim for the American creation of NATO and the Organization of American States (OAS), although the latter is a political forum rather than military alliance.

If change is constant, the longer an alliance exists, the more likely it is oriented toward past rather than present challenges and opportunities. Alliances themselves can prevent positive change by freezing rivalries and conflicts. While alliances provide states with greater potential military resources, they take away their members' diplomatic flexibility. Alliance building is a type of arms race, with a similar escalation of perceived threats and tensions. One alliance's creation is likely to spark the creation of an opposing alliance, thus possibly worsening the threat the first alliance was originally created to deter. If war breaks out, the destruction and death can become as widespread as the alliance itself.

Napoleon once said, "I'd rather fight than join a coalition." The difficulty in coordinating the strategy and tactics of an alliance at war are vast and often unmanageable. The more states in an alliance, the weaker the influence of any one state on the alliance's policies and the greater the difficulty in reaching decisions. Napoleon and many other leaders have found that the advantages of fighting alone with a unified and decisive command outweigh the added troops and resources that alliances can provide.

Historically, alliances have been ephemeral, arising and dissolving with perceived threats. Most governments recognize that in a constantly changing world they have no permanent friends or enemies, just national interests that must be preserved. Today's friend can be tomorrow's enemy. One of four wars between 1815 and 1965 were fought between allies![27]

CONSEQUENCES

What is the ultimate source of national power? Traditionally, military rather than economic power was considered the more important component of national power. As Machiavelli put it, "the sinews of war are not gold, but good soldiers; for gold alone will not procure good soldiers, but good soldiers will always procure gold."[28]

No longer. As the United States and former Soviet Union discovered to the former's tripling of its national debt during the Reagan years and the latter's self-destruction, overinvesting in a huge military industrial complex may actually diminish rather than enhance national power in an ever more interdependent world. Military power was traditionally used to seize wealth; today, most countries create wealth and then divert no more than a token fraction to the military while investing most of it in the industries and technologies that can create more wealth.

Military power becomes increasingly irrelevant to most conflicts in an ever more interdependent world in which all states are ever more tightly bound as both the system's beneficiaries and prisoners. In his book *The Rise of the Trading State*, Richard Rosecrance argued that increasingly economic rather than military means are the primary source of national power. He contrasted military states like the United States and Soviet Union with trading states like Japan and Germany, and concluded: "Since 1945, a few nations have borne the crushing weight of military expenditure while others have gained a relative advantage by becoming military free-riders who primarily rely on the security provided by others. While the United States spent nearly 50 percent of its research and development budget on arms, Japan devoted 99 percent to civilian production."[29]

Yet military power is still a key component of national power for many governments. Although international wars dwindle in number, internal wars still plague dozens of countries. Those countries that face a geopolitical threat at once face the challenge of determining just what kind and how much of a military to have. Too much or the wrong kind of hard military power can weaken rather than bolster national power. As always, the key is mustering and mastering the appropriate resources of hard and soft power, known as smart power.

CHAPTER 2

Why Nations Go to War and Stay at Peace

We make war that we may live in peace.

Aristotle

There has never been a good war or bad peace.

Benjamin Franklin

War is the central problem of international relations.[1] For as long as humans have existed, they have been killing one another; throughout the modern era, they have been doing so in increasingly well-organized, large-scale, and devastating ways. The human and material destruction of war in the twentieth century alone is incalculable. Why do nations go to war or stay at peace?

Every war has its own unique set of causes, which are invariably multiple, complex, and interrelated. Wars have been fought either exclusively or in some combination to gain or defend territory; security; wealth; national, religious, cultural, racial, and/or ideological identity and values; political dynasties; colonies; independence; allies or other friendly states; empire; hegemony; freedom of the seas; endangered citizens; or national honor. Wars have also been fought to weaken or destroy rivals; retaliate against the aggression of others; preempt an imminent or inevitable attack; avenge insults or past losses; fill power vacuums before someone else does; or maintain alliance credibility.[2] And these are merely some of the more prominent reasons for war.

To determine the reasons for any particular war, let alone the general phenomenon, one must tap into such fields as psychology, sociology, history, economics, political science, religion, biology, demography, ecology, philosophy, and decision making—to name the more obvious. As Quincy Wright puts it, "A war, in reality, results from a total situation involving ultimately almost everything that has happened to the human race up to the time the war begins."[3]

Given that array of reasons, is it possible to discern any underlying patterns that lead states to war or keep them at peace? Of course, there are some. War, essentially, arises from conflict. Wars do not occur unless one or more sides in a conflict are convinced that their vital interests are threatened and are willing to use violence to protect those interests. Not surprisingly, most wars are fought by neighbors. In their book *War and Reason*, Bruce Bueno de Mesquita and David Lalman analyzed 700 geopolitical conflicts between pairs of states from 1815 to 1970. They reach the not-quite-earth-shattering conclusion that leaders will take their states to war when they think they will win and then wield the strategy that makes winning most likely. Wars often result when leaders miscalculate their chances for winning.[4] At times, the wars of a historic period and geographic region may display a distinct patterns of causes. Throughout Europe's modern era, for instance, the central reasons for war changed dramatically from religion (1519–1648) to dynastic rule (1648–1789), and then to revolution and nationalism (1789–1945).

How do we determine just why any particular war erupted? The best way is to sort out all the possible reasons by importance (primary, secondary, and tertiary) and time (long, intermediate, short). That framework can be used to analyze the reasons for any war at any time in history, if there is enough accurate information. Scholars, of course, will debate whether a potential cause was of primary, secondary, or tertiary importance, and just when to divide time into long-term, intermediate-term, and short-term phases before the war begins. The same framework can be flipped to analyze the results of any war, starting with the short-term. Quite often the results of one war are among the reasons for the next war.

Given the virtual universality of war, can we ever expect violent conflict between or within states to end? Many answer "no," maintaining that wars are perfectly natural and are simply a violent means to resolve conflict: "War is a means for achieving an end, a weapon which can be used for good or bad purposes. Some of these purposes for which war has been used have been accepted by humanity as worthwhile ends; indeed, war performs functions which are essential in any society. It has been used to settle disputes, to uphold rights, to remedy wrongs... One may say... that no more stupid, brutal, wasteful, or unfair method could ever have been imagined for such purposes, but this does not alter the situation."[5] Traditionally, a state's ultimate sovereign power was the ability and right to wage war. Karl von Clausewitz considered war merely an extension of diplomacy by other means and rejected any limits to the violence of battle: "War is an act of force, and to the application of that force there is no limit."[6]

Yet others argue that although wars grab the headlines, throughout history most states have been at peace most of the time. From the mid-nineteenth century through today, states have signed a series of treaties limiting war's justifications, weapons, targets, consequences, and in the twentieth century actually outlawed aggressive war itself. Since 1945, international laws of war and international organizations such as the United Nations that have tried to uphold them have combined with the world's ever denser webs of interdependence to significantly reduce the number of international wars waged around the world. Nearly all states strictly obey the restrictions on weapons and behavior; the ranks of "rogue states" are thin and diminishing. As the world becomes ever more interdependent economically and politically democratic, international war will just as steadily diminish as its economic and political costs rise and benefits fall. Despite these changes, war will remain a scourge for many peoples around the world, though increasingly within rather than between states.

War's increased moral and practical obsolescence should reduce the range of reasons why states go to war. In his book *Man, the State, and War*, Kenneth Waltz points out that all theories of war find their source in the character and behavior of one of three areas: human nature, the nation-state, and the international system.[7] We will use that typology for our discussion below.

WAR AND HUMAN NATURE

Nature, Nurture and War

Humans are territorial animals who struggle to take, keep, and expand property. But is violence innate (nature/hereditary), learned (nurtured/socialized), or some combination of the two? These views are propounded respectively by the Social Darwinian or Realist, Behavioral, and Psychoanalytical schools of thought.

The so-called Realist or Social Darwinian paradigm assumes that human nature is forever fixed and flawed, a belief that can be traced to the biblical notion of original sin and human evil. War, thus, is inevitable. Waltz agrees: "Our miseries are ineluctably the product of our natures. The root of all evil is man, and thus he is himself the root of the specific evil, war."[8] Or, as Albert Einstein put it in a letter to Sigmund Freud, "Man has within him a lust for hatred and destruction...It is a comparatively easy task to call this into play and raise it to the level of a collective psychosis."[9]

After studying aggression in various animal species, Konrad Lorenz concluded that humans were "killer apes," one of the few species that kills its own kind.[10] Aggression comes from and is essential to evolution. Charles Darwin theorized that life evolved from a few simple species to millions of complex species through a survival-of-the-fittest struggle as each attempted to adapt to hostile environments. "Social Darwinism," popularized by Herbert Spencer and others, argued that nations, like animal species, were engaged in a perpetual war of all against all in which the stronger conquered the weaker. A constant struggle to survive has always characterized human existence, from the simplest hunter-gatherer groups that persisted for hundreds of thousands of years to the complex nation-states of today. Progress comes from competition as the strong and more advanced vanquish and exploit the weak.

Thus imperialism is natural and even moral because it allows "superior" peoples to subdue and civilize the "inferior" ones. During the late nineteenth century and the 1930s, governments used Social Darwinism to justify their imperialism. As Hitler put it, "Nature knows no political boundaries. First she puts living creatures on this globe and watches the free play of forces. She then confers the master's right on her favorite child, the strongest."[11]

Others—behavioralists—argue that societies rather than genetics shape how humans see and act. Thus human aggression is learned rather than innate.[12] Some environments promote and others inhibit aggression. Wars are fought by governments, not individuals, and, therefore, are political cultural inventions rather than biological imperatives.[13] An Adolf Hitler or Saddam Hussein can skillfully use ideology, religion, and/or nationalism to whip a population from passivity into aggression, and channel that collective hate, fear, creed, and greed into imperialism. "Behavioralism" also distinguishes sporadic acts of violence by individuals and small groups from war organized and conducted by states.

Most humans have an existential and psychic need to identify with something greater than themselves such as God or some other powerful force. During the modern era, the nation has become the primary source of identity for many. Jack Levy explores the connection between human psychology, nationalism, and war: when people "acquire an intense commitment to the power and prosperity of the state and this commitment is strengthened by national myths emphasizing the moral, physical, and political strength of the state and by an individual's feelings of powerlessness and their consequent tendency to seek their identity and fulfillment through the state, then assertive and nationalist policies are perceived as increasing state power and are at the same time psychologically satisfying for the individual and, in this way, nationalism contributes to war."[14]

Psychological and sociological theories of war, particularly the innate aggression school, have been criticized on several grounds. If humans are innately aggressive and that aggression leads to war, why then are not men at war all or most of the time? In reality, peace mostly prevails among states and humans. While conflict among humans is inevitable, violence inherently is not. Studies of primitive societies find as many peaceful as violent ones.[15] Though humans are certainly capable of violence, they seldom commit it and instead resolve most conflicts peacefully. Most humans use rationality to check their aggressive drives. A human drive to cooperate with others is far more important than the drive to vanquish them. The aggression of states or individuals may well be deviant rather than natural behavior. Although some peoples like the Germans and Japanese are commonly thought to be more aggressive than others, studies have debunked that belief.[16]

There is not necessarily a link between human and state aggression. Wars can occur even when the respective populations are disinterested or opposed, just as wars can be averted through skilled diplomacy even when the respective populations feverishly demand it.[17] Some argue that for every leader who dragged a reluctant populace to war, one may find a reluctant leader who was pushed into war by an eager populace.[18] Yet one study of twenty-five wars found no case "precipitated by emotional tensions, sentimentality, crowd behavior, or other irrational motivations."[19]

Sigmund Freud uses a psychoanalytical approach to bridge the diametrically opposed Social Darwinian and Behavioral views. In his book *Civilization and Its Discontents*, he argues that aggression is only one of many often contradictory innate drives within humans including a compulsion to preserve oneself and perpetuate one's gene pool (eros), to have a family (paternalism), to extinguish one-self (thanatos), to cooperate with (fraternalism) and help others (altruism), and to take advantage of and surpass others (egoism). How those drives are expressed varies from one person and situation to the next. The fundamental drive, however, is survival. Allowing one's innate aggression to prevail is ultimately self-destructive since it will provoke others to eliminate the aggression that threatens their own existence. Thus cooperating with others is the best survival strategy for nearly all people nearly all the time. To that end individuals "sublimate" their aggressive, brutal, greedy drives by diverting them into figuratively and literally constructive behavior. The result is civilization.[20]

Misperception, Escalation, and War

The decision to wage war is rarely taken lightly, even among the most belligerent governments and peoples; few have ever wanted to risk destruction even for popular political ends. Yet most states have experienced war's horrors. What explains the discrepancy?

Some argue that most wars happen because of mutual misperceptions about the other's intentions and power.[21] Misperception's root is the human tendency to simplify information; people see what they want to see and hear what they want to hear. There is only so much that any human or group of humans can comprehend. Instead of trying to understand the world's complexities, decision makers and the public cling to and become trapped by a collection of simplistic prejudices and stereotypes.

Misperceptions can involve a range of images, attitudes, and behaviors, including a government's angelic self-image and diabolical image of the rival government and people; overconfidence in one's military power and disregard for that of the other; missed signals that show the other side's peaceful intentions or willingness to compromise; and lack of understanding or empathy for the other's interests. As the conflict unfolds, communications break down or were limited from the start. Governments and their peoples project their fears, ambitions, and capabilities on their rivals. In conflicts and particularly in a crisis, governments tend to assume the worst about one another's intentions, power, and goals.

"Mirror image" occurs when each side

> believes the other to be bent on aggression and conquest, to be capable of great brutality and evil-doing, to be something less than human...To hold this conception of the enemy becomes the moral duty of every citizen, and those who question it are denounced...The approaching war is seen as due entirely to the hostile intentions of the enemy.[22]

Tragically, mirror images often become self-fulfilling prophecies as each side interprets the other's actions in the worst way and then counters them accordingly, resulting in spiraling tensions and saber-rattling. Even the most innocent of the rival's actions are interpreted in the worst way. The result is an existing gap between image and reality that worsens with a conflict. The tenser a situation, the greater the human tendency to stereotype themselves and their opponents, thus making compromise increasingly difficult. Governments tend to believe their own propaganda about themselves and their rivals.

Statesmen often have several audiences; their domestic constituents, their foreign rivals, and the international community. Misunderstandings can arise when governments send different messages to different audiences. Even authoritarian governments can become the prisoners of public expectations. Once a government draws a line in the sand for a domestic audience, it often feels compelled to stick to it even if it might secretly prefer to be more flexible toward its rivals. As conflicts escalate, states get trapped in a game of "chicken" with their rival in which they charge each other, hoping the other will give way. The result is often war, as neither side wants to step aside and compromise. Governments misperceive the military capabilities and intentions of their rivals. Once a decision for war is made, leaders convince themselves and their publics that they will enjoy a quick and easy victory. However ,that is rarely the case.

Misperceptions themselves are not the cause of war. Real conflicts over vital issues must be present for either side to consider war as a means to resolve them. Often the different sides in a dispute understand each other's intentions and capabilities quite clearly, yet war occurs anyway because one or both sides made a "rational" decision that they could prevail through force.

War and the Nation-State

Ideology and War

Men often go to war over ideas. The better organized those ideas and the more fervent their claim to be the one and only truth, the more frequently such ideologies provoke wars. Ideologies can be both secular and religious.

Some ideologies may not overtly be about God but inspire in their followers beliefs akin to religious zeal and structure. Communism and fascism have often been called secular religions as they promoted visions of class and national struggles that justified aggression and brought to power charismatic leaders who championed those crusades. Communism, after all, was an ideology that demanded world revolution and wars of national and class revolution. The variants of fascism in Japan, Germany, and Italy all justified aggression for the greater glory of that nation and the authoritarian state that personified it.

At various times, most religions have been interpreted in ways that provoke crusades against peoples of other faiths, and even warred against their own members who proposed alternative interpretations of sacred scriptures. Although Jesus was a pacifist, the religion of Christianity has been interpreted by some of its followers to inspire wars against nonbelievers. For two centuries, from 1095 when Pope Urban II called for the first crusade against the "infidel" Muslim Arabs who had conquered the Holy Land, to 1291 when Acre, the last crusader bastion in Palestine fell, the Catholic princes of Europe obeyed Rome's orders and launched seven major campaigns. A series of blood-soaked religious wars between Catholics and Protestants plunged much of Europe from the revolt of the Anabaptists in 1525 until the Treaty of Westphalia in 1648. Western imperialism was usually justified in part as an attempt to bring Christianity to benighted peoples elsewhere. But other religions have provoked wars just as vicious. The Bible's Old Testament reveals how the Israelites warred continually and sometimes committed genocide against neighboring peoples. Islam's Koran explicitly calls on its adherents to wage Jihad or holy war against infidels and assures martyrs in those struggles a prominent place in heaven.

Islam, Jihad, and Bloody Borders: The Huntington Thesis

In his book *The Clash of Civilizations*, Samuel Huntington noted that "Islam has bloody borders." Is that true? If so are Islam's borders any bloodier than those of other creeds?

Islam does distinguish between "the land of Islam" (*Dar al-Islam*) and "the land of war" (*Dar al-Harb*), and insists upon an incessant struggle between the two, although at times a temporary truce (*Dar al-Suhl*) can suspend fighting for a while. Islamic *jihad* or holy war has two meanings—one is a war against infidels and the other a struggle by believers to purge themselves of sin. In the Muslim world, mosque and state are one, guided by the "Sharia" or Islamic law, which is rooted in the Koran or theology of Mohammad and "Hadith" or elaboration of that theology, which in turn is interpreted and administered by the "Ulema" or religious scholars and followed by the *ummah* or community of believers. Ever more Muslim governments, clerics, and adherents are anti-Western and deplore what they believe is the poisonous spread of liberalism to their societies (*gharbzadegi*). Iran's fundamentalist leaders, since coming to power in a 1979 revolution, are only the most outspoken Islamist government in their hatred of the West and especially the United States.

Those animosities are nearly 1,400 years old. Mohammad, Islam's founder, was a warrior as well as a prophet. His successors spread

Islam through conquest as Arab armies swept across the Middle East, Southwest Asia, North Africa, and the Iberian Peninsula. That initial burst of imperialism lasted a century. It was followed for several centuries by the brilliant flowering of Arab civilization in philosophy, theology, literature, and architecture. Ironically, while Europe was plunged into the "dark ages," it was Arab scholars who preserved, studied, and transmitted Greek philosophy to the West and thus inadvertently helped spark the Renaissance. When Arab imperialism reached its limits, other converts to Islam, most notably the Turks, carried on the struggle. But once Islam was well established, it expanded more by the genuine conversion of people who believed they had found the truth, than by conquest.

Today Islam is the world's fastest growing religion in converts and births with over 1.5 billion people around the world professing that faith. Although the number of Christians is larger with nearly 2 billion, Islam may well surpass Christianity in numbers someday. Of the fifty-seven countries with predominantly Muslim populations, the three largest—Indonesia with over 240 million adherents, Pakistan with 180 million, and Bangladesh with 160 million—are far from Islam's birthplace in the Arabian peninsula.

While Islamist terrorists, especially suicide bombers, make headlines, nearly all Muslims lead peaceful, productive lives just like nearly all people of other faiths. Tragically, Islam is among several religious creeds characterized by "bloody borders" at some point in their expansion. Christianity may lack Islam's theology for war but historically it has at times waged war just as enthusiastically for converts and other spoils. Yet, like Islam, Christianity has more recently expanded mostly from peaceful rather than forced conversion. The followers of both religions are split among a vast spectrum of groups that interpret their faith ranging from the most joyfully liberal, tolerant, and peaceful to the most harshly conservative, puritanical, and aggressive.

Nonetheless, Huntington supported his assertion that

> Islam has "bloody borders" with hard data. Muslim states were involved in 76 of 142 international crises between 1928 and 1979, and, more recently in 1993 waged war in 28 of 59 conflicts within or between civilizations. Of the six wars "in which over 200,000 people died, three (Sudan, Bosnia, and East Timor) were between Muslims and non-Muslims, two (Somalia, Iraq-Kurds) were between Muslims, and only one (Angola) involved only non-Muslims."

Huntington argues that Islam's propensity for war will only worsen in the in the future because of a population explosion among Muslims. The number of young people demanding jobs will increasingly outstrip the supply. The result will be worsening poverty, despair, and rage. Muslim governments will be tempted to vent that rage against enemies within or across borders.[23]

Ideologies have at times been a major cause for some wars, but are rarely the sole cause for any war. Other forces invariably motivate a state or group of states with one ideology to attack a state or group of states with an opposing ideology. Indeed just because state share an ideology may not prevent them from warring against each other. Ideals of communist brotherhood were not powerful enough to prevent the Soviet Union and China from fighting a border war in 1969, or China from invading Vietnam in 1979. Christian states have warred repeatedly against one another as have Muslim, Hindu, and Buddhist states respectively against others sharing the same faith.

Separatism, Irredentism, and War

Conflicts between "nationalism" and "multinationalism" are the heart of ever more geopolitical issues.[24] More established and newly independent states alike are faced with the problem of realizing "out of many, one" (*E Pluribus Unum*), the motto of the United States. Governments from Nigeria to China and from Iraq to the Congo are struggling to promote a new cultural identity that spans numerous distinct cultural identities. In many of these nation-states people are forced to choose between loyalty to one's government and loyalty to one's traditional identity, which may be shaped by national, ethnic, racial, religious, tribal, familial, linguistic, cultural, or some combination of forces.

These unification efforts often fail. Virtually every one of the 192 sovereign states has significant minorities that either currently or potentially demand independence or merger with a similar group in a neighboring country. Nationalism can spark a war for independence within a state (separatism), or a war by one state to "liberate" those of the same nationality in a neighboring state (irredentism).

Nationalism has destroyed all the great modern empires. The most prominent nationalist struggles of the early modern era were that of the Dutch against Spain in the late sixteenth century, America's against Britain in the late eighteenth century, and Spanish Latin America's against Spain in the early nineteenth. A wave of over a hundred "people's liberation" broke up the British, French, Dutch, American, Portuguese, and Japanese empires from 1945 through the 1970s. Symbolically, the third wave began on November 9, 1989, with the fall of the Berlin Wall, and led to the liberation of Eastern Europe and the collapse of the Soviet Union. Nationalism continues violently to tear apart dozens of countries around the world.

The reason for those conflicts is simple enough. The boundaries of modern nation-states were often drawn with complete disregard for the identities of the inhabitants. Frontiers grouped different nationalities, who were often enemies, and separated similar nationalities. Africa is the most glaring example. At the Berlin Conference of 1885, the imperial powers satisfied their conflicting claims to different regions simply by drawing lines across a map of the continent. Today Somalia is the only country with no significant minority national group, although that unity did not prevent it from plunging into civil war in the early 1990s.

The number of potential international conflicts is partly related to the number of nation-states, especially if newly independent countries carry deep animosities toward the neighbors that formerly suppressed them. If so, in the future we could return full circle to an era of international wars.

"Irredentism" has been a major cause of war. In 1938, Hitler seized Czechoslovakia's Sudetenland province to "liberate" the 3 million ethnic Germans living there. The North Vietnamese fought the United States and South Vietnam (1954–1975) as much to reunify the country as to impose communism on the South. However, economic as well as nationalist motivations can prompt a state's irredentist claims for neighboring territory. Hitler not only rejoined the Sudeten Germans to the fatherland, but also took over two-thirds of Czechoslovakia's industrial capacity. Iraq's attempts to swallow Kuwait in August 1990 had as much to do with taking the latter's oil as joining two separate Arab populations.

The global system upholds two conflicting values—"self-determination" and stability. The world becomes increasingly unstable as more people with national identities demand autonomy or outright independence. Those demands often result in war. Thus will civil rather than international wars increasingly make the headlines.

Wars for National Cohesion

Conflict is inseparable from life. When two or more groups spar over an issue, the solidarity of each is often enhanced. Conflict between groups can be a safety valve that releases hostility caused by conflict within groups.

Sometimes a government may deliberately square off with another just to divert the population's attention from internal problems and divisions. That strategy of provoking the "rally around the flag" effect is known as "wag the dog" after a film of the same name. According to the "scapegoat theory," war with others "is sometimes the last chance for a state ridden with inner antagonisms to overcome these antagonisms, or else break up indefinitely."[25] For example, in 1861, Secretary of State William Seward encouraged President Lincoln to pick a fight with Britain to reunite the Southern states with the United States and prevent the Civil War. The decision by Argentina's government to invade the British Falkland Islands in 1982 may have been largely an attempt to divert the public's attention from economic stagnation and political oppression at home. One motive for President Saddam Hussein's 1990 decision to send his army into Kuwait may have been to sublimate the Sunni-Shiite and Arab-Kurdish strife within Iraq.

How common is this cause of war? Different studies reach different conclusions over how often "scapegoating" occurs. One study revealed that over half of all international wars between 1823 and 1937 were preceded by serious conflicts in one or more of the states.[26] Most other studies, however, found little correlation.[27] The resort to war to heal internal divisions relative to the number of countries torn by internal conflict is minute.

The cement holding healthy societies together is shared values, traditions, behavior, and ambitions, not fear of government repression or foreign attack. From a practical point of view, the scapegoat strategy is risky. If a nation is already divided, a government's decision to go to war would most likely weaken its cohesion and ability to fight. While a victory may help repress divisions, a defeat will only exacerbate them.

War aside, do governments use foreign conflicts to heal internal conflicts and strengthen their own legitimacy? Sometimes. For example, some American presidents have been known to whip up an international crisis or terrorist threat in an election year, particularly when the economy or their party's popularity is ailing, to distract people from their problems and rally them around both the flag and their leader.

Wars from National Incohesion: Civil and Uncivil Wars

More commonly, civil or internal wars lead to international wars. "Civil wars" occur when one group—class, religious, ethnic, regional, and so on—either tries to takeover or escape from a brutal, corrupt, exploitive government dominated by another group. The rebellion is usually inspired, organized, and justified by an ideology, be it religious, nationalism, communism, democracy, or some other. Rebel and government leaders struggle to win popular support ("hearts and minds") by presenting themselves as saviors and the other as vicious enemies. "Uncivil wars" are violent struggles by groups simply to rob, rape, and murder anyone in their way, and carve out a criminal empire usually funded by smuggling illegal drugs like cocaine, heroin, or marijuana. Cambodia's Khmer Rouge used an extreme version of communism to justify genocide; most simply wield terror without comment as in Sierra Leone, Sudan, or Liberia. Civil wars fall generally into two types, "state control wars" when rebels try to capture the government and "state formation wars" when they seek independence. Uncivil wars are "failed state wars" whereby criminal groups take advantage of the inability of a government to govern. Regardless of what type afflicts it, a state torn by war offers an opportunity for other ambitious states and/or groups to intervene on one side to advance their interests.

Civil wars are the most common armed conflicts. More than 85 percent of all wars between 1945 and 1976 were civil wars. Most of these were extremely destructive—ten of the twelve bloodiest wars of the past 200 years were civil wars. Of those relatively few international wars since 1945, most occurred when a great power got involved in a civil war. There were 161 civil wars with over 1,000 deaths between 1816 and 1988. Civil wars mostly occur in poor countries. In 2010, there were no international wars but internal wars raged in twenty-seven countries.[28]

Civil wars can become international wars when the government and/or antigovernment forces receive outside help. That was almost inevitable during the Cold War as Washington, Moscow, and sometimes other governments lined up behind the side that seemed to best represent their interests—even if that interest involved simply bleeding the material, human, and emotional resources of the enemy side. For example, during the 1980s, Washington sponsored guerrilla forces against pro-Soviet regimes in Afghanistan, Ethiopia, Angola, and Nicaragua. Ideally, Washington wanted the pro-Soviet regimes toppled and Soviet advisors and troops removed. But usually the United States was content with forcing the Soviets to commit even more resources to maintain their position. Over the years, Moscow played the same game against American efforts to supports of governments in Vietnam, El Salvador, and Israel, to name a few. Sometimes a power will justify intervening in another state to prevent its subversion by the other side, as Moscow did when it crushed democratic forces in East Germany (1953), Hungary (1956), Czechoslovakia (1968), and Poland (1980), and Washington did when it toppled unfriendly governments in Iran (1953), Guatemala (1954), the Dominican Republic (1965), and Grenada (1983).

In the post–Cold War era, the United Nations has intervened in ever more civil or uncivil wars. In 2010, there were peacekeeping missions in fourteen countries torn apart by violence. Sometimes a peacekeeping mission that simply tries to maintain a truce between warring sides becomes a peace enforcement mission that uses force to restore order, as happened unsuccessfully in Somalia in 1993 and successfully in Kosovo in 1999.

Liberal Democracy, Illiberal Democracy, and War

In his 1795 essay "Perpetual Peace," Immanuel Kant argued that humans are naturally inclined to peace; democracies are more peaceful than dictatorships; and the number of wars will diminish as more countries become democratic.[29]

It is true that genuine liberal democratic countries have never warred against each other.[30] The implications of this are profound. Jack Levy states that the "absence of war between democracies comes as close as anything we have to an empirical law in international relations."[31] It follows that as more states become democratic, the possibility of war decreases accordingly, and if all states were genuine democracies, war would cease to plague humankind, thus fulfilling Kant's dream of a "perpetual peace."

Encouraging as the propensity for peace among democratic states is, Levy points out that "democratic states have been involved proportionately in as many wars as non-democratic states."[32] For example, of the fifty wars studied between 1816 through 1865, liberal democratic states were involved in nineteen and started eleven.[33] Another study concluded that democracies are actually less militaristic than authoritarian states.[34] According to Michael Doyle, the reason for continued armed conflict between democratic and authoritarian states is that "the very constitutional restraint, shared commercial interests, and international respect for individual rights that promote peace among liberal societies can exacerbate conflicts in relations between liberal and non-liberal societies."[35] However, as increasing numbers of states become democratic, we can expect to see the numbers of international wars decline.

And then there are the so-called illiberal or crony democracies that tend to be as aggressive as dictatorships and more so than liberal democracies.[36] Such states in transition from dictatorship to democracy may have elections but lack other essential institutions like a justice system and free press that investigates, exposes, and punishes corruption or the abuse of public power for private gain by the political and business elite. Democratic institutions are not enough for democracy; they will wither and die unless they are rooted in a liberal culture that promotes civil rights, liberties, duties, majority rule, minority rights, and equal protection before the law.

So why are illiberal or crony democracies more inclined to war? What often happens is that a majority votes for a charismatic leader and populist party that promises much more than they can deliver and uses power not to promote national interests but only to benefit themselves. The subsequent corruption empties the treasury and devastates the economy. Ever more people are enraged and the appeal of any opposition parties or leaders swells. The government may declare a state of siege or martial law that suspends free expression and institutions. Then, to distract the populace, the government may square off with a neighboring country over some real or contrive conflict.

War—civil and/or international—often results.

Development and War

Many studies have shown that there is a close correlation between wealth and violence. Before 1945, richer countries had more resources to go to war so they did so more often than poorer countries. Since then, with access to modern weapons often supplied by rich countries, poor countries have tended to war more than the rich. Rich countries in which most people enjoy middle-class lifestyles do not war with one other.[37]

The lack of wars between rich countries represents a major change in international relations. Traditionally, the richer a country the more it warred against rich and poor countries alike. Throughout the modern era, Europe was the world's richest and most war-torn region, accounting for 65 percent of all wars in the sixteenth and seventeenth centuries, and 59 percent of all wars between 1816 and 1945, or one every one and a half years. Since 1945, Europe has been one of the more peaceful regions on earth, with only two wars occurring outside the communist bloc nations, both involving NATO and Serbia.[38]

The wealthier a country, the more it can financially afford to go to war. Yet offsetting that are the greater psychological and political constraints for doing so. Today there are over 800 million people in the Organization for Economic Cooperation and Development (OECD), often known as the rich country's club. The OECD's thirty members. Shared values and needs account for peace among those countries. Most of the OECD states are liberal democracies and all are ever more interdependent. The benefits of international trade and investment far exceed any costs. Peace between these states is not simply war's absence but the complete lack of a perception among the leaders and public in each country that war could go on between them, and thus no preparations to do so. Thomas Friedman explains that phenomena with his "golden arches theory" of international relations. According to Friedman, a country symbolically reaches middle-class status when the first McDonalds opens. Although countries with McDonalds did go to war in 1999 when NATO fought Serbia, Friedman insists on the general truth of his theory.[39]

During the Cold War, the economic development and interdependence among the OECD countries was accelerated by the challenge posed by their common enemy, the Soviet Union. These countries could contain the Soviet threat by creating a grand economic and military alliance. Yet none of the OECD countries ever fought the Soviet Union.

The world's wealthiest states have no desire to war against each other because the costs would be too great. Yet that does not inhibit them from at times warring against poorer countries when vital interests are at stake.

Economic Interest Groups and War

Interest groups shape national interests; the more powerful an interest group, the greater its ability to substitute its interest for the nation's. Some argue that "military industrial complexes" are the most powerful interest groups in the United States, Russia, China, and other great powers. The military along with the businesses and politicians, which benefit from and support it, have a vested interest in ever more military spending and war itself. That argument was perhaps best expressed by George Bernard Shaw's play, *Arms and the Man*, and Bob Dylan's song, "The Masters of War." Military industrial complexes constantly try to justify and expand their existence by exaggerating or outright fabricating threats. Throughout the Cold War, the military industrial complexes of the United States and Soviet Union fought any attempts to limit arms races, military intervention overseas, or the peaceful resolution of conflicts.

Nonetheless there is little evidence for the military industrial complex theory of war. Most wars have not been fought primarily for economic gain.[40] War has rarely conferred direct economic benefits upon the participants. In any national economy, war benefits only a few industries while hurting most. Thus, most business leaders prefer peace to war. Often many profits from war go to those in neutral counties who sell to both sides.

Military industrial complexes may not be as omnipotent as their critics maintain. Other factors are much more important in explaining the reasons why countries with large military industrial complexes go to war.

War and the International System

The Power Balance, Imbalance, and War

Many theorists maintain that wars explode not from the quirks of humans or the states in which they live, but from the configurations of power in the international system itself. Few concepts of international relations are cited more frequently and interpreted more widely than "the balance of power."

Ernst Haas found seven distinct ways of using the term "balance of power."[41] Three involve how power was distributed and the subsequent relations among states: (1) any distribution of power; (2) an equilibrium of power; and (3) hegemony of power. Two concentrate on the notion of an equilibrium of power having two very different impacts on international relations and war: (4) stability and peace; and (5) instability and war. The two final uses of the term claim that either (6) states will always attempt to strengthen their national security by countering the power of others and thus try to maintain an equilibrium in the international system (universal law of history), or (7) whether or not they do, they should (prescriptive).

The classic balance of power system operates on the rather simple notion that "the enemy of my enemy is my friend." Few concepts of international relations have been as thoroughly explored. In the premodern era, Thucydides, Kautilya, Sun Tzu, Polybius, and Machiavelli all analyzed the concept in depth, and urged their governments to apply it to policy. The "classic" system requires a half dozen or more states relatively similar in population and territory size; limited geographical area; a shared political culture among national elites; no fixed alliances; the tendency for most states to combine to offset any aggressor state or coalitions of states; the absence of ideology as a motivation for expansion; the preservation of defeated states in the system; the recognition that it is in all their interests to maintain the system; relatively slow means of transportation and communication that inhibit rapid mobilization and attacks; relatively limited means of mass destruction; the absence of international organizations that inhibit the actions of states; and a consensus among the governments of each state as to the system's rules. Power is not balanced for all states. The great powers ally, fight with, and preside over more numerous midsized and small states.

Historically, the classic balance of power existed only from 1648 to 1792. Other eras had only some of those characteristics. Nonetheless, analysts have tried to characterize each era's distribution of power as multipolar, bipolar, or unipolar. Analysts, however, differ over whether the distribution of power should be defined by states or alliances.

The debate between A.F.K. Organski and Hans Morgenthau exemplifies the difficulty in achieving a consensus over just what the balance of power means and how to apply it.[42] To Organski, the balance of power simply means the constantly shifting distribution of power among individual states (Multipolarity), while Morgenthau maintains that the balance of power refers to shifting alliances of states rather than power among individual states (bipolarity).

One way to finesse this problem is to distinguish between polarity or the distribution of power among states, and polarization or the alliances among states. Thus the system can be bipolar in structure, but multipolar in the power distribution among states, a framework that can be applied to both world wars and the Cold War. While the post-1945 system remained bipolar in polarization, the system's polarity became increasingly multipolar. States usually ally against threats rather than power per se. For example, the United States continued to hold predominant power throughout the postwar era, but the West European states chose to ally themselves with Washington in NATO rather than offset America's power by allying with Moscow because the Soviet Union rather than United States posed the genuine threat. However, since the Cold War's end NATO continues not just to exist but to expand even without a clearly defined threat against its members.

Is a balanced or imbalanced power system more susceptible to war? Some argue that power imbalances rather than balances make war more likely. When one state has more power than others, it is more likely to go to war because it has a greater chance of winning.[43] Others argue that the more egalitarian the power distribution the

more states feel they could win a war against their rivals, and thus war
is more likely

> an even distribution of political, economic, and military capabilities
> between contending groups of states is likely to increase the prob-
> ability of war; peace is preserved best when there is an imbalance of
> national capabilities between disadvantaged and advantaged nations;
> the aggressor will come from a group of dissatisfied strong countries;
> and it is the weaker, rather than the stronger, power that is most likely
> to be the aggressor.[44]

Both arguments are partially right. A study of all wars between
1820 and 1965 found that there was no correlation between the power
balance and war.[45] When power was distributed relatively equally war
was likely 50 percent of the time, and when it was unequally distributed it was likely 46 percent of the time. There was a difference
between nineteenth-century wars, which were more likely when there
was an imbalance of power, and twentieth-century wars which were
more likely when there was a relative power balance. "Wars of rivalry"
are more likely when there is a power balance; "wars of opportunity"
when there is a power imbalance.[46]

Those who maintain that a power balance increases the chance for
war differ over whether a bipolar or multipolar system is more unstable.
There are those who argue that in a bipolar world each side focuses its
attention on the other and counters every move the other makes. The
increased tension and arms races inevitably make war more likely. In
contrast, the proliferation of issues and actors in a multipolar system
tends to defuse tensions and thus the chance of war. Destabilizing
arms races are more likely in a bipolar than multipolar system. Others
argue just the opposite, and point out that the multipolar system of
the early twentieth century led to two world wars while the post-1945
bipolar system remained at peace. Multipolar systems involving three
powers, they argue, are much more unstable than a bipolar system
because of the tendency for two to ally against the third.[47]

Who is right? One study of all wars of the past five centuries found
that wars were less likely in a multipolar system but far more bloody
because they involved far more people.[48] Though no general wars
like the Napoleonic era or the twentieth century's two world wars
occurred during bipolar periods, wars were more likely.

Whether the global system is predominately multipolar or bipolar,
war is more likely when that power distribution is changing. Power is
more than possessing troops, tanks, and missiles. The size and quality of the two sides' respective populations, industries, geographies,

natural resources, technological levels, and, most importantly, political wills and national cohesions, all of which shape the power calculus. Karl Deutsch argues that whenever

> there is a major change at any level—culture and values, political and social institutions, laws, or technology—the old adjustment and control mechanisms become strained and may break down. Any major psychological and cultural, or major social and political, or legal, or technological change in the world thus increases the risk of war, unless it is balanced by compensatory political, legal, cultural, and psychological adjustments.[49]

Many theorists believe the most important shifts in regional or global power balances are technological and economic. Organski and Kugler maintain that "war is caused by differences in the rates of growth among the great powers and...the differences in rates between the dominant nation and the challenger that permit the latter to overtake the former."[50] One side's introduction of a new weapon system can dramatically shift the power balance. For example, the English won the Hundred Years War as much with the long bow as anything else. While larger states are more aggressive than smaller states, the distribution of military technology can supply smaller or poorer states with an ability to wage war that they formerly did not have.[51]

Hegemonic Stability, Long-Cycles, and War

Some see international relations shaped not by a balance of power but by a hierarchy of power. The great powers struggle for power, and eventually one emerges from a war to become a hegemon or dominant state in the system, until sooner or later that power declines and is surpassed by another. The concept of the rise and fall of hegemons, or "hegemonic stability theory" as it is known, is closely linked to the "long cycle theory" of history.[52]

Of all the distributions of power throughout history, unipolar systems such as those of Roman, British, and American hegemony have been relatively more peaceful because other states lacked enough power to challenge the prevailing system. An era of hegemony, however, is hardly free of violence. During America's post–Cold War global hegemony, the United States warred twice against Iraq, against Yugoslavia, and against Al Qaeda and its affiliated terrorist groups in

Afghanistan and elsewhere, while wielding military power in attempts to change the political systems of Somalia and Haiti.

Historically, hegemony has been a short-lived one as other states usually rise up to challenge the hegemon. Shifts in economic and technological power, which contribute to wars, are seen to reoccur in long cycles, generally of a century. The hegemonic wars of the modern era would include "(1) the Italian Wars (1494–1517), from which Portugal emerged as the world power; (2) the War of Dutch Independence (1585–1609), leading to the rise of the Netherlands as a world power; (3) the Wars of Louis XIV (1689–1715), which gave way to British leadership; (4) the French Revolutionary and Napoleonic Wars (1792–1815), which renewed the world-power role of Britain; and (5) the two World Wars of this century (1914–39), which marked the transition of the United States to world power."[53]

Joshua Goldstein nicely summarized the rise and fall of hegemons and other great powers: "Countries rebuilding from war incorporate a new generation of technology, eventually allowing competition with the hegemonic country. For these reasons, each period of hegemony gradually erodes. Recurring wars, on several long wave upswings, eventually culminate in a new hegemonic war, bringing another restructuring of the core and a new period of hegemony."[54]

Most studies, however, do not find a war cycle for nations; Jack Levy's findings are especially critical of the concept.[55] Even if these long cycles ever existed, hegemonic wars are increasingly unlikely as the world becomes ever more interdependent.

Arms Races, Alliances, and War

In an anarchical global system, states must rely on themselves for their own security. "If you want peace, prepare for war" has been the guide for statesmen throughout history. The power balance or peace through strength theory, however, can lead to arms races that destabilize international relations and make war more rather than less likely. Arms races occur when states become trapped in a "security dilemma."[56] One state perceives a foreign military threat so it builds up its forces. In seemingly alleviating its own security problem it simultaneously threatens the security of the other state, which responds by building up its own forces. The first state then reacts by further enlarging its forces, and the arms race spirals indefinitely. Arms races are easy to begin, very difficult to end, and often end in war.

Often there may be no hostile intent in an arms race, but each state becomes a prisoner of its own fear and distrust for the other and the possibly dire results of not keeping up. Each side sees only the other's offensive capabilities and not its defensive intentions. Thus the race continues. The concept of the "prisoner's dilemma" has been applied to this situation.[57]

Arms races occur both because of international rivalries and domestic politics. Which is more important? Choucri and North argue that

> The primary importance of domestic factors...does not preclude the reality of arms competition. Two countries whose military establishments are expanding largely for domestic reasons...almost certainly will become acutely aware of each other's spending. Thereafter, although spending may continue to be powerfully affected by domestic factors, deliberate military spending may be over specific military features and may be a very small portion of total military spending.[58]

Do arms races tend to end in war? Scholars exploring the question have reached different conclusions.[59] One study of great power arms races since 1815 found that most have ended in war.[60] Another study that examined thirteen arms races in the nineteenth and twentieth centuries concluded that only five ended in war.[61] A more pervasive study of arms races between 1816 and 1980 cited only 20 percent were followed by war.[62] Finally, there was the study that uncovered no example of an arms race being the primary cause of any war.[63]

Who are we to believe? Arms races themselves may be difficult to define. Just because rival states annually increase their military budgets does not necessarily mean they are engaged in an arms race. Domestic politics and military industrial complexes may be more important in determining the amount and priorities of a nation's military budget than the international power balance. States may build up their arms yet not feel they are "racing" against others, and thus tensions remain low. The study that "found" that most arms races ended in war only analyzed those in which the participants increased their spending in direct response to that of their rivals. Clearly some arms races do lead to war while others are substitutes for war.[64]

Arms races are symptoms rather than causes of war. Genuine arms races do not occur unless those countries already have deep conflicts. Arms races exacerbate existing conflicts; they do not create them. While the mere possession of weapons is not enough to start a war, the more powerful a government's military forces, the more inclined it might be to use those weapons in a conflict.

A state's military power is less important than what it intends to do with those forces. States with good relations do not engage in arms races. As Hans Morgenthau put it, "Men do not fight because they have arms. They have arms because they deem it necessary to fight."[65]

Regardless of whether they end in war or not, arms races consume enormous amounts of human, scientific, industrial, financial, and political resources that could be invested more profitably elsewhere. If a war does occur, it will probably be more destructive than if an arms race never preceded it. Although most people would agree that "guns don't kill, people do," the proliferation of guns certainly increases tensions that may result in war. It also makes war more likely since in a crisis, leaders might feel more confident backing their position with force.

Alliances, like arms races, can exacerbate conflicts and make war more likely. Nations obviously can augment their power by allying with other states. Alliances are formed when its members anticipate the strong possibility of war. Alliances can be destabilizing because

> First alliances look menacing; hence it is likely that they will cause others to scramble for allies of their own, and therein raise tensions to a new, more dangerous level. Second, alliances are entangling; they can drag members into conflicts which do not affect their vital interests; Finally, alliances are sanguineous; their very existence means that even if a nation's armies are beaten and its leaders can see that resources are inadequate to sustain further combat, it would be encouraged to continue fighting by the hope of aid from its allies. In sum, whereas some theorists and statesmen advance the proposition that alliances sustain peace, others echo Sir John Frederick Maurice's lament that "if you prepare thoroughly for war you will get it."[66]

Do allies make war more or less likely? Alliances seem no more likely to cause a war than arms races. A study of 256 international conflicts between 1815 and 1965 concluded that wars were just as common whether or not an alliance was involved, although it did find that being in an alliance made smaller powers more likely to go to war.[67] Minor powers with great power allies went to war in 42 percent of conflicts; without such allies they went to war only 17 percent of the time. An even more comprehensive study of the past five centuries reached the same general conclusions.[68]

One study concluded that alliances decreased the chance for war throughout the nineteenth century, increased it in the twentieth century up through 1945, and decreased it thereafter.[69] Another study, which spanned from 1495 to 1975, found that most alliances led to war within five years of their formation, except between 1815 and 1914 when no wars followed within five years of an alliance's formation.[70] Alliances, like increased arms, may not be a war's underlying cause but aggravate existing tensions and thus make war more likely. In both studies, the most important effect was whether or not the alliance stabilized relations.

Interdependence, Security Communities, and War

The reasons why the world's wealthiest states do not war against each other may have less to do with their wealth than the interdependence among them. The members of the European Union, North American Free Trade Association (NAFTA), and OECD have created what Karl Deutsch would call a "security community" or

> a group of people which has become "integrated." By integration we mean the attainment, within a territory, of a "sense of community" and of institutions and practices strong enough and widespread enough to assure...dependable expectations of "peaceful change" among its population. By sense of community we mean a belief...that common social problems must and can be resolved by processes of "peaceful change."[71]

That is not to say that there are no conflicts among the twenty-seven European Union, three NAFTA, and thirty OECD countries. Geoeconomic disputes are rife, yet are handled diplomatically with no thought of using military force.

Although security communities are most common between ideological allies, they can also exist between countries that are ideological rivals. A security community evolved between the United States and Soviet Union after 1945 as the crises, saber-rattling, and brinksmanship of the 1950s were eventually transformed into the detente and restraint of the 1970s and 1980s. The superpowers continued to compete across the global geopolitical chessboard, but avoided any direct confrontation after the 1962 Cuban missile crisis. They bolstered this "crisis-avoidance" understanding with more than a dozen conventional and nuclear arms control treaties. With the collapse of the Soviet Union's communist regime and empire, Russia and the other newly independent countries are being slowly drawn into the interdependent global economy, a trend that will only strengthen the prevailing peace.[72]

Mutually Assured Destruction (MAD) was the basis of the American-Soviet security community. Gilpin writes that

> it was not until after 1945 that the threat of an all out military conflict (including the use of nuclear and thermonuclear bombs) became catastrophic so that such wars as did occur took on a more limited character. The risks of trying to take new territory through military invasion mounted while the alternative of development through rational industrial and trade policies heralded new rewards for a peaceful strategy. This shift...has largely escaped notice in the study of international politics.[73]

The greater the world's economic, nuclear, and environmental interdependence, the lower the chance for war. According to Rosecrance,

> a new "=trading world" of international relations offers the possibility of escaping such a vicious cycle [war] and finding new patterns of cooperation among nation-states...the benefit of trade and cooperation today greatly exceeds that of military competition and territorial aggrandizement. States, as Japan has shown, can do better through a strategy of economic development based on trade than they are likely to do through military interventions in the affairs of other states...the new world that is unfolding contrasts very sharply with comparable periods of major historical transition. Unlike those earlier periods, no major new military threat is likely to replace the old one anytime soon.[74]

International Law and War

International law outlaws aggressive war. While some may scoff at the effectiveness of international law in deterring war, others argue that "statesmen nearly always perceive themselves as constrained by international principles and rules that prescribe and proscribe behavior," and that these "international norms are more important than countervailing power in constraining states."[75]

How effective has international law been in deterring war? It is difficult to say with certainty. One sign of its increasing importance is the fact that most governments will rigorously claim that they are following it even as they are accused of breaking it.

Environmental Catastrophes and War

No matter how much modernity appears to seal off humanity from nature, they are inseparable. If humans destroy nature, they will destroy themselves. An array of interrelated environmental catastrophes—the population explosion, global warming, the ozone layer depletion, deforestation, desertification, and biocide—threaten to do just that. That could lead to ever more violence within and among nations as people compete ever fiercely for diminishing resources like water and land that ultimately sustain human life.

The most dire predictions of the horrendous impact of those catastrophes on humanity does not come from an environmental organization. The U.S. Defense Department issued a report in 2004 that foresaw global warming unleashing ever worsening calamities in the decades ahead including cities flooded by rising sea levels, megadroughts, hundreds of millions of environmental refugees, pestilence, economic collapse, and war, all of which threaten not just America's national security but its very survival.[76]

The report recommended that the United States lead an international effort to combat global warming and related environmental crises. That "inconvenient truth" exposed as a myth those who insist that global warming was either a myth or was not a serious problem and thus nothing should be done about it. Because that science-based analysis conflicted with its ideological assertions, the administration of George W. Bush tried to bury the report by stamping it top secret. We know about it only because a courageous whistleblower leaked a copy to the press.

What is clear is that the United States and other industrial nations have identified those catastrophes, but have failed to take the systematic and decisive measures that might mitigate their potential to unleash ever more violence around the world.

CONSEQUENCES

Although each war has its own unique set of causes, we can make some general observations. The behavior of states is shaped by the international system of which they are a part. In a global system with no government, every state ultimately must fend for itself. At any given time in history, some countries are largely satisfied with the international status quo, while others wish to change it, sometimes by violent means. Wars occur because governments and peoples perceive them as being useful for resolving conflicts. "War," as Karl von Clausewitz famously pointed out, "is simply the continuation of politics by other means."

Yet there are signs that war is becoming an increasingly unimportant part of international relations as interdependence thickens and the costs of war soar while its benefits plummet. Despite that favorable trend, it is unlikely that war will ever entirely disappear. Though international wars have diminished, civil wars continue to tear apart some states. People will continue to kill one other as long as they perceive a need to do so.

CHAPTER 3

Warfare in the Twenty-First Century

The adversaries of the world are not in conflict because they are armed. They are armed because they are in conflict and have not yet learned peaceful ways to resolve their conflicting national interests.

Richard Nixon

When the enemy advances, we retreat; when the enemy halts, we harass; when the enemy seeks to avoid battle, we attack; when the enemy retreats, we pursue.

Sun Tzu

We are marrying a first world force with a fourth world army.

Colin Powell

Every gun that is made, every warship launched, every rocket fired signifies, in the final sense, a theft from those who hunger and are not fed and those who are cold and are not clothed.

Dwight D. Eisenhower

This is a game of wits and wills. You've got to be adapting constantly to survive.

General Peter Schoolmaker

WAR AND INTERNATIONAL RELATIONS

War has traditionally been the engine of history, bearing with it the direct or indirect fate of everyone on earth. War can redraw maps, topple, or bolster regimes; redistribute, destroy, and create wealth; enslave or liberate nations; and inspire in its participants the noblest or vilest deeds. War or the threat of war has been the most power-ful force shaping international relations. Prussian King Frederick the Great captured that reality when he proclaimed: "Diplomacy without armaments is like music without instruments."[1]

War, many argue, is natural and inevitable. As Hans Morgenthau put it,

> Men do not fight because they have arms. They have arms because they deem it necessary to fight. Take away their arms and they will fight each other with their bare fists...The elimination of certain types of weapons altogether would have a bearing upon the technology of warfare...It is hard to see how it could influence the frequency of war.[2]

Thus if you want peace you must prepare for war. Others argue that if you prepare for war you will probably get it.

Wars can be fought between sovereign states (interstate), between sovereign states and a nonsovereign people struggling for independence (imperial or colonial), between groups within a sovereign state (intrastate, civil, or uncivil), and between a state or states and a transnational group or groups (transnational).

But are all armed conflicts wars? War, like so much else in life, is in the mind of the beholder. The Correlates of War (COW) project at the University of Michigan, which has been studying war since 1963, uses the arbitrary threshold of 1,000 or more combat deaths to designate a war. By that standard there were 79 international and 281 internal wars between 1816 and 1990.[3] But that rules out hundreds of other violent conflicts, including the American invasions of Grenada in 1983 and Panama in 1991; those Grenadians and Panamanians caught in the crossfire might beg to differ with that scholarly definition. A broader definition of war obviously yields different results. By defining international war as any time two or more states use armed forces violently along or beyond their borders, 269 wars involving 591 states broke out between 1945 and 1988 alone, of which the great powers started one of four.[4]

War is as old as history and undoubtedly as old as humankind. Throughout the 5,500 years of recorded history, the broader definition of war finds over 14,500; wars have occurred an average 94 of every 100 years. During the industrial era, wars steadily diminished as a proportion of the states in the system: 1816–1848, 33 wars and 28 states; 1849–1881, 43 wars and 39 states; 1882–1914, 38 wars and 40 states; 1915–1944, 38 wars and 40 states; and 1945–1988, 43 wars and 117 states. In all, only 20 of those 172 years were peaceful! Traditionally aggression paid. Between 1495 and 1985, the attackers won 58.1 percent of the time, or 51.5 percent between 1495 and 1799, and 69.2 percent between 1800 and 1985. However, that upward trend was reversed in the 1980s when only 18 percent of aggressors won their wars.[5]

During the modern era, wars between the great powers diminished, but when they erupted, they tended to include more troops, countries, people, casualties, destruction, and territory. Seventy-five percent of all great power wars between 1495 and 1980 occurred before 1735. Peace through strength may not be a foolproof means of security. More than half or five of the nine wars engulfing great powers between 1815 and 1965 involved militarily weaker countries attacking stronger ones that were building up their military power. Nationalism and ever more efficient means of enlisting, training, supplying, and sending men to the front consumed ever more of a country's population. Before 1800, only about 3 of 1,000 people (0.3 percent) in a country directly participated in its wars. During World War I, one of seven draft-age men (14 percent) was in uniform. Increasingly costly in lives and destruction, the wars of the twentieth century alone killed over 100 million and destroyed trillions of dollars of property.[6]

Stunning changes have happened since 1945 in where and how wars are fought and who fights them. With twenty-nine major wars between 1600 and 1945, Europe was the world's most violent region. Then the guns fell silent on the continent until the 1990s when civil and international wars broke out as Yugoslavia broke up into six countries. Before 1945, the advanced industrial countries were the most belligerent both against themselves and less developed states; since then war has been confined mostly to the Third World, especially the Middle East, Africa, and Asia. Until 1945, 80 percent of wars were conventional international wars; since then 80 percent have been unconventional or guerrilla intrastate wars.[7]

Those trends march into the twenty-first century. What explains those changes? For most advanced industrial nations, as economic interdependence deepens, national and international interests increasingly mesh, and war's potential financial and moral costs rise to unacceptable levels. War, thus, has become inconceivable between prosperous, democratic industrial countries. When an industrial country does fight a war, it is almost inevitably against a poorer country.

Only four of the thirty members of the Organization for Economic Cooperation and Development (OECD), the rich countries' club, have warred since 1945. The United States has fought major wars against North Korea and its ally China, North Vietnam, and Afghanistan, two wars against Iraq, and minor wars against Grenada and Panama. The British fought Egypt, Argentina, and twice Iraq, and waged a colonial war in Malaya. The French also fought Egypt and colonial wars in Vietnam and Algeria. South Korea fought North Korea. While nearly all the other OECD members have sat on the sidelines, a few have contributed token numbers of troops to those wars. Beyond the OECD, the Soviet Union fought only one major war in Afghanistan and minor wars with Hungary and China, while China fought a major war against the United States in Korea along with shorter border wars against India and Vietnam.

Even those countries that avoid direct involvement in war cannot escape its consequences. Every country on earth devotes some measure of money and people to self-defense, although how much varies enormously. Today one of every twenty dollars spent worldwide feeds the military. With globalization, the fallout from a distant war may not be obvious but nonetheless can ripple through financial markets, UN Security Council debates, refugee camps, aid organizations, defense budgets, oil prices, and the minds of countless television viewers or newspaper readers far beyond the actual battlefields.

WAR, TECHNOLOGY, AND STRATEGY

Over time people have devised more effective means of destroying lives, property, governments, societies, and environments. For the first several thousand years of history, bows and catapults were the most powerful delivery systems. During the fourteenth century in Europe, gunpowder was first used for crude muskets and cannon, and improved versions of these weapons systems shaped warfare for the next 500 years. Then, during World War I, the introduction of warplanes and dirigibles allowed the first massive air bombardments. The experiments in air warfare during World War I, which killed thousands of people, led to massive carpet- and fire-bombing of cities during War World II, which killed millions of people. The first missiles were developed and used by the Germans during World War II when their V-2 rockets could deliver a one-ton bomb more than a hundred miles away. These first rockets were inaccurate, however, and were mostly targeted on large cities.

World War II ended with the most horrendous weapon of all when the United States dropped atomic bombs on Hiroshima and Nagasaki, forcing Japan's government to abruptly and unconditionally surrender. America's nuclear monopoly was fleeting. The Soviets tested their first nuclear bomb in 1949; since then seven more states have become nuclear powers. Nuclear bombs were delivered by planes until the late 1950s when Submarine Launched Ballistic Missiles (SLBMs) and International Continental Ballistic Missiles (ICBMs) cut the time to target from hours to minutes.

Some of the more recent developments have been just as dazzling. Television viewers during the Persian Gulf War safely witnessed the performance of a vast array of high tech weapons, including sea-launched conventional cruise missiles that flew hundreds of miles and then precisely down the air shafts of bunkers they were programmed to hit. Conventional weapons are becoming increasingly powerful:

> a bomber can drop 50 or more bombs of 500–1,000 pounds each... a single cluster bomb detonates into several hundred bomblets. Fuel air explosives disperse fuel into the air and then detonate the fuel cloud. Both in lethality and in area covered, so-called conventional weapons today approach small nuclear weapons in destructive power.

They are also ever more accurate. During the 2003 Iraq War, the United States launched 750 cruise missiles and dropped 15,000 precision-guided and 7,500 unguided bombs; in all, the precision rate was 68 percent rate compared to only 9 percent in the previous war against Iraq.[8] Some of these new conventional weapons pack the destruction of small nuclear weapons without the radioactive fallout and thus might make them obsolete.

How wars are fought depends on what technologies are available. There was a time when men killed one another with nothing more sophisticated than sticks and stones. Imagine in ancient days the advantage won in combat by the people who invented the sling, the bow and arrow, the chariot, or the catapult, or first mounted a horse, melted ore together and pounded out a sword, fashioned a stirrup to a saddle, or raised a sail to a mast. Each invention revolutionized warfare and gave the innovators an advantage over their enemies.

Any advantage in tactics or strategy that one side has over another can be an example of "asymmetrical warfare." That edge can result from applying cutting-edge technologies to warfare or old technologies in new ways. A stunning example of asymmetrical warfare occurred on September 11, 2001, when nineteen terrorists using nothing more than box-cutters and penknives hijacked four airliners and turned those passenger jets packed with aviation fuel into flying bombs that destroyed the twin World Trade Center towers and part of the Pentagon.

A technological edge, of course, is fleeting. Inevitably, others master the new ways of killing. At times countries create but fail to capitalize on technologies that can change the nature of warfare and the distribution of power. China, for instance, first invented gunpowder, but it was Europeans who developed that technology into weapons so advanced their wielders could literally rule the world, at least for a while.

Unchallenged naval power is among the array of key pillars of American military hegemony. Starting in World War II, the United States inherited Britain's title as the world's greatest naval power and has held for over six decades since. All the world's navies combined could not equal the power of America's fleets and the personnel who man them. The backbone of American naval power are 16 aircraft carriers, each packed with a squadron of fighter-bombers, scores of cruise missiles, and 5,500 strong crews, and escorted by a dozen other warships. They enable the United States to project power in every sea and adjacent shores around the world. During World War II, aircraft carriers rendered obsolete cannon-studded battleships, whose various versions had ruled the waves for hundreds of years. What new technologies and strategies could eventually send aircraft carriers to the scrapyard? How would those new weapons affect international relations?

Of course, simply wielding cutting-edge weapons is not enough to win wars. Technology determines both strategy and tactics, or how to get to (and sometimes from) a battlefield and what to do when you get there. Some leaders are more skilled at creatively preparing for and waging war than others, and that is often the most crucial reason for victory. But war depends on much more than weapons, warriors, tactics, and leaders. Soldiers, sailors, and, more recently, aircrews must be fed, clothed, and sheltered. Traditionally, those peoples who raised more crops and livestock could feed more troops. Those who produced more leather, wool, metal, canvas, and lumber, and fashioned them into sandals, shields, wagons, and tents enjoyed a huge advantage over their enemies.

Revolutionary technological changes in production, communications, and transportation have greatly expanded war's destructiveness and reach. The industrial revolution began in the eighteenth century as inventers and entrepreneurs developed new technologies for making and moving masses of goods and services, including those vital for waging war. At that revolution's heart was mass production on a hitherto unimaginable scale run by machines driven first with such energy resources as water and coal, later by oil and natural gas, and more recently by uranium.

The application of steam power to machines that made things eventually was applied to machines that moved things. The result was railroads and steamships that cut journeys across vast continents or oceans from months to weeks. Automobiles were born from the refinement of oil into gasoline and the invention of the internal combustion engine. The harnessing of electricity allowed people to send messages first by telegraph and then telephone and finally radio. All those new ways of organizing, making, and sending things were applied to war. In rapid succession, inventors proudly unveiled the machine gun, submarine, airplane, tank, aircraft carrier, and, most ominously, atomic bomb, each of which revolutionized war's scale, strategy, and destructiveness.

The industrial revolution brought more than just new ways of killing. Mass nationalism, ideologies, communications, and transportation allow governments the ability to mobilize virtually everyone for war as a soldier, supplier, or supporter. Most countries have highly professional militaries that are prepared to fight on short notice.

Starting in the late twentieth century, inventors and entrepreneurs gave birth to the technologies and techniques of what is called the postindustrial age. A revolution in microelectronics allows us to process and send ever more knowledge ever more quickly via faxes, satellites, cell phones, and the Internet, all of which flow from computers. The power of computers is said to double every eighteen months. The first computer was made during World War II and was as big as a house. A computer today can fit in the palm of one's hand. Supercomputers can crunch billions of data in seconds.

The result is the latest revolution in warfare, a revolution so far mastered only by the United States. With the collapse of the Soviet empire and communism, the United States emerged during the 1990s as the world's sole superpower. Minicomputers and satellites have rendered once "dumb" weapons increasingly "smart," which allows war to become a deadly video game for ever more Americans in uniform. The strategy involves widening the "information gap," allowing American forces to be all-seeing and all-knowing while blinding their enemies. Electromagnetic pulses (EMPs), high power microwaves (HPMs), and computer viruses followed up by "smart" missiles and bombs destroy with pinpoint accuracy first the enemy's "command, control, communications, and intelligence" system (3CI), then its supply depots and transportation lines, and finally its troop concentrations. That "shock and awe" power and strategy allowed the United States to inflict devastating defeats on conventional enemy armies in Yugoslavia, Afghanistan, and Iraq with few or no battle casualties.

And that is only the revolution's beginning. The United States is developing cutting-edge technologies that could completely revolutionize its military and warfare, enabling America to leap so far ahead of its rivals that its hegemony will endure for generations. The technology now exists to have a pilotless air force. Once the huge expense of manned aircraft is eliminated, the air forces will cost a fraction of today's squadrons of F-16s, F-18s, and F-117s, and the newer F-22s and F-35s. A F-22 fighter bomber costs over $500 million; an unmanned drone $15 million! The most advanced drones, known as Reapers, are packed with scores of cameras tracking potential enemies and battlegrounds in different directions, along with a dozen Hellfire missiles. Advanced technology will revolutionize naval power as well. Aircraft carriers will become as obsolete as battleships as they are replaced by dozens of small, fast, semisubmerged, stealth "arsenal ships" packed with more firepower but manned with 50 rather than 5,500 sailors. An aircraft carrier costs over $5 billion; an arsenal ship $500 million! In space, microsatellites can destroy the enemy's satellite fleet and thus wipe out vital links in that country's communications and intelligence systems. Advanced technology can even revolutionize the ground war. Networks of satellites, unmanned combat aerial vehicles (UCAVs), cell phones, laptops, enemy-detecting sensors, killer-robots, and laser-guided weapons give small, elite bodies of troops unprecedented ability to know where enemy troops are, and then dash by air and ground through gaps in the lines to encircle and destroy them. Battles will be won with ever fewer combat troops or "boots on the ground," as ever leaner but more muscular Davids systematically hack apart blind blundering Goliaths.

Thus does the United States have the ability to revolutionize its military and economic power at a fraction of current personnel and costs. As the defense budget plummets, tens of billions of dollars could annually be invested much more productively elsewhere in the economy, pay down the skyrocketing national debt, and/or returned to taxpayers. American economic and military superpower could be unchallengeable for the foreseeable future.

That "revolution in military affairs" (RMA), however, is moving at a snail's pace. If the United States can do all that, why is it not doing so? The answer is politics. That military revolution that could vastly strengthen American national interests threatens the careers, profits, and prestige of all those in the military industrial complex, which includes the people in and out of uniform who directly or indirectly work in the defense bureaucracy and industries, along with the politicians who represent them, and the stockholders who profit from them. They have enormous power to block any changes that adversely affects them while getting American taxpayers to fund bases, weapons, and units of often dubious strategic worth. Will the United States be like China several centuries ago, inventing technologies that rivals revolutionize and thus convert themselves into superpowers?

Double-Edged Swords: Military Spending, Power, and Security

Military power can be a double-edged sword. Under some circumstances it may actually undermine rather than enhance a nation's security. When states become trapped in arms races that consume an ever greater amount of resources, war can become more rather than less likely, and thus render the state more rather than less vulnerable to destruction. And even when soldiers and weapons are never used, they become an enormous financial, human, economic, and technological drain on that country.

Since 1930, military spending has exceeded world population and economic growth. Richard Rosecrance dramatically reveals the ever-rising costs of defense: "in constant dollar terms, tanks went from less than $50,000 per unit in 1918 to more than $2,000,000 in 1980. Fighter planes that cost less than $100,000 in 1944 rose to at least $10,000,000 per copy forty years later." In 2008, global military spending was $1.47 trillion, of which America's $711 was 48 percent of the total or nearly half (see box below).[9]

Who's Side Would You Rather Join? A Giant among Dwarfs: America, Allies, Friends, and Foes

Add up the defense spending in each category. Do America and its allies face any significant threat from any or all of its potential foes? Of course, military spending can only give an impression of potential power. Much depends on whether that country's military has any ability to project destruction beyond its borders. Even more important is whether or not its leadership is committed to aggression. Capacity plus will equals power.

Country	Amount of Military Spending		WMD
	1999	2008	
United States	288.8	711.1	N
Leading Formal American Allies			
Japan	41.1	41.1	
Britain	34.6	55.4	N
France	29.5	54.0	N
Germany	24.7	37.8	
Italy	16.2	30.6	
South Korea	11.6	24.6	
Taiwan	10.7	7.7	
Brazil	10.3	16.2	
Turkey	8.9	11.6	
Australia	7.2	17.2	
Netherlands	7.0	9.9	
Israel	6.7	10.6	N
Canada	6.7	15.0	
Spain	6.0	14.4	
Greece	3.8	7.3	
Poland	3.2	6.2	
Friendly Nonaligned			
Russia*	55.0*	70.0	N
China*	37.5*	121.9	N
Saudi Arabia	18.4	29.5	
India	10.7	22.4	N
Pakistan	2.7	4.2	N
Vietnam	0.9	2.4	
Egypt	.2	4.3	
Kuwait	3.0	3.5	
Libya	1.3	0.5 (2005)	PS
Unfriendly			
Iran	5.7	6.3 (2003)	P
Syria	2.9	5.9 (2003)	
North Korea	1.3	5.5 (2002)	N
Cuba	0.8*	0.6 (2005)	

Sources: Center for Defense Information, 1999, 2008.

Notes: The amounts are in billions of dollars.

* denotes 1998 funding.

N—nuclear weapons

WMD—weapons of mass destruction

P—program to develop nuclear and possibly chemical and biological weapons

PS—program to develop WMD suspended

Selling arms is big business, but who gets what usually depends as much on political loyalty as on the ability to pay. Military budgets and arms exports tend to rise together. Until 1991 the Cold War was the most important reason. Washington and Moscow filled the arsenals of their immediate allies in NATO and the Warsaw Pact, respectively, and those of scores of more ephemeral potential and actual "allies" and "friends" throughout the Third World. When one superpower began to aid a side in a regional or national conflict, the other superpower would inevitably feel compelled to begin aiding the other side. The United States still targets many of its weapons sales to friendly countries in the Middle East in order to maintain the power balance against its foes. The other great powers—Britain, France, and China—also became big arms dealers during the Cold War and remain leading arms merchants.

While politics was the primary motive for these sales during the Cold War, profit has become the most important reason since then. Weapons exports are big business and, for poorer countries like Russia and China whose governments often own those industries, an excellent cash cow. Since the Soviet Union's breakup, Russia, Ukraine, Georgia, and other former "republics" have been selling off even their most advanced and secret weapons systems for hard currency. Many of those sales have gone to aggressive states like Iran, North Korea, Serbia, and Syria, which threaten their neighbors. China has been severely criticized for selling missile technology to Iran, Pakistan, and North Korea, a practice it may have stopped under American pressure in 1998. A more insidious problem involves hundreds of unemployed Soviet bloc scientists gaining jobs in Iraq, Iran, North Korea, and other countries trying to develop nuclear, chemical, and biological weapons (table 3.1).

After the Cold War, the United States surpassed Russia to become the world's largest arms merchant.[10] Several reasons explain that shift. About half of all the money owed the former Soviet Union for weapons is considered uncollectible, so Moscow tends to demand hard currency rather than "I owe you"s for their hardware. UN arms embargos on Libya, Iraq, Bosnia, Croatia, and Serbia cost the Soviet Union and its successor state Russia $7 billion in lost sales in 1992 alone. When former members of Moscow's Warsaw Pact of Eastern European states joined the North Atlantic Treaty Organization (NATO), they shifted their buying from Russia to the United States and other Western suppliers. In addition to a lack of credit, spare parts, and service, Russian sales are further inhibited by the inferior quality of many Russian military products. Potential buyers watched American weapons and equipment destroy Russian weapons and

Table 3.1 Merchants of Death?: The Top
Ten Arms Exporters, 2000–2009

Country	billions of dollars
United States	$65.178
Russia	$54.446
Germany	$18.439
France	$16.349
Britain	$10.214
Netherlands	$5.564
China	$4.928
Italy	$4.318
Sweden	$4.271
Ukraine	$3.964

Source: Stockholm International Peace Research Institute.

equipment during the wars against Iraq in 1991 and 2003. That quality gap is steadily widening.

America's military industrial complex contracted by nearly half between 1989 and 2000 before nearly tripling in size since then. The military industrial complex weathered that initial contraction through huge economies of scale fueled by Pentagon procurements, consolidations, and applications of cutting-edge technologies. Today America's military industrial complex is a generation or so beyond its most sophisticated rivals. American weapons and equipment producers have achieved a virtuous cycle of production, sales, profits, investment, research, development, and more production. The greater the sales, the greater the economies of scale that lower costs and raise profits, which in turn allows even more investments in research and development, which allows even more sales. The more sophisticated a weapons system the greater the long-term dependence of the buyer on the manufacturer's spare parts and technicians. Because the research and development costs for many weapons are so high, the loser in a competition for markets might well become bankrupt.

Nonetheless, American exports of weapons can be and often are a double-edged sword for national security. At times those weapons are used to threaten or attack the United States or its allies. More often the influx of weapons can destabilize a country or region by raising tensions and the capacity to resolve conflicts with force. Increasingly, America is in an arms race with itself. The Defense Department justifies developing new weapons systems to fight potential but usually highly unlikely enemies armed with the previous generation of American weapons.

Global arms sales will continue for very good reasons. As engineers keep devising better ways of killing, they render obsolete existing weapons and thus create the need for their replacement. Thus arms races are fueled as much by new technologies as politics and profits. And, of course, there could not be sellers without buyers. The wealthier a country the more arms it can afford to import. There would not be any arms exports if governments did not have real or imagined internal and international enemies that they hope to deter or defeat with more numerous and advanced weapons. While many Third World governments import arms to counter perceived international threats, most use them against their own peoples, and some buy merely for the prestige that modern weapons bring regardless of their military utility. Arms sales and aid are closely related. States often sell their weapons at a loss or outright donate them to gain influence with the recipient, grab market share from their rivals, and thus strengthen their own military industrial complex.

Military power is supposed to make countries more rather than less secure; it is valuable only when it actually deters or defeats real enemies. The larger and better equipped a country's military, the more likely its government might use it to resolve a conflict. Over 50 million people have died in wars in the Third World since 1945, and the international arms trade was a major contributor both to the large number of wars and deaths.[11]

Militarization's indirect costs are just as enormous. Even if arms are never used, by spending ever more money on the military, a government can actually undermine rather than enhance national security. As President Eisenhower put it, the

> problem in defense spending is to figure out how far you should go without destroying from within what you are trying to defend from without…Every gun that is made, every warship launched, every rocket fired signifies, in the final sense, a theft from those who hunger and are not fed, from those who are cold and are not clothed. This world in arms is not spending money alone. It is spending the sweat of its laborers, the genius of its scientists, the hopes of its children.

Or as Eisenhower's chairman of the Council of Economic Advisors, Arthur Burns, put it,

> The real cost of the defense sector consists…not only of the civilian goods and services that are currently forgone on its account; it

includes also an element of growth that could have been achieved through larger investment in human or business capital.[12]

Studies have shown that generally the higher a country's military budget as a percentage of gross national income (GNP), the lower its manufacturing productivity growth:

> inter-country comparisons suggest that high military expenditures have curtailed productivity growth...heavy defense spending seems to have a particularly important impact on dampening capital formation and investment, which in turn reduces economic growth in the long run.

One study compared the impact on employment of one billion dollars. A billion dollars worth of guided missiles created only 21,392 workers, the lowest of 6 different employment categories. That same amount of money would create 21,783 railroad equipment workers, 26,145 solar energy and energy conservation workers, 26,459 public utility construction workers, 27,583 housing workers, and 31,078 mass transit workers. Overall, a billion dollars spent on construction creates 100,070 jobs or 1.3 times more than the 75,710 defense jobs created by those same dollars.[13] And those construction jobs are largely productive—increasing a nation's efficiency and wealth. Much of the money spent on the military is nonproductive—millions of able-bodied men and women sit in barracks around the world rather than use their brains and muscle to develop their countries. Because they consume rather than produce, the impact of their spending is inflationary. In all, there is a trade-off between guns and butter— the more a country spends on the military, the more it hurts itself economically.

Of the two superpowers, the Soviet Union collapsed largely because of the enormous resources it poured into the military over decades to the neglect of everything else. Though the United States did not collapse, America's economic growth, productivity, savings and investments ratio, and per capita income are among the lowest, and its infant mortality, life expectancy, low birth weight babies, per capita spending for education and health are among the worst of the democratic industrial countries.

An obsession with military spending traps scores of Third World countries into a vicious cycle in which poverty and stagnant growth led to political instability, which prompts governments to spend scarce resources on more arms that further inhibits development, causing greater instability, more military spending, and so on. For every dollar the Third World spends on defense, it loses 25 cents of economic investments and 20 cents of agricultural output; therefore, as military spending rises, economic growth declines. By one estimate, the Third World loses 187 million human years of income for its total annual military spending; the industrial countries lose 56 million human years annually. There are eight times more soldiers than doctors in the Third World, and thirty times more is spent on the military than education.[14]

INSURGENCY AND COUNTERINSURGENCY WARFARE

War in the twenty-first century will almost invariably erupt from "failed states" rather than great powers, from within rather than between states, and from stateless rather than state-backed terrorist networks. The result will be ever more "insurgency" and "counter-insurgency" warfare as rebels and governments try to destroy each other.

Insurgencies or guerrilla wars like the ones the United States and its allies have been fighting in Afghanistan and Iraq since the respective 2001 and 2003 invasions are asymmetrical in ends and means. A government wins only by destroying the rebels while the rebels win by not losing. Sun Tzu offers a timeless insurgent strategy: "When the enemy advances, we retreat; when the enemy halts, we harass; when the enemy seeks to avoid battle, we attack; when the enemy retreats, we pursue."[15]

Mao Zedong elaborated that concept in his three-stage strategy for winning a "people's war" or mass revolutionary movement against an oppressive government.[16] During the first stage, the rebels launch hit-and-run attacks by small units of a dozen or so troops against the country's military and economic infrastructure like public buildings, military bases, bridges, power stations, and so on. That at once wears down the enemy and provokes the government into brutal counter-measures that alienates ever more people and drives them into the arms of the rebels. Gradually the insurgents increase their strength in numbers, organization, and presence across the country. During the second stage, the rebels launch surprise attacks by hundreds of troops against government soldiers, while increasing the number of small-scale attacks. The goal is to isolate the government's army in bases and cities by asserting control over ever more rural regions and mobilizing the peasants, while steadily and stealthily infiltrating the cities to organize resistance. During the final stage, the rebels stage large-scale assaults by tens of thousands of troops against the enemy forces and destroy them one by one. So far the insurgencies in Afghanistan and Iraq are in the first stage.

An insurgent victory depends as much on winning "hearts and minds" or popular support as it does firefights. Indeed, military and political success are inseparable. The rebels have two parallel strategies, one to destroy the enemy and the other to construct a new society on the ruins of the old. As the insurgents try to destroy the existing political system, they try to create a shadow parallel political system of governmental, economic, educational, and social institutions that provide humanitarian relief and eventually develop the country.

How can a government best counter that insurgency strategy? Although each rebel movement is different and thus demands a different strategy to defeat, every strategy will include varying types and amounts of both reform and repression. The government must simultaneously seek out and destroy the guerrillas militarily while economically, politically, and socially developing the country that will reduce popular support for the guerrillas.

Sun Tzu identified the foundation for those twin policies of repression and reform: "Know your enemy; know yourself." People do not rebel for frivolous reasons. For a government to understand why rebels are trying to overthrow it is to understand its own weaknesses, pathologies, and follies. If done right, reforms at once strengthen the government and weaken the rebels. Most governments cannot defeat an insurgency by themselves—they need foreign sources of money, arms, and advisors. But ultimately, a state triumphs in a guerrilla war by the same means as the rebels—winning "hearts and minds" and "nation-building." Essentially, if the government can build up a country faster than the insurgents can tear it down, then it is winning; otherwise it is losing. For insurgents and counterinsurgents alike "clear, hold, and build" is the winning strategy.

The essence of that strategy is articulated in the Department Department's 2006 counterinsurgency manual that turns inside out the traditional assumptions about how to defeat an insurgency. The Pentagon has discarded the old "search, destroy, and withdraw" strategy because it tends to provoke more rather than less support for the insurgency. The new strategy emphasizes winning over the "hearts and minds" of the population, which is best achieved when military and civil forces work together to "clear, hold, and build" a country one district or region after another. General David Petraeus was one of the authors of the counterinsurgency manual, whose ideas he implemented in the so-called surge in Iraq, which sharply reduced the level of violence.[17]

The key lessons from that manual were expressed as Zen-like paradoxes:

1. Sometimes the more you protect your force, the less secure you may be.
2. Sometimes the more force is used, the less effective it is.
3. The more successful the counterinsurgency is, the less force can be used and the risk must be accepted.
4. Some of the best weapons do not shoot.
5. Sometimes doing nothing is the best reaction.
6. The host nation doing something tolerably is normally better than us doing it well.
7. If a tactic works this week, it might not work next week; if it works in this province, it might not work in the next.
8. Tactical success guarantees nothing.
9. Many important decisions are not made by generals.

The counterinsurgency campaigns in Afghanistan and Iraq will never succeed with military means alone. The United States is in a classic battle for "hearts and minds" in both countries, a war that can be won only if force is mixed with persuasion. The White House must somehow establish regimes with broad popular support. Legitimacy for the new regime will come only if it is broadly representative and, more importantly, ever more efficient at supplying enough food, water, shelter, electricity, jobs, and safety for people so that their lives gradually improve. And, ultimately, only the leaders of those countries can accomplish that.

The insurgents, meanwhile, are trying to tear down what the Americans and their allies are trying to build up. They do so by blowing up infrastructure like electric power plants, bridges, pipelines, police stations, and office buildings while killing those who collaborate with the foreigners. The goal is to raise the costs in blood and treasury for the United States and its allies so high that they abandon their mission. Most of the guerrillas are animated by Islamic concepts of *jihad* or holy war, and hope to establish fundamentalist Muslim regimes in both countries.

Not all internal wars are fought for what the insurgents in Afghanistan and Iraq believe is such a noble cause. A "civil war" occurs when a group wants either to depose a government and take its place or secede from a state and form a separate state. Civil wars thus are fought by political groups, whether organized as parties or movements that field armies and seek legitimacy or the legal and popular right to rule. In contrast, an "uncivil war" is about destroying the state and plundering the country in an endless orgy of robbing, raping, maiming, and murdering. Uncivil wars often involve one group driving into exile or destroying the culture of a hated group ("ethnic cleansing") or outright mass murder ("genocide"). During the 1990s and beyond, that mass slaughter was most notorious in Bosnia, Sierra Leone, Liberia, Somalia, Rwanda, Burundi, Kosovo, and the Congo. Uncivil wars, thus, are fought by criminal gangs or bloodthirsty mobs that seek illegitimate riches by shops, farms, and the only sources of large-scale wealth a poverty-stricken country might hold such as gold mines, oil wells, or opium fields.[18]

The ultimate source of most internal wars stretches back to the late nineteenth and early twentieth centuries when the imperial powers drew lines across maps of Africa, Asia, the Middle East, and Eastern Europe without regard for the peoples living in those lands. The result was to tear apart nations, religions, tribes, and clans into separate realms, which usually included their ancient enemies. The colonial power kept the peace but often exacerbated those animosities by playing off groups against each other.

With independence, those pent-up hatreds often exploded. Ironically, the Cold War between the United States and Soviet Union helped restore order in many newly independent states, although their machinations sowed chaos in others. The superpowers competed for control over those states by backing movements, parties, and/or factions. The Cold War's end contributed to the rise of uncivil wars. After the Soviet Union and communism collapsed, Moscow was unable and Washington was unwilling to patronize all of their respective clients. That loss of money was compounded by ideological upheaval and economic implosion. Throughout the Third World, socialism was discredited as an ideology while liberalism failed to take root in those illiberal cultures. The only thing most of the countries had in abundance were stockpiles of weapons. Countries become locked into a vicious cycle of worsening poverty, chaos, and violence. The result in dozens of countries is a failed state and anarchy, or a war of each group against all others for diminishing sources of wealth.

THE SOURCE OF FUTURE WARS?

States have gone to war for many reasons. When is the last time people killed each other for fresh water? Perhaps not since nomadic enemy bands converged at a desert spring. But future wars over water may not be far off.

Globalization has steadily raised the costs and reduced the benefits of war. The world's peoples are so interdependent economically, technologically, and culturally that negotiations rather than violence are the only rational way to resolve conflicts in nearly all international relations among the 192 nation-states. So what is worth fighting for? In 1991, the United States allied with thirty-seven other states to drive Iraq from oil rich Kuwait. Could water ever be as geopolitically vital to national interests as oil? In ever more countries it already is.[19]

The world's amount of fresh water is naturally limited while the planet's population will continue to soar from 6.6 billion today to perhaps 9.5 billion by 2050. Already about 500 million people in 30 countries suffer severe water shortages; by 2025, 2 of every 3 people on the planet or about 5 billion people will suffer from moderate to severe water shortages. That may be an underestimate. Today, in China alone over 300 northern and western cities of 50,000 people or more each have pumped their aquifers nearly dry; the water table beneath the capital Beijing has plummeted over 100 feet in the past 40 years. Bangkok, Thailand's capital, is sinking as people drain the aquifer beneath their feet. If the Ogallala Aquifer that runs under most of America's Great Plains continues to dwindle at the present rate, hundreds of thousands of people will be forced to abandon their prosperous farms, ranches, and towns within a generation; indeed, over 50 million Americans live in arid regions dependent on water from elsewhere. A gallon of water at an American supermarket now costs less than a gallon of gasoline. What will be the relative costs of water and gas a decade from now?

Ever more water is too foul to consume. Over 2.6 billion people or two out of five drinks, baths, and cooks with water laced with chemical, human, and animal wastes, many of which cause cancer and other diseases. As water sources disappear, demand for its use for industry, agriculture, and humans rises, and that cocktail of vile and sometimes deadly pollutants thickens.

All that is disastrous enough for countries whose swelling populations get most of their water from their own territories. But billions of people depend on water drawn from rivers, lakes, and aquifers linking two or more countries. For now most of these common water sources remain abundant enough to fulfill the demands of different peoples upon them. Yet in many regions of the world like the Jordan, Tigris, and Euphrates rivers of the Middle East, the Nile and Niger rivers of Africa, or the Indus of South Asia, to name a few of the most contentious, the demands for fresh water are rapidly exhausting the existing supply. Wars have erupted in those regions over territorial, ethnic, and/or religious disputes. Water will most likely be another potential catalyst for war there and increasingly elsewhere in the years ahead.

Perhaps the most likely water war will break out in the Middle East. Since its creation in 1948, Israel has fought five wars with surrounding Arab states that, until recently, vowed to destroy that Jewish state. The Arab-Israeli standoff is further complicated by the reliance of Israel, Lebanon, Jordan, and Syria on the Jordan River. Israel currently takes 95 percent of that river's waters. Israel's population has increased sixfold since independence. Although Israeli farmers have mastered drip agriculture, which maximizes water efficiency, the increased demands of farmers, factories, businesses, and households is rapidly outstripping all available surface and aquifer water sources. Seawater has seeped into and polluted some aquifers as they are drawn down, compounding the shortages. By 2009, Israel's water supply fell as low as 45 percent below demand. Meanwhile, neighboring states are growing just as rapidly in population and are clamoring for a greater share of the Jordan River and other regional water sources for themselves. Will the next Israeli-Arab war be over water?

Yet dwindling water supplies for ever more thirsty people along with the demands of agriculture, industry, sanitation, and so on is only one of a web of interrelated global environmental crises that threaten our future. While people may eventually war over water, we may simply commit slow suicide if not enough is done to arrest other crises like global warming, ozone layer depletion, desertification, deforestation, species extinction, and the population explosion. Those will be the most persistently vital issues of war and peace in the twenty-first century and beyond.

Consequences

Throughout history, war or the threat of war has been an intricate and often dominant part of international relations. As warfare changes so too does international relations, and new technologies drive the changes in both. New weapons—gunpowder, the tank, submarines, atomic bombs, computer viruses—can dramatically shift the nature of warfare, and in turn, the distribution of power. Can that link among war, technology, and international relations ever be broken?

Conventional wars between states will become increasingly rare for two related reasons. Until recently launching a war was a viable option for policymakers. States once shamelessly used war to steal territory, people, and wealth from others. But as the global web of interdependence among states thickens, the costs of buying what one wants from others plummets while the costs of stealing soars. Globalization has reached a point where states are so thoroughly integrated with one another that to war against others militarily means warring against oneself economically. Thus war between states is increasingly unthinkable for all but one state in the global system. America's military has become so powerful with state-of-the-art training, logistics, intelligence, command, control, communications, firepower, and movement that it can swiftly pulverize virtually any other army in a conventional fight. That in turn reinforces the swelling economic reasons for other states to desist from doing so.

However, unconventional or asymmetrical warfare most likely will ravage ever more countries in the decades ahead. Warfare is increasingly asymmetrical in two ways, one ageless and the other recent. Guerrilla warfare is as old as humankind; American hyperpower emerged only recently with the Cold War's end. The American invasions of Afghanistan in 2001 and Iraq in 2003 exemplify those two types of asymmetrical warfare. With precision bombing followed by fast moving, hard-hitting, high tech armed special operation forces in Afghanistan and massive ground forces in Iraq, the Americans swiftly crushed within weeks the conventional forces protecting the authoritarian regimes of both countries. But those exhilarating conventional war victories were followed by stalemates as the remnants of those defeated forces rallied and, bolstered by thousands of fresh volunteers from across the Muslim world, launched guerilla wars against the occupiers. Within months in both Afghanistan and Iraq, the number of Americans killed surpassed those who died in the initial assault. And guerilla wars continue to sputter on in both those countries.

How will technology affect warfare in the twenty-first century? That remains to be seen. Until then we can only speculate about cyberwarfare and other new technologies. One thing is certain, the dynamic relationship among war, technology, tactics, and strategy will remain unbroken.

CHAPTER 4

Terrorism and Counterterrorism

Why do they hate us?

> *George W. Bush*

One man's terrorist is another man's freedom fighter.

> *Ronald Regan*

The difference between the revolutionary and the terrorist lies in the reason for which each fights. For whoever stands by a just cause and fights for the freedom and liberation of his land ... cannot possibly be a terrorist.

> *Yasser Arafat*

IN THE EYES OF THE BEHOLDER?

What is terrorism? We all think we know it when we witness it either before our eyes or via television—the shattered burned out buildings, vehicles, and bodies; the weeping or stunned survivors; the vows of vengeance. For Americans in particular, the image of terrorism is forever associated with jetliners exploding into the World Trade Center towers.

Yet terrorism is among those concepts that want a clear definition. Like so much in life, it is in the eyes of the beholder. Ronald Reagan popularized the notion that one person's terrorist is another's freedom fighter. Why else would some people on the planet condemn and others cheer the September 11 attacks on the World Trade Center and Pentagon that left 3,000 people dead? Were those people killed in a legitimate act of a just war or murdered in an act of pure evil? As Yasser Arafat put it,

The difference between the revolutionary and the terrorist lies in the reason for which each fights. For whoever stands by a just cause and fights for the freedom and liberation of his land...cannot possibly be called a terrorist.[1]

The U.S. State Department defines terrorism as "the use or threatened use of violence for political purposes to create a state of fear that will aid in extorting, coercing, intimidating, or otherwise causing individuals and groups to alter their behavior." To this can be added the definitions that terrorism "is ruthless and does not conform to humanitarian norms, and that publicity is an essential factor in terrorist strategy." Finally, most would agree that terrorism is targeted against noncombatants. Vladimir Lenin put it more succinctly: "The purpose of terrorism is to inspire terror."

Terrorism thus is the threat or use of violence by a group or individual against noncombatants in a struggle to achieve political goals. Violence against public institutions and personnel by armed, uniformed men may not be considered terrorism; violence against civilians certainly is. International terrorism occurs when two or more countries are the supporters, targets, and/or refugees of a terrorist group. Criminal and political terrorists differ in motivation if not tactics. While criminals use terror to extort money or other forms of wealth from their victims, political groups use terror to discredit, change, and, ideally, destroy entire political systems.

Who commits terrorism? Terrorism can be one tactic of many used by a broad political movement struggling for independence or revolution. Terrorism can be the sole means of a tiny, close-knit group to assert its views, whatever they may be. Terrorism can even be the vile acts of an individual. While many terrorists operate against states, some are employed by states to terrorize their own or foreign citizens. The United States, Soviet Union, Israel, Libya, Syria, Iraq, Cuba, and Iran, to name a few, have all supplied, trained, and/or led groups that launched terrorist attacks against other states. Finally, totalitarian or authoritarian regimes frequently use terror to intimidate their own citizens into compliance.

Though terrorism is as old as humanity, the term as such was coined by Edmund Burke during the French Revolution to denote the state's "reign of terror" against its enemies within the country and among exile groups conspiring abroad. Modern organized terrorism against a state emerged in the late nineteenth century among either "anarchists" who believed that governments should be abolished and people allowed to live together in self-regulating communities, or "nihilists" who believed that the world lacked meaning or morality and thus any behavior was justified. In the early twentieth century some nationalist groups like the Serbian Black Hand or Irish Republican Army (IRA) employed terrorism as one means to the end of independence. After taking power in Russia in 1917, the communists wielded terrorism both to foment revolution abroad and consolidate the revolution within. After World War II, terrorism was part of many national liberation struggles in the Middle East, Africa, and Asia, most notoriously in Palestine, Algeria, Cyprus, Kenya, and Vietnam. From the 1960s through the 1980s, Palestinian groups conducted more international terrorist attacks than any other movements. Before the 1979 Iran revolution, sixty-two of sixty-four terrorist groups were secular nationalist and/or socialist and only two were religious. Since then ever more groups have emerged to fight for Islamic fundamentalism and other religions. By 1995, twenty-six of fifty-six international terrorist groups were religious; those groups accounted for 25 percent of all attacks and 58 percent of all fatalities.[2] Al Qaeda became the world's most widespread and deadly group during the 1990s and into the early years of the twenty-first century. The American-led efforts against Al Qaeda after September 11 have severely eroded it as an organization. Today Hezbollah, founded by Iran in Lebanon in 1982, is the world's most powerful transnational political movement that uses terrorism as one of its tactics.

States once were the primary source of shelter, training, intelligence, and money for terrorist groups. However, since the Cold War ended, most states have either abandoned or downsized their support for terrorism. The reason is simple—the costs grew and benefits dropped for doing so. Even before September 11, the United States retaliated against state sponsors of terrorism with economic sanctions, covert operations, and occasionally even military strikes. Of those states listed by the State Department in 2001 as sponsors of terrorism, Libya, Cuba, Syria, North Korea, and Iraq had either cut back or ended the practice while only Iran persisted in massively aiding Islamist groups, especially Hezbollah. Typically some American "friends" like Pakistan and Saudi Arabia were not on State Department list; factions within those governments unofficially supplied extensive financial, intelligence, and political support to the Taliban and Al Qaeda.

Terrorist groups today seek support primarily not from strong states but from the dominant faction vying for power within failed or failing states such as Lebanon, Afghanistan, Yemen, Somalia, and Iraq. Al Qaeda, for instance, successively allied with Mohammed Aidid's clan in Somalia, the Taliban in Afghanistan, anti-American forces in Iraq, and the Pashtun people of Pakistan's lawless Northwest Territory.

Globalization certainly makes terrorism easier. Even a terrorist group that is located within a country fighting against its government can use Internet or airlines to garner money, information, and recruits. And nearly all well-publicized destructive terrorist acts reverberate internationally, whether they provoke a drop in trade, tourism, or stock prices not just to that country but throughout the region, heightened security vigilance and costs, and copy-cat attacks.

"Old," "New," and "Hybrid" Terrorism

All terrorists have a cause whose advancement they believe is worth threatening or destroying people and property to achieve. Scholars of terrorism have recently distinguished among "old," "new," and "hybrid" types. As with all other concepts, those distinctions raise questions—how do you define and apply them? What the three versions share is the targeting of civilians. They differ, however, over the purpose of that terrorism.

"Old terrorism" was one of several related means used by a group to win some specific political end like overthrowing a government, liberating a people, and/or fomenting a revolution. Terrorism helped publicize their cause and intimidate their enemies and the population. Yet they restrained themselves from killing too many or too often for fear that they would provoke condemnation rather than win sympathy. They also got most of their money, training, intelligence, and, often, shelter from states. The IRA, African National Congress (ANC), and Palestinian Liberation Army (PLO) exemplify "old" terrorist groups, which—having largely won their wars—try to transform themselves from guerrilla movements into political parties and their leaders from revolutionaries into statesmen. Of those three groups, the PLO and ANC now head governments recognized even by their former enemies, while the IRA signed a peace treaty which, among other goals, recognizes its political legitimacy.

Hamas and Hezbollah, which respectively fight for the liberation of Palestinians and Shiite Lebanese, would also be considered "old terrorists." Both are political movements with terrorist organizations that seek to take over and rule countries. Hezbollah was founded by Iran and continues to receive money, arms, and other support from Iran and Syria. Ironically, the creation of Hamas was actually assisted by Israel, which hoped to use it as a counterweight to the PLO; Hamas gets support from Iran, Syria, and many radical or fundamentalist Muslim states. Both movements have made enormous progress in their goals. In 2006, Hamas won a majority in the Palestinian parliament and now governs the Gaza Strip. Hezbollah is an accepted member of Lebanon's political landscape and in 2010 held 14 of 128 seats in the parliament.

"New terrorism" has no end but terror itself—terrorism for terrorism's sake. The American Symbionese Liberation Army, Italian Red Brigade, German Red Army, and Japanese Red Army communist/anarchist groups, which embarked on robbery and murder sprees during the 1970s; Unabomber Ted Kaczynski; and the Japanese cult Aum Shinrikyo, which set off in Tokyo's subways sarin nerve gas canisters that killed a dozen people and wounded 5,000 others in 1995, all proclaimed vague revolutionary slogans, but were apparently motivated more by the sheer sadistic thrill of having the power to destroy lives and property. As for state terrorism, North Korea's government never gave any reason for detonating bombs that murdered half of South Korea's cabinet in 1985 and blew up a South Korean airliner in 1986. When terrorism is unaccompanied by specific realistic demands it is the new type. Yet, by that definition, "new terrorism" is quite old since it would include Russian anarchists and nihilists of the nineteenth century.

So on which side of that conceptual fence does Al Qaeda stand? Actually Al Qaeda straddles that fence with characteristics that are a "hybrid" of old and new terrorism. Al Qaeda has a clear political agenda, a characteristic of old terrorism. Osama bin Laden, Al Qaeda's leader, has repeatedly vowed ultimately to destroy Israel, drive American power from the Middle East, and inspire Islamic revolutions in all Muslim countries. Yet the reality that those goals are unlikely at best gives Al Qaeda a new terrorist tinge. And, unlike Hezbollah and Hamas, Al Qaeda is not a mass political movement that uses terrorism as one of any array of tactics. As an organization, Al Qaeda remains dedicated solely to terror operations, although it does try to inspire a broader movement that fights for its political goals.

Some analysts add other points to the definition of new terrorism. For instance, if those groups that try to get and use weapons of mass destruction are placed under that rubric, then Al Qaeda and Aum Shinrikyo were new terrorists while Kaczynski, the Symbionese

Liberation Army, Red Brigade, and Red Army were old terrorists. Those states that have used weapons of mass destruction against civilians include Japan, which wielded biological weapons against the Chinese during World War II, the United States, which dropped two atom bombs on Japan during World War II, and Iraq, which used chemical weapons against Iran and a Kurdish revolt. If weapons of mass destruction include dropping incendiary and high explosive bombs on civilians, then Japan, the United States, Britain, the Soviet Union, Italy, and Germany would top that list. Likewise, if new terrorism includes the ability of an individual, group, and/or state to build networks and launch attacks around the world, then clearly Al Qaeda and Hezbollah fit that definition while the other groups are excluded.

Yet another distinction between old and new terrorism is the terrorist's attitude toward his or her own death. In the old version, terrorists sought to survive to commit repeated attacks and eventually see their cause triumph. "New terrorism" includes those who kill themselves while killing others. That would include nearly all Islamist terrorist groups along with the Tamil Tigers of Sri Lanka.

Religious fundamentalism is thought by some to characterize new terrorism, although the use of terror by some fanatical sects is as old as religion itself. The words zealot, assassin, and thug originated as the respective names for Jewish, Muslim, and Hindu terrorists in the premodern era. Murder and even genocide is certainly easier to commit in the name of "God" against an "evil" target.

Most people find the notion that God endorses terrorism repulsive. Yet many sacred texts including the Bible and Koran contain passages that can be cited by terrorist sects to justify slaughtering their enemies. The Christian Identity movement believes that the world's "end of time" is near; when the end comes, an apocalyptic struggle will erupt between the "true Christians" who represent good and all others who are demonized as evil. Jewish terrorist groups such as Chai, Kach, Gush Emunim, and Kahane believe that God granted them "Eretz Israel" or the Great Israel of the Bible, and thus they can expel all Palestinians from that land and exterminate those who resist. Islam means submission to God; a Muslim is someone who submits; and that submission involves getting others to submit, ideally with persuasion, but if necessary with a *jihad* or holy war by *Mujahideen* or holy warriors and *fedayeen* or commandos against infidels. Some Muslim leaders have openly espoused terrorism, often by declaring a *fatwa* or holy order; Sheik Omar Abdel-Rahman issued just such a fatwa for terrorists to bomb the World Trade Center in 1993. Osama bin Laden issued fatwas in 1996 and 1998 calling on Muslims to war against the United States, Israel, and other Western powers, which would include killing civilians and soldiers alike.

WHO BECOMES A TERRORIST?

Why do some individuals, groups, and/or states resort to terrorism?[3] The motivations divide into whether old or new terrorism prevails. A further distinction can be drawn between "revolutionaries" and "reactionaries"; while both are fighting against the contemporary world, the former fights for some ideal future world and the latter fights to restore some ideal past world. Regardless of the group's goals, virtually every act of terrorism is said to be a strategy of the weak against the strong.

Can anyone become a terrorist? Clearly not. Only a tiny sliver of humanity trods the terrorist path. So what drives those who do? The popular notion that poverty, despair, and oppression are breeding grounds for terrorism is not true. While billions of people around the world exist in misery, only thousands ever join terrorist groups, and only hundreds actually commit terrorist acts. Rich countries like the United States, Germany, and Japan have unwittingly bred terrorism while scores of poor countries around the world are free of that scourge. Likewise religious fundamentalism is said to cause terrorism. Here again only a radical fringe of the fundamentalists actually commit such acts.

The typical terrorist is believed to be young, poor, single, uneducated, alienated, and volatile. While certainly many do fit that description, reality, as usual, is more complex. Nearly all of the nineteen September 11 terrorists were middle class, in their late twenties or thirties, and university educated, while some even had wives and children. Most of America's right-wing terrorists are middle class, church-goers, and family men, if extremely ill-schooled. Many terrorists are born into families of affluence and privilege; the most notorious, Osama bin Laden, was the son of a billionaire!

Nonetheless, those who are jobless, poor, ignorant, and desperate are more likely to become terrorists than those who are not. Ayatollah Ruhollah Khomeini, who led Iran's Islamist revolution, exclaimed: "My soldiers are still infants." What he meant was that in Iran and throughout most of the Islamic world, with half of those populations under twenty years old, a demographic time-bomb is ticking away that will lead to the explosion of many actual bombs. As the populations in those countries race ever further ahead of existing let alone meaningful jobs, ever more young people will search for some ideology or movement to give their lives meaning and enemies against whom to vent their despair and hatred.

The relative handful of people who do choose to join terrorist groups and commit terrorist acts do so for unique combinations of psychology and circumstances. They combine rage against an enemy, devotion to a cause, iron will, and the opportunity to act. Virtually no successful terrorist is a psychopath or someone raging without reason. Terrorist organizations shun the "crazies" for very practical reasons— they are nearly impossible to control and can jeopardize the group's operations and security. They look instead for calm, patient, pliable, introverted people who do what they are told and do not stand out in a crowd. One recruiter explained to a potential recruit "that terrorist activity did not consist of throwing bombs; that it was much more minute, difficult and tedious than might be imagined; that a terrorist is called upon to live a rather dull existence for months at a time, eschewing meeting his own comrades, and doing most difficult and unpleasant work—the work of systematic observation."[4] That perfectly describes the September 11 terrorists along with countless others.

What would motivate someone to commit suicide for a political cause? Islamist groups like Al Qaeda, Hezbollah, Hamas, Islamic Jihad, and the Al-Aksa Martyrs Brigade promise that those men who martyr themselves will be rewarded with automatic ascent to heaven where seventy-one beautiful virgins await the hero, seventy relatives can later reside, and all the strict rules of Islamic law (Sharia) including the prohibition of alcohol, are suspended for eternity. That is not a bad incentive for believers. Yet there are ever more Islamist women suicide bombers for whom such incentives do not apply. Nor do the Tamil Tigers offer any other-worldly rewards for martyrs. The explanations for each suicide terrorist involves a unique and complex mix of incentives and coercions.[5]

Lone terrorists are rare; terrorism is almost always a group activity. Most groups are organized in a classic pyramid structure composed of cells of a half dozen or so people. The members of each cell work together as a team but for security reasons seldom know anything about the members or activities of the other cells above, below, or parallel to theirs. Thus if a terrorist is captured and interrogated, he can reveal only details of his immediate comrades and operations.

Yet, here again, we can distinguish old from new terrorism. "Old terrorism" was organized in a hierarchy of power headed by a single leader. "New terrorism" is organized as a network of affiliated groups around a core founding group, with each autonomous in recruitment, finance, and operations. Al Qaeda evolved organizationally from a pyramid into a network. The catalyst was the American-led counter-attack that routed Al Qaeda from Afghanistan and destroyed scores of its cells elsewhere around the world. Though Al Qaeda as an organization was diminished, Al Qaeda as a movement is more popular and powerful than ever as ever more groups organize themselves and commit terrorism in its name.

Another type is known as "leaderless resistance." The idea was pioneered by American environmental and right-wing terrorists during the 1990s and is ideal for the Internet age. The strategy involves advancing a cause by avoiding rather than joining groups. A movement's ideas and tactics are circulated through Internet messages and Web sites anonymously. People act alone or with a few trusted true-believers, strike, lie low until the subsequent investigation and beefed up security relaxes, and then strike again.

Ends and Means

Revolutionary movements that wield terrorism do so to advance several related goals: they seek to demonstrate their power; publicize their cause; damage the enemy's economy, military, bureaucracy, and/or morale; reveal the government's impotence; provoke the government to overreact with brutal measures that alienates rather than reassures the population; and thus inspire ever more people to shift their loyalties to the movement. As such, changing people's minds is more important than inflicting damage. To force fundamental change—a government's overthrow, independence, and/or revolution—terrorism must be one among many tactics wielded by a well-organized group with ever more soldiers, administrators, financiers, and popular support.

Terrorists often target a prominent symbol of a country with destruction. Plots were thwarted to blow up the Statue of Liberty and Eifel Tower. Al Qaeda clearly chose the World Trade Center and Pentagon to attack on September 11 because they symbolized American economic and military power. The destruction of the World Trade Center was far more than symbolic; it blasted a $100 billion hole in America's economy as well as murdered nearly 3,000 people.

At times an attack may be more "expressive" than "programmatic," meaning the group is motivated more by venting rage than advancing an agenda. They strike out with blind fury that murders, maims, and devastates. The result of an expressive attack is often to provoke hatred rather than sympathy from most people for the terrorists, and determination rather than intimidation from the government to eliminate the group.

Terrorists can choose from a spectrum of weapons to hurt those they hate. They naturally use what they can get that will work best under specific and changing circumstances. Although terrorism is as old as humanity, technological advances have expanded the repertoire of available tactics from the preindustrial reliance on knifings, kidnappings, poisonings, arsons, bludgeonings, and threats to do any or all of that to shootings, bombings, cyberattacks, and detonating weapons of mass destruction (WMD).

Bombs are the weapon of choice for about half of all terrorist attacks. The reason is simple—it is the safest to pull off. A bomb can be planted well ahead of its explosion, allowing the terrorist ample time for a getaway. They also can be strewn virtually anywhere and set off without warning. The explosion of one small bomb can terrorize entire populations. The most destruction caused by a terrorist bomb was that thrown by the Serbian nationalist Gavril Princep at Austrian Archduke Franz Ferdinand; it sparked a crisis among Europe's great powers, which erupted into World War I and led to 16 million deaths.

Suicide bombing is a relatively new phenomenon. Hezbollah initiated the practice in Lebanon during the early 1980s. The nineteen Al Qaeda terrorists who hijacked four airliners on September 11 and turned them into bombs was the most horrific and destructive suicide bombing to date. Yet the record for suicide bombers is held by a radical Hindu rather than an Islamic group. From 1980 to 2003, the Tamil Tigers committed 76 of 315 suicide bombings, or more than 13 Islamic groups, which wielded that tactic.[6]

Though most likely any terrorist group might dream of getting their hands on weapons of mass destruction like nuclear, biological, chemical, or radiological bombs, only Aum Shinrikyo actually did so with sarin gas, and Al Qaeda is known to have unsuccessfully tried to purchase a nuclear backpack bomb and deadly radioactive material. Making, buying, or stealing weapons of mass destruction is impossible for most groups and extremely difficult even for Al Qaeda or Hezbollah with their respective global networks of agents, sympathizers, and hundreds of millions of dollars. The most likely scenario for triggering a weapon of mass destruction is to fly an airliner into a nuclear or chemical plant.

The most successful terrorist groups manage to keep a step or two ahead of their enemies. When governments thwart one tactic, they master another. For instance, when officials responded to hijackings with metal detectors, the terrorists switched to planting plastic explosives in luggage. When officials began using explosive-sniffing dogs, Al Qaeda came up with the idea of arming hijackers with penknives and box-cutters. When officials responded by searching hand-luggage and confiscating anything sharp that could conceivably be used as a weapon, Al Qaeda dispatched Richard Reed with explosives packed in his shoes. Now passengers are required to offer their shoes for inspection before boarding. Most recently, Al Qaeda talked a follower into placing a genital shaped bomb in his underpants. Mercifully, that plot too was thwarted, and, to prevent similar attacks, airports are installing machines that render a person naked in the eyes of the screener. What will Al Qaeda think of next?

Acts of terrorism and the organizations that commit them must be financed. As state-sponsored terrorism declines, groups must organize themselves like corporations to survive and ideally thrive. Money can come from many sources. Ever more groups have seemingly legitimate businesses, which earn profits and charities that take donations. Then there are blatantly criminal means of making money like smuggling and theft. Terrorists can steal money by robbing banks, kidnapping people for ransom, or demanding "taxes" or "protection money" from unwilling but intimidated businesses and families. As the word implies, "narco-terrorism" combines drug smuggling and terrorism, a strategy most notoriously practiced by Columbia's two communist guerrilla groups, ELN and FARC, and Al Qaeda and the Taliban in Afghanistan.[7]

Passing money and messages can involve the most traditional face-to-face meetings or the most cutting-edge high technology methods. Since electronic banking can be monitored, ever more groups use the "hawala" method that involves the whispered exchange of a promise to repay with a code word in one location, often a small business in an innocuous urban neighborhood, and then that whispered magic word for the money in another location, usually a different country. Although the account books are adjusted, no other paper trail links the deal. At the opposite end of the technological spectrum is for computer wizards to embed messages in the pixels or hundreds of thousands of dots of images on computer screens, which can be whisked around the world in a split second with a few taps on a keyboard. Those messages are virtually impossible to detect let alone decode.

Training is just as essential to terrorism. Recruits must be taught such vital skills as how to spy, evade detection, and escape when detected; how to extract information by theft, observation, persuasion, and/or coercion; how to keep silent even under torture; how to receive and pass coded messages through the Internet, dead-drops, telephone, radio, or advertisements; how to make, plant, and detonate bombs; how to kill calmly and swiftly with guns, knives, kicks, punches, and snaps of necks.

Mastering the art of propaganda is yet another key skill. Terrorism is a type of politics, and to varying degrees and ways all politics involve theater. The better a group markets its image, the more recruits, money, information, shelter, and popularity it will attract, and thus the better the odds of realizing its goals. That task is obviously easier if the terrorists claim to champion a religion or nationality with which many people already identify. Yet even ideologies that are obscure or unpopular at first can generate widespread support with the right marketing strategy.

Like politicians, terrorists try to manipulate the mass media so that it projects a favorable image of their cause and acts. Governments often try to censor the print and electronic media from reporting attacks or interviewing leaders. The fear is that such reports encourage more support for the terrorists and more terrorist attacks.

The best propaganda sells the group as Robin Hood–like champions of the people and merciless warriors against their enemies. To be truly effective, a group must back up its image with action. Hezbollah, Hamas, and the Taliban have excelled in that strategy in Lebanon, Palestine, and Afghanistan, respectively, where they have established shadow governments that provide work, clean streets, combat crime, and manage a range of other problems far more effectively than the corrupt, inept governments that are supposedly in charge. Not surprisingly, ever more people in those countries see Hezbollah and Hamas as legitimate movements and governments.

How to Fight Terrorism

How can terrorism be contained, reduced, and ideally eliminated?[8] A counterterrorist strategy is an intense, mostly covert, long-term concerted campaign by the threatened nation's diplomats, spies, cops, and accountants working among themselves and with their foreign counterparts to understand, uncover, and eliminate the enemy. That campaign has two broad interrelated elements: boosting the security of vulnerable vital national interests and improving the means of understanding, watching, and attacking terrorist groups and their sources of money, arms, and training. Both these elements depend on one essential commodity—information. The first step in the war against a terror group is understanding why it exists. That involves unraveling not just the group's leaders, ideology, organization, membership, operations, and strongholds, but also the broader political and socioeconomic context that nourishes it. If the "why" can be eliminated, the group will wither on the cut vine.

There is a golden mean between doing too much or too little. Governments should not overreact by imposing draconian measures that end up alienating the population and magnifying the terrorist group's importance and appeal. Nor should governments allow themselves to be paralyzed and thus appear weak and ineffectual, and even worse being bullied into granting concessions.

Governments counterterrorism mostly by using various means to get information on plots, plotters, and their sources of money, arms, and shelter, and then apprehending the terrorists and putting them on trial for their crimes. They also try to deter attacks by enhancing security at potential terrorist targets like government buildings, military bases, energy grids, transportation networks, and other essential infrastructure. If terrorists believe they will be caught before they get to a target, they might not attempt a strike in the first place.

A controversial tactic known as "rendition" involves capturing suspects, taking them to a safe location, and interrogating them. Renditions are usually conducted with the cooperation of the government of the country in which the suspect is nabbed. The controversy comes when someone is rendered illegally and taken to another country where confessions are coerced through torture. Separate illegal CIA renditions in Italy and Germany resulted in trials in those countries, although no agency personnel ever appeared in court or suffered penalties.

Even more controversial and rare are the so-called wet operations or assassinations of suspected terrorists. From the 1970s through 2002, CIA was forbidden from such actions. The Mossad, Israel's foreign intelligence organization, is not so constrained. Over the decades, Mossad has conducted scores of "hits" against known or suspected terrorists. Although most succeeded, a few misfired disastrously. In 1997, for instance, two Mossad agents were captured in Amman, Jordan, when they tried to kill an Hamas leader with the rather awkward method of injecting poison in his ear. To win their release, the Israel government agreed to free from prison the spiritual leader of Hamas, Sheik Ahmed Yassin, along with seventy-one other Palestinian terrorists. Then, in February 2010, a twenty-six person team assassinated a top Hamas leader in a luxury Dubai hotel. Although the team scattered to safe havens overseas shortly after the hit, parts of their operation were caught on tape and their passport photos broadcasted around the world. That publicity has ruined each team member's ability to operate internationally. Thus that successful assassination came at a very high price: the highly trained individuals who pulled it off must be confined to desk jobs for the rest of their careers.

If better security and intelligence is clearly essential to bolstering counterterrorism, it is equally clear what not to do. The legacy of their hero Ronald Reagan notwithstanding, conservatives in the United States vow never to compromise or negotiate with terrorists. Is that an effective strategy? Realists reply that it depends; every terrorist group is unique and thus a strategy must be tailored to fit the exact threat posed by each. What works with fighting one group may fail against or actually aid another group. In one case the best strategy may well involve unrelenting attempts to identify, capture, and kill the members. In another case, negotiation, compromise, and conciliation may be the best strategy. For instance, Columbia's government decided to attack rather than bargain with the M-19 group of terrorists that captured the Supreme Court in 1979. Over a hundred people, including most of the justices, died in the assault. Peru's government did the same thing when the Tupac Amaru group took over the Japanese embassy and held seventy-two hostages in 1996. Yet the Peruvian assault succeeded for several reasons. First, they were patient. They gathered intelligence and waited while the terrorists gradually relaxed their vigilance and fell into a predictable routine. The subsequent assault with Special Forces was minutely planned to infiltrate the compound and attack while the terrorists had set aside their weapons to play their daily game of soccer in the embassy compound. The soldiers killed all the terrorists and freed all the hostages.

As with any other endeavor, there is usually strength in numbers. Perhaps the most important reason why America's war against Al Qaeda has succeeded in diminishing that group's personnel, operations, and shelters is that the United States has worked closely with over ninety countries around the world to those ends.

The international community is mostly united against terrorism. From 1963 through today, thirteen international treaties have been ratified dealing with various dimensions of terrorism under the auspices of the United Nations, and since 1971 seven other treaties by regional international organizations. Those treaties have gotten most of the world's nation-states to work closely together to dry up sources of terrorist finance, weapons, and refuges. Economic sanctions against state sponsors of terrorism have had mixed results: Libya eventually renounced terrorism and its WMD program, while Iran continues those practices while denying that it does so.[9]

Finally, there is the "drain-the-swamp" nation-building strategy that tries to transform failed or failing states that can be breeding grounds for terrorism. The American-led efforts in Afghanistan and Iraq are the most explicit recent examples of that strategy. Whether those efforts succeed will not be known for a generation or two at best, given the devastation, poverty, violence, and traditionalism those countries have suffered.

THE DILEMMAS OF AMERICAN COUNTERTERRORISM

Counterterrorism clearly begins at home. But where does home begin in an ever more globalized world? With vast oceans east and west, and weak friendly neighbors north and south, the United States has not been threatened with foreign invasion since 1814. Yet, as the horrendous bombings of 1993, 1995, and 2001 illustrated so clearly, America is vulnerable to vicious attacks by terrorists born within and beyond the nation's borders. Imagine being the Homeland Security director for the United States, a continental sized realm with over 300 million people of whom tens of millions are legal and illegal aliens; long undefended frontiers; thousands of airplanes landing and hundreds of ships docking from abroad every day; tens of thousands of shipping containers piled up at ports or being trucked across the country; an economy dependent on an ever denser global computer network, trade for one of every five dollars of wealth generated, and foreign oil for six of ten barrels consumed; a permissive culture for owning guns, explosives, and volatile chemicals, and committing violence; and a hyperpluralist political system where the richest and most powerful interest groups take most of the spoils.

What is Washington doing to counter this real and continuing danger to the United States?

Although the Homeland Security budget for 2010 was over $50 billion, many of those responsible for security at scores of cities, ports, airports, power plants, electrical grids, and borders complained that they got only a fraction of what they needed to do their jobs. What are America's vital interests, which are the most vulnerable, and how are they vulnerable? If you were the Homeland Security director, what would be your priorities? What tough decisions would you have to make over who receives and who is denied the money they demand? Is there a trade-off between freedom and security, and, if so, where would you draw the line?

The mission of tracking and intercepting terrorists is daunting. That is the foremost mission of the Directorate of National Intelligence (DNI), which was established in 2005 to unite the efforts of fifteen intelligence organizations within the American government. Of those organizations, the CIA and FBI are the most powerful. Until the DNI was created, the CIA was responsible for acting as the system's hub that collected information from both its own sources and from the other members, analyzed it, and then distributed those reports to key institutions and policymakers. Assisted by the CIA and other institutions, the FBI leads the efforts of apprehending terrorists, ideally before they have struck.

But gathering and analyzing intelligence on terrorists is extremely difficult. Those groups are increasingly adept at using low and high tech methods to evade surveillance, often speak languages in which few Americans are fluent, and are protected by fiercely loyal clan, tribal, or religious cultures where outsiders are immediately spotted. Somehow the CIA and other intelligence agencies must become better at penetrating those cultures in which terrorist groups thrive. Training and infiltrating case officers with no official cover into those alien cultures is an extremely risky and time-consuming venture. Another dilemma involves what the CIA euphemistically calls "special activities." Those can include "black bag jobs" of stealing secrets or planting listening devices, spreading disinformation, and committing acts of sabotage and even assassination. Authorizing such an operation is a very tough choice. The chances and consequences of getting caught must be weighed against the mission's hoped for benefits.

Compounding those challenges was the crusade of George W. Bush and his fellow conservatives in Iraq, which provides the perfect model of what not to do about movements like Al Qaeda. Contrary to the claims of the Bush administration, Iraq posed no threat to its neighbors, let alone the United States before the American invasion on March 19, 2003. Saddam Hussein regime may have been among the world's most brutal, but it neither nurtured weapons of mass destruction nor Al Qaeda. The conservative crusade in Iraq may not have found any nuclear, chemical, or biological weapons, but it has provoked Islamist extremism and war against the United States and its allies in Iraq, destabilized friendly governments like Jordan, Egypt, Pakistan, and Saudi Arabia, enhanced the power of enemies

like Iran and Syria, and drained enormous amounts of American
wealth, power, prestige, and honor.

CONSEQUENCES

Can a war against terrorists be won? History reveals that terrorism
can be contained, diminished, and outright destroyed or converted.
Yet, while terrorism cannot be successfully attacked until it is understood, the motivations for some terrorist groups and individuals defy
easy analysis. Old terrorism is rooted in failed states, new terrorism
in failed psyches. It is possible to win a war against the former with
better security, intelligence, retaliation, and incentives. Yet deterrence
clearly is not effective against zealots willing to blow themselves up in
truck bombs or fly airliners into sky-scrappers. Terrorism will exist as
long as people are so alienated from society and themselves that they
believe that violence is the only path to salvation. And all it takes is
that one nondescript man carrying a suitcase, test-tube, or computer
thumb with a very unusual load.

The fears of being a terrorist victim have increased since
September 11 among Americans and many other people around the
world. Just what are the odds of being killed or wounded in a terrorist attack? There were 11,650 acts of international terrorism from
1968 to 2001. Although over 10,000 people died in those attacks,
85.5 percent of those attacks were nonfatal while another 8 percent
resulted in only one death. Thus two or more deaths occurred in only
6.4 percent of all attacks. Indeed there were not even any injuries in
82 percent of all attacks. Of the 678 attacks that took place within the
United States, 93.9 percent resulted in no fatalities or grievous property damage. Before September 11 and excluding the 1996 Oklahoma
City bombing, less than a hundred people died on American soil.
During those same years the populations of the United States and
world rose respectively from 200 million to 300 million and from 4.5
billion to over 6 billion. The odds of being a terrorist victim are long
indeed![10]

Those Americans who fight or fear terrorism can take heart at
some realities. First of all, aside from Al Qaeda's attacks on Americans
within and beyond the United States, most attacks by other groups
and individuals have been relatively limited in numbers, deaths, and
destruction. That, of course, is no comfort to those who have lost relatives, friends, and property from attacks. Still, the United States can
remain relatively safe if it funds and deploys the full array of sensible
counterterrorist measures. There have been no significant attacks by

Al Qaeda or other terrorists groups against the United States since September 11. That certainly does not mean that another will not happen. But the chances of that diminish as Al Qaeda's power erodes under the unrelenting counterterrorist efforts of the United States and over ninety allies around the world.

Although Al Qaeda's global network of members, supporters, and money is unprecedented, history is not on its side. Every terrorist group has sooner or later stopped executing terrorist attacks and almost always dissolves. A study of thirty-one groups that existed from the 1950s through the 1980s found that a group's average active operational life expectancy was six and a half years, although many continued to issue the occasional manifesto long after they lost most of their followers and gave up terrorism. Another study found that 90 percent of terrorist groups last less than a year; of the 10 percent that survive that the first year, half dissolve within a decade. Although each group had its own unique set of reasons for doing so, usually the government became more effective at the strategy of crushing and/or co-opting the terrorists. As with any other stressful career, even the most committed terrorist can experience emotional "burnout" and then drop out. Harsh realities can expose a group's delusions. The attacks provoke public rage against rather than support for the group. Donations from supporters dry up. The constant danger and despair erode morale. Government policies meet some or all of the group's demands. When all that happens, the group must reinvent itself or die. The IRA has existed since 1916 and the PLO since 1964 because they have been flexible enough to adapt to changing circumstance, including setting aside terrorism when it was appropriate to do so.[11]

Yet, though terrorist groups come and go, terrorism is as old as humanity, will undoubtedly be around as long as humanity survives, and may ultimately be the reason for its extinction.

CHAPTER 5

Weapons of Mass Destruction

*It may be that we shall by a process of sublime irony have reached a
stage where safety will be the sturdy child of terror and survival the
twin brother of annihilation.*

Winston Churchill

*Today every inhabitant of this planet must contemplate the day
when this planet may no longer be habitable. Every man, woman,
and child lives under a nuclear sword of Damocles, hanging by
the slenderest of threads, capable of being cut at any moment by
accident or miscalculation or madness.*

John F. Kennedy

*I know not with what weapons World War III will be fought, but
World War IV will be fought with sticks and stones.*

Albert Einstein

The Shadow

Since the first human used a stone to crack open a nut through the
latest generation of supercomputers, the development of technology
has benefited humanity in an infinite number of ways. Imagine life
without just three types of technology we have mastered—chemicals,
biotechnology, and nuclear energy. Chemicals can render foul water
fit to drink, prolong the shelf-life of perishable foods, and purge our
own bodies of deadly germs. Biotechnology can create plants that
flourish in deserts or cows that yield three times as much milk as their
ancestors. Nuclear energy can light our homes, cook our food, and
warm our bodies.

Yet technology can literally be a double-edged sword. Many of
the same technologies that enrich our lives also carry with them
the capacity to destroy us. During the twentieth century chemical

weapons like mustard gas and sarin killed or maimed hundreds of thousands of people in acts of terrorism. So far only Japan has waged large-scale biowarfare but may have killed millions of Chinese during World War II. In 2001, the right-wing American terrorist who sent anthrax-laced letters through the mail killed five people and forced the shutdown of contaminated buildings including part of the U.S. Senate. The atomic bombs dropped on Hiroshima and Nagasaki at once ended World War II in the Pacific and killed over 200,000 people—since then we have all existed under the shadow of a genocidal mushroom cloud. As if those methods of the mass destruction of people and property were somehow inadequate, governments and terrorist groups will soon try to stock their arsenals with directed energy weapons (DEWs).

Here, we explore the key concepts, developments, and paradoxes of weapons of mass destruction, with an emphasis on the nuclear arms race and its control.

THE NUCLEAR CROWN OF DESTRUCTION

Nuclear power is still the deadliest weapon of mass destruction. At the peak of the nuclear arms race the world groaned under the weight of perhaps 50,000 nuclear weapons with the destructive power of 1 million Hiroshima atomic bombs or 1,600 times the "firepower released in World War II, the Korean War, and the Vietnam War that killed 44,000,000 people."[1] Although a series of arms control treaties between the United States and Russia has cut that number, enough nuclear weapons remain to wipe out most of humanity immediately while the radioactive fallout and "nuclear winter" would most likely soon kill everyone else.

The destructive power of nuclear weapons is mind-boggling. One "kiloton" equals 2,200 pounds of TNT. The atomic bomb dropped on Hiroshima was equal to 20 kilotons or 44,000 tons of TNT. One "megaton" equals 2.2 million pounds of TNT. One B-52 bomber alone carries 25 megatons of nuclear explosives or 12.5 times the destructive power of all bombs dropped during World War II![2] A cruise missile launched from a submarine can fly 1,500 miles and explode with 13 times the destructive power of the Hiroshima bomb. ICBMs are the most destructive nuclear weapons of all. An ICBM fired from Nebraska can travel 8,000 miles at 15,000 miles per hour to explode with 300 times the destructive power of the Hiroshima bomb (table 5.1).[3]

Table 5.1 Nuclear Weapons by Country, 2010

	Stockpiles	Operational	ICBMs/ Warheads	SLBMs/ Warheads
Russia	14,000	5,192	430/1,605	176/624
United States	5,400	4,075	488/764	288/1,728
France	348	348	26/26	48/288
China	240	193	0	12/12
Britain	185	160	0	48/144
Israel	80	?	0	0
Pakistan	60	?	0	0
India	50	?	0	0
North Korea	10	?	0	0

Source: The Nuclear Information Project.

A nuclear explosion includes three elements: initial blast, thermal or heat, and radiation. A 1-megaton bomb can destroy all brick buildings within four miles and burn human flesh up to nine miles of ground zero. A 10-megaton bomb can destroy up to nine and burn up to twenty-four miles. A 100-megaton bomb can destroy up to eighteen and burn up to seventy miles. The explosion's intense heat creates a fire storm that sucks in oxygen and hurls out vast winds that vaporize virtually everything around. A 100-megaton nuclear bomb could cause fire storms up to seventy-five miles away. The radiation fall out of a 10-megaton bomb could spread to 100,000 square miles. Human exposure to 100–200 roentgens of radiation would cause vomiting, nausea, and weakness, and almost inevitably cancer and genetic mutations. Exposure of over 200 roentgens can cause death for most people either immediately or shortly thereafter. The psychological effects would be devastating for those who escaped direct injury, but understood that their society and all they cherished was forever destroyed.[4]

The nuclear threat may be more insidious than a nuclear war. Accidents have left at least fifty nuclear warheads and nine reactors strewn across the world's oceans. The Chernobyl meltdown rendered a huge swath of Ukraine uninhabitable and spewed radiation that drifted worldwide. Twice as much radiation as Chernobyl has been released as nuclear waste into Lake Karachay from the nearby Chelyabinsk nuclear warhead production plant, making it the most polluted spot on earth. Any one standing on its shores without protective clothing would die instantly.

The nuclear threat comes not just from bombs or generators with nuclear cores. A "dirty nuclear bomb" is composed of radioactive materials packed around conventional explosives; its detonation in a crowded city center would probably not kill many people but would wreak enormous economic damage since that district would have to be abandoned for years or even decades as the contamination slowly subsided.

Nuclear Tests: 1945–2009

Even if a nuclear war never again occurs, we all carry with us evidence of the nuclear arms race. The fallout from every atmospheric nuclear test since 1945 has drifted around the world, and all human beings have a cocktail of radioactive elements in their bones. In all, between 1945 and 1998, the 6 nuclear powers conducted 2,050 nuclear explosions at 35 sites, an average of 1 every 9 days. From 1945 until the 1963 "Limited Test Ban Treaty," 424 nuclear bombs were exploded in the atmosphere, an average of 23.6 times a year. China and France refused to sign the treaty, which banned tests in the atmosphere, underwater, and in space. Between 1963 and 1991, France conducted 41 atmospheric tests and China 23, for a combined average of 2.4 times a year. The total number of nuclear tests in the atmosphere and below ground are given in table 5.2.

Table 5.2   Nuclear Weapons Tests

Country	Number of Tests
United States	1,030
Soviet Union	715
France	210
Britain	45
China	45
India	3
Pakistan	2
North Korea	1

Source: Arms Control Association.

What purpose do these vast nuclear forces, and all the testing, tens of thousands of scientists and engineers, trillions of dollars and foregone development opportunities they consume, serve?[5]

Many people argue that, paradoxically, nuclear arsenals preserve the peace. By the late 1950s, the United States and Soviet Union had each accumulated enough weapons to annihilate the other, a situation known as mutually assured destruction (MAD) and the essence of nuclear deterrence. Early in the nuclear age, Winston Churchill captured the paradoxes of deterrence: "it may be that we shall by a process of sublime irony have reached a stage where safety will be the sturdy child of terror and survival the twin brother of annihilation."[6]

"Deterrence" occurs when the other side does not attack because it believes it would lose far more than it would gain—nuclear deterrence involves the fear of being destroyed as a civilization. To wield deterrence, a state needs two essential elements: capability and credibility. Capability includes not just a large and survivable nuclear force but also a "C3I" (communications, control, communications, and intelligence) system that can survive a nuclear attack and a leadership with the political resolve to retaliate. To deter a foreign attack in the first place, it must clearly communicate its military capacity and resolve to any potential enemies, and prove its credibility by not failing to use that power when its interests are threatened. Only then does it have deterrent power. Psychology is as important to deterrence as hardware.

Nations possess nuclear weapons to deter other nuclear powers from attacking them. Nuclear power is effective only in how convincingly its holders can threaten its use, and in how rationally and carefully national decision makers analyze the costs and benefits of their actions. Deterrence cannot be a bluff because it just might be called. Deterrence has failed if nuclear power is actually used.

The Nuclear Arms Race

Amidst World War II, five nations—the United States, Germany, Japan, Britain, and the Soviet Union—raced to create an atomic bomb. The United States won, a controversial victory only if the alternatives are dismissed. Code-named the "Manhattan Project," America's $2 billion effort was the only one among the five great powers with the scientific, financial, and material resources vital for the bomb's creation. On July 16, 1945, near Alamogordo, New Mexico, American scientists exploded the world's first atomic bomb.

President Harry Truman received word of the successful test while he was meeting with Prime Minister Winston Churchill and Premier Joseph Stalin at Potsdam, Germany. These Allied leaders were discussing the strategy for defeating Japan and determining the postwar world's fate. Truman realized that with the atomic bomb the war could be won quickly without the estimated loss of half a million American lives necessary to invade and defeat Japan (as well as tens of millions of Japanese who were determined to fight to their death), and the need for the Soviet armies that Stalin had promised would soon attack Japanese forces in China and Korea. Truman casually mentioned to Stalin that the United States now had an atomic bomb. The Soviet dictator was not visibly moved by the news; his spies had already passed on the word along with secrets that would be essential to the Soviet testing of a bomb four years later. The United States dropped an atomic bomb on the Japanese city of Hiroshima on August 6. Soviet forces attacked the Japanese army in China on August 8. An atomic bomb was dropped on Nagasaki on August 9. On August 14, Japan announced that it would surrender.

The nuclear age began with the United States possessing unprecedented, literally earth-shattering power. But America also faced unprecedented, devastating dangers. What if a potential enemy like the Soviet Union got its hands on nuclear weapons?

Having released the nuclear genie from its bottle and realizing its horrors, the Americans unsuccessfully tried to stuff it back inside. In March 1946, the Truman White House submitted the "Baruch Plan," named after its author Bernard Baruch, to the United Nations Security Council. Under that plan, the United States would give up its atomic power to the United Nations if all other countries agreed never to develop such weapons and to open their scientific facilities to international inspection. The Soviets vetoed that plan with the fear that the United States would still retain knowledge of how to manufacture such bombs. Moscow then offered to give up its own nuclear program but only if Washington first surrendered its atomic weapons and technology. Truman refused. The nuclear race continued.

The Truman administration reasoned that it did not matter if the nuclear genie was out of the bottle as long as the United States controlled it. With a monopoly over atomic power, the United States could deter any attack on its vital interests and defeat any enemies should war break out. After America's wartime alliance with the Soviet Union broke down into a Cold War in 1947, nuclear weapons became central to America's containment policy.

Although the Soviet Union exploded its first nuclear bomb in August 1949, the United States had an overwhelming superiority in the number, quality, and delivery of nuclear weapons for the next decade. Moscow had nuclear bombs but lacked the means of delivering them. Soviet bombers had enough fuel only for a one-way trip to the United States, and America's air defense system of radar and interceptors would probably have wiped out such an attack before it reached the country. In contrast, American B-36 bombers based in

Britain, Italy, Japan, and Alaska could quickly reach most of the Soviet Union. Nuclear technology advanced steadily during this period. The first bombs were fission ("atomic bomb"), but they were rendered obsolete in 1952 when the United States tested its first fusion ("hydrogen bomb" or thermonuclear) bomb. The Soviets exploded their own hydrogen bomb the following year.

American nuclear strategy during this period was based on "deterrence" of a Soviet invasion of Western Europe, Japan, or the Middle East. The United States played the game of "brinksmanship" in which it would go to the "brink" of war in order to force the Soviets to back down. If war broke out and Moscow attacked the West, then Washington would respond with the "massive retaliation" of all its nuclear arsenal against the Soviet Union. Since slow flying bombers were the only means of delivering the nuclear payload, the targets would be relatively accessible Soviet cities and industries, a strategy known as "countervalue."

Although this strategy was an integral part of American policy from 1947, it became explicit following the North Korea attack on South Korea in 1950 when American Secretary of State John Foster Dulles announced that henceforth any communist attack on the West would be countered "in a manner and at a place of our own choosing," implying strongly that Washington would retaliate with nuclear weapons against the Soviet Union even if it was not directly involved militarily in that communist aggression. The Eisenhower administration rattled its nuclear saber against North Korea and China during negotiations for an armistice for the Korean War in 1953, and to deter a threatened Chinese attack on Taiwan's islands of Quemoy and Matsu in 1957.

American nuclear superiority clearly began to erode when the Soviet Union in 1957 was the first to launch an intercontinental ballistic missile (ICBM) and place its Sputnik satellite into orbit. Although the United States successfully launched both an ICBM and satellite shortly thereafter, the Soviet ability to target ICMBs across America appeared to be a significant shift in the nuclear power balance. Psychologically, Americans perceived themselves to be vulnerable and in danger of losing their lead. The 1960 American presidential election was fought and won partially over the issue of a "missile gap" the United States supposedly suffered with the Soviet Union. In reality, the Soviet Union would not achieve genuine nuclear parity with the United States for another decade. The Soviets had many nuclear bombs but were unable to deliver more than a handful at that time. It was estimated that a full nuclear exchange would have resulted in as many as 50 million Soviet deaths but "only" 5–10 million American deaths.

As the Soviets began to catch up in the nuclear arms race, Washington shifted its nuclear war strategy from massive retaliation to "flexible response." Henceforth, if the Warsaw Pact attacked West Europe, the United States would use nuclear weapons only if the Soviets appeared on the verge of winning a conventional war. But rather than launch ICBMs against Moscow, the United States would use tactical nuclear weapons against Warsaw Pact armies in Central Europe. If the Soviets responded by using their own tactical nuclear weapons, the United States would escalate to regional nuclear weapons that could hit targets in Eastern Europe and the western Soviet Union. Only if Moscow matched that escalation would Washington launch ICBMs at targets across the Soviet Union. With the highly accurate and fast ICBMs, the United States now targeted Soviet missile silos and command and control centers rather than cities and industries, a strategy known as "counterforce."

The flexible response strategy had several flaws. Most basic was the question of whether the United States could control a step-by-step escalation up the "nuclear ladder," from conventional to tactical, regional, and finally strategic levels. A "counterforce" strategy depends on striking first. Clearly there is no point in targeting the other side's silos and then wait for them to fire first, because if you retaliate you would simply be destroying empty silos. If one side either explicitly or implicitly declares a first-strike strategy, then both must adhere to the logic of either "use 'em or lose 'em" that in turn exacerbates tensions and the chance for nuclear war in a crisis. Not surprisingly, Moscow rejected Washington's flexible response strategy and maintained that it would massively retaliate against the United States itself even if Washington exploded just one nuclear device on the battlefield of Central Europe.

And while there was little question that Washington would retaliate if Moscow fired nuclear weapons at the United States, there was doubt whether it would be willing "to trade Chicago for Hamburg." In other words, the flexible response strategy dictated that if Moscow dropped a nuclear bomb on Hamburg, the United States would respond by destroying a comparable Soviet city like Minsk.

Was flexible response credible? Many Soviets and others thought Washington was bluffing in its determination to uphold its "extended deterrence" strategy for Europe, as opposed to its "basic deterrence" of protecting solely the United States. If a Soviet attack on Hamburg was followed by an American attack on Minsk, Moscow would certainly retaliate by striking an American city like Chicago. Faced with this probability, an American president might well abandon Europe to a Soviet takeover rather than risk the nuclear devastation of the United States. After leaving the presidency, Jimmy Carter admitted that if faced with this dilemma, he would have backed down rather than escalated the nuclear war. Henry Kissinger also asserted that extended deterrence involves "strategic assurances that we can not possibly mean or if we do mean, we should not execute because if we should execute, we risk the destruction of civilization."[7] Thus nuclear deterrence worked both ways; an American attack on the Soviet Union was deterred, and, in turn, a Soviet attack on the United States.

There are "first-" and "second-"strike nuclear abilities and weapons. A "first-strike" capability means a country can strike first and destroy most of the enemy's nuclear force so that it would not retaliate with its remaining forces because it would then suffer a nuclear attack on its cities. A country has a second-strike ability if it can absorb an enemy first strike and then retaliate and inflict "unacceptable damage" to the enemy, which Secretary of Defense McNamara defined in 1964 as the ability to destroy half of Soviet industry and a quarter of its population. As will be seen, the United States may well have a first-strike capability and most certainly has a second-strike ability. Arguably, despite its vast array of nuclear weapons, the Soviet Union and its successor, Russia, has neither.

Washington has a "triad" strategic force built upon on "first-strike weapons" like ICBMs, which are fast and accurate but, in their fixed silos, vulnerable to an enemy attack, and "second-strike weapons" like bombers, which can either directly drop nuclear bombs or fire air-launched cruise missiles (ALCMs), and submarines with sea-launched ballistic missiles (SLBMs). Nuclear bombs launched from bombers and submarines are slower and less accurate, but also less vulnerable to an attack. Cruise missiles are the most versatile nuclear weapons since they can be launched by submarines, surface ships, bombers, and land-based systems. First-strike weapons are best used in a counterforce strategy against the enemy's ICBM silos and headquarters while second-strike weapons are better targeted against an enemy's cities and armies. There is some overlap between second and first-strike weapons. An ICBM in a hardened missile silo could survive an enemy strike and retaliate, while SLBMs are now as fast and accurate as ICBMs, and thus have first-strike capabilities with the relative invulnerability of a second-strike weapon.

Although by the late 1960s, there was a rough parity in the number of warheads, there was and remains an asymmetry in the superpowers' types of nuclear weapons and delivery systems. About 80 percent of America's strategic nuclear weapons remain in second-strike delivery systems—sea-based and air-based (one third each), and only a third in land-based ICBMs. Thus, in a nuclear war, Washington could launch a first strike with its ICMBs against Russian missile silos and bomber bases, while using its attack submarines and aircraft to destroy Soviet nuclear submarines. Even though some Russian nuclear forces would probably survive an American attack, Moscow would probably not retaliate, knowing that the United States would use its second-strike SLBMs and bombers against Russian cities.

Although Moscow also has a triad system, its ICBM leg is overwhelmingly the largest with 60 percent of the total strategic warheads, while air-based account for 10 percent and sea-based 30 percent. None of the Russian triad legs is considered very sturdy. The Russian bomber command is thought incapable of penetrating American air defenses and its submarine fleet is vulnerable to American attack submarines and aircraft. Russia's ICBMs are thought to be less accurate than America's, with a circular error probability (CEP) of 1,000 feet, which means half would probably fall within and half beyond 1,000 feet of the target, and most would fail to destroy a hardened silo; that compares to 265 feet for America's ICBMs. And Russia's nuclear forces are much more vulnerable than Washington's. In a war, Moscow might feel compelled "to either use or lose" its entire system, particularly its most vulnerable ICBM force. However, Moscow has ruled out a first strike since it is deterred by America's vast second-strike capability.

Several technical factors further deter an ICBM first strike by either side. One is the probability that missiles flying over the Arctic would be drawn slightly off course by the magnetic north pole. Second, even if the ICBMs are able to directly strike their targets, the explosion of one bomb would throw out an immense electromagnetic pulse (EMG) that would knock all other incoming missiles off course and might well destroy them in flight. Building thousands of dummy silos, the real ones while camouflaging can make accurate first strike targeting nearly impossible. Electronic countermeasures can jam the sensitive guidance systems of the incoming missiles and shove them off course. Finally, both sides have already hardened their missile silos to survive an impact of 2,000 pounds of explosives per square inch.

Calculations of the nuclear balance and appropriate strategies were complicated by the development of multiple warheads or multiple independently targetable reentry vehicles (MIRVs) during the 1970s. Of America's strategic nuclear force, a Minuteman III can carry up to three MIRVs, a D-5 Trident submarine SLBM eight MIRVs, and a MX (Peacekeeper) missiles ten MIRVs. The Soviets have a similar MIRV system. MIRVs simultaneously weakened American and strengthened Soviet deterrence. The more Moscow MIRVed its ICBMs and SLBMs, the greater the chance that enough nuclear forces would survive an American first strike and thus could retaliate against American cities. Knowing this, Washington would hesitate before launching a first strike, even at the tactical level.

America's submarine fleet is particularly formidable. A submarine armed with 20 MIRVed D-5 Trident SLBMs could devastate 160 targets across Russia. The D-5 SLBM can be used as both a first- and second-strike weapons. It is as accurate as an ICBM and far less vulnerable to an enemy attack. Yet it has its drawbacks. A Trident submarine's wake, even deep underwater, can be detected by satellite and its engine noises picked up by listening devices. In wartime, communications between the commander-in-chief and the submarine fleet would be tenuous at best, which is why submarine commanders are given the discretion or permissive action link (PAL) to fire their SLBMs without a direct command under certain circumstances.

While the number of nuclear warheads increased steadily until the late 1980s, their individual destructive power has been decreasing since the 1960s. Today, America's total warhead destructive power is only a quarter its 1960 level, while Moscow's is about one-third. Increased accuracy negated the need for immense payloads. Now that theoretically both American and Russian missiles can strike within 1,000 feet of their target, they no longer need to be equipped with enough megatons of explosives to devastate everything within 20 or so miles. Another reason is the development of conventional weapons with as much destructive power as small nuclear bombs but without the radioactive fallout, thus rendering the latter obsolete.

Ronald Reagan won the presidency in 1980 partly from his claim that there was a nuclear "window of vulnerability" with the Soviet Union, and his promise vastly to increase American military power, which would include regaining nuclear superiority over the Soviet Union and the ability to "win" a nuclear war. Despite Reagan's claims, there was no more a "window of vulnerability" in 1980 than there was a "missile gap" claimed by Kennedy in the 1960 election. Although the Soviets had a greater number of ICBM missiles and warheads, or more equivalent megatons (EMT) of explosives, that advantage was more than offset by the greater accuracy or hard-target kill (HTK) capacity of American ICBMs and its second-strike superiority in SLBMs, bombers, and cruise missiles. By placing its ICBMs in super-hardened sites, America's land-based missiles were relatively protected, which helped deter a Soviet first strike upon them. And only a third of America's nuclear bombs were atop land-based ICBMs, while ICBMs made up 60 percent of the total Soviet nuclear forces. Without a first-strike and perhaps a second-strike capability, it was the Soviets who suffered the "window of vulnerability" to a first strike.

The idea of winning a nuclear war, known as the "nuclear utilization theory" with the appropriate acronym of NUT, was the opposite of MAD's premise that there would be only losers in a nuclear exchange. Those who advocated NUT claimed that by increasing America's ability to win a war, they strengthened deterrence and thus lessened the actual chance of war. MAD advocates countered by arguing that the opposite would occur, that in a crisis the White House would be more inclined to pull the nuclear trigger than retreat from the brink. Henry Kissinger dismissed NUT by pointing out "What in the name of God is strategic superiority...What can you do with it?" Faced with such criticism by realists and dropping public support, Reagan eventually began saying "a nuclear war can never be won and should never be fought." For a dozen years the concept of winning a nuclear war was shelved until George W. Bush took the White House. His administration reembraced NUT as a strategy, but for public relations purposes preferred to call it the much more reassuring unilateral assured destruction (UAD).

Actually, America's nuclear war fighting plan contains elements of NUT and MAD. NUT advocates applaud the flexible response strategy, which involves fighting a nuclear war through first strikes at each nuclear level. America's nuclear forces, however, are heavily weighted in favor of second-strike weapons, which MAD advocates favor because they are the essence of deterrence. In an all-out war, the Pentagon has targeted not only Russia's nuclear forces, but also 65 percent of its industrial power and 35 percent of its population. That strategy thus contains both counterforce and countervalue targets.

Although Reagan appeared to renounce NUT, he championed a concept that theoretically gave the United States the ability to destroy the Soviet Union in a devastating nuclear first strike. In March 1983, Reagan unveiled his Strategic Defense Initiative (SDI) program, which he claimed would shield the United States from a

Soviet attack and make "nuclear weapons impotent and obsolete." As part of a vast public relations campaign to sell the program, the Reagan administration ran television commercials with a little girl's voice describing a child's drawing of the world in which Soviet missiles exploded high in space while Americans with smiling faces survive below.

The initial SDI scheme would have involved at least three different ballistic missile defense (BMD) layers in space between the Soviet Union and United States, and a fourth stationed on ground in the United States. The first defense layer would be parked in space directly above the Soviet ICBM silos to destroy as many as possible during their relatively slow-moving, easily tracked "boost phase" before the MIRVs are released in space. Another layer would counter the "busing phase" where the cone releases the MIRVs along with such decoys as metal flakes and infrared aerosols to reflect laser beams. A third layer would counter the "midcourse phase" where the MIRVs disperse toward their separate targets and their speeds reach the highest levels. The ground-based fourth layer would target those remaining missiles in their "terminal phase" when they reentered the atmosphere. Each layer would fire a barrage of lasers or particle beams at the incoming ICBMs.

Reagan's scheme was attacked from several directions. SDI was seen by nearly all experts along with Moscow as the most destabilizing system yet devised. The Soviets argued that SDI would give the United States an overwhelming first-strike advantage. In a crisis Washington could attack Soviet ICBMs, SLBMs, bombers, and command and control centers, and then use SDI to destroy any remaining missiles that Moscow launched in retaliation. Moscow threatened to counter SDI by building thousands of more ICBMs in super-hardened bunkers that could withstand an American first strike and overwhelm the SDI system. Or the Soviets could avoid the expense of building more missiles by simply putting hundreds of decoys in their existing ICBMs. The SDI satellites would be overwhelmed by having to fire at hundreds of targets, only a fraction of which were actual nuclear warheads. A final Soviet option was to deploy anti-satellite weapons (ASAT), park them in space beside SDI, and detonate them before launching a first strike. It would cost the Soviet Union a small fraction to neutralize or overwhelm SDI compared to what it would cost the United States to build it. The closer the United States got to deploying SDI, the more incentive the Soviets would have to strike first. Moscow also stepped up its own SDI research.

In addition to this argument, American critics pointed out that SDI would cost at least $500 billion and possibly $1 trillion, consuming scarce resources that were desperately needed for investment elsewhere in the economy. Most scientists, including in the U.S. Office of Technology Assessment, argued that the technological obstacles to SDI were insurmountable; SDI would require the ability of a bullet to hit another bullet traveling as fast as 30,000 miles per hour. Furthermore, there was no means of testing it if it should become operational, and it would have to work perfectly the first time. Just how could those satellites generate enough energy to shoot a laser beam hundreds of miles through space to penetrate a hardened steel missile cone?

Advocates could only sheepishly shrug and mention a few ideas like nuclear reactors or space mirrors to use solar energy. But knowledgeable scientists dismissed those ideas as fantasies given current technologies. It would take only thirty minutes for an ICBM fired from Siberia to run the SDI gauntlet and obliterate New York. And an operational system could be easily destroyed by Soviet ASAT weapons or overwhelmed by decoys. Even if it worked, the space shield against an ICBM attack would not protect the United States against an attack by SLBMs, cruise missiles, or bombers. In addition, SDI would violate the 1972 Anti-Ballistic Missile Treaty. America's allies complained that the scheme could protect the United States while they would remain vulnerable to an attack. Finally, no government would ever conceivably order a nuclear attack on the United States because it would face nuclear devastation in retaliation; dictators in Moscow, Beijing, Pyongyang, or Tehran might be homicidal but they are not suicidal. In other words, deterrence rendered Star Wars completely unnecessary. Thus SDI would spark an endless nuclear arms race, which would deepen tensions, economically bankrupt both sides, increase the chance for war, and not even protect the United States from a nuclear attack. In all, the experts warned that SDI was at best a financially crippling "Star Wars" fantasy and at worst made a nuclear holocaust much more likely.[8]

From 1983 to 2001, the "modest down-payment on the future" promised by Reagan for SDI had cost American taxpayers over $95 billion and some of their best scientists, technicians, and laboratories, while the program remained stuck in the theoretical stage. Reagan's original $500 billion scheme for protecting population centers had been rejected as unfeasible and the goals shifted to protecting ICBM sites. In the late 1980s, SDI advocates shifted from the layered defense system to a "brilliant pebbles" scheme involving thousands of small nonnuclear satellites in orbit, which would ram incoming missiles. But that idea too was shelved as technologically impossible. The next versions were the ground-based Theater High Altitude Area Defense (THAAD) and the Navy Theater-Wide Defense (NTWD), which have the more modest goal of shooting down a few rather than hundreds of incoming missiles, although it is supposed to protect all of the United States. Those technologies are called "kinetic kill devices," which simply means slamming a missile into a missile. Both systems have failed most of their tests to date, either from technical reasons or because the Pentagon rigged the results.

Despite the mounting bills and failures, SDI will not die. A coalition of politicians motivated by pork-barrel politics and Reaganite ideology succeeded in resurrecting scaled-down versions. When tests fail, rather than give up, adherents simply demand more money. After taking office, President George W. Bush committed the United States to deploying by 2020 a system of space-, air-, sea-, and land-based interceptions whose total cost is conservatively estimated at $225 billion. Defense, technology, and science experts blasted Bush's missile defense scheme as a system that cannot work against a threat that does not exist. Nonplused by that barrage of criticism, Bush lived up to his promise to deploy the first part of the system by 2004, the year he ran for reelection, even if the system failed all its tests. Critics dubbed Bush's a "scarecrow defense."

For now Star Wars remains a technological "Holy Grail." But that may not forever be an impossible dream. Within a generation the vision of a limited missile defense just may be realized by utilizing "directed energy" technologies.

Nuclear Arms Control

"Vertical proliferation" occurs when one country diversifies its types and increases its numbers of nuclear weapons, such as has occurred between America and Russia; "horizontal proliferation" occurs when new countries acquire nuclear weapons. Regardless of who owns them, the possession of nuclear weapons has clear benefits and costs. Nuclear weapons can bring a country more prestige, allies, power over others, independence, and security from attack.

They also suck up scarce resources, undermine economic development, spark one's adversaries to get or increase their own nuclear weapons, and make the owner a nuclear target in the event of war.

Security or Insecurity: Pakistan, the Bomb, and Development

Does heavy military spending help or harm a country's development? Do nuclear weapons make a country more or less secure? As always, the answers to such questions depend on circumstances. Take Pakistan, for example. Pakistan faces a perennial threat from its neighbor India. India's 1.3 billion mostly Hindu people dwarf Pakistan's 180 million nearly all Muslims. Those religious differences exacerbate geopolitical conflicts that exploded into war between the two countries in 1947, 1965, and 1971. How did Pakistan fare in these wars? Pakistan fought India to a draw in first two wars, but in the third lost its province of Bangladesh, which broke away and became an independent country.

Many animosities sparked those wars, the worst being the fate of Kashmir, which caps the northern end of both countries. India occupies two-thirds of Kashmir whose population is two-thirds Muslim. Pakistan owns the rest. Both sides claim all of Kashmir. In between the three wars, small-scale fighting has periodically flared along the Line of Control (LOC) splitting Kashmir between Pakistan and India, with about 25,000 people having been killed.

To counter India, Pakistan's government maintains not just a large conventional military but also has developed nuclear weapons and missiles. In May 1998, India tested five and Pakistan six nuclear weapons, along with missiles capable of devastating the other. India had previously tested a nuclear weapon in May 1974. The tensions eased somewhat when, in February 1999, the two countries signed the Lahore Declaration whereby they pledged to avoid nuclear war and negotiate a solution to Kashmir.

Are Pakistan and India locked into a security dilemma whereby steps taken to build up one's military actually make war not only more likely but also more destructive? Can spending too much or too little on the military actually provoke the attack a country wants to deter?

It is difficult and often impossible to measure just what benefits high military spending bring a country, especially ones as poverty-stricken as India and Pakistan. The costs of military spending, however, are easier to calculate. Pakistan's government spends ever more on a military that it cannot afford. Two-thirds of Pakistan's government goes to the military and debt servicing. In 2009, the government's foreign debt surpassed $40 billion. Pakistan's economy is an ever more fraying basket case. The country runs perennial trade deficits that are paid for only by borrowing ever more money.

Pakistan's nuclear tests imposed enormous costs on the country. The direct costs of its nuclear program are not public knowledge. Although the IMF and the United States imposed economic sanctions on both countries after their tests, they hurt Pakistan worse. The Pakistani rupee plunged 25 percent in value, raising the country's import bill another $3.5 billion, and sending inflation and unemployment soaring while remittances from Pakistanis living abroad dropped. Thus was an already poverty-stricken country rendered more so.

Pakistan and India alike are abysmally poor, respectively ranking numbers 136 and 128 with scores of 0.527 and 0.602 (on a scale of 10 with 10 the highest), respectively, in the United Nations Development Program's 178 country ranking of human development in 2008. With a purchasing power parity (PPP) of $2,069, the average Pakistani was poorer than the average Indian with $3,113. In 2008, India's GDP of $3.362 trillion dwarfed Pakistan's $336 billion.

Islamic fundamentalism is growing ever more popular in Pakistan as the government remains corrupt, inept, and brutal, while most people are getting poorer. Islamist militants are warring against the government, conducting ever more terrorist attacks, and overrunning ever more of the country. The second worst case scenario would be for an Islamist revolution to overthrow Pakistan's pro-Western government and get its hand on as many as fifty nuclear weapons. The worst case would be for an Islamist terrorist attack on India to spark a crisis that would erupt into first a conventional and then nuclear war that would kill tens of millions of people and devastate both countries.

Although it would take decades for Washington and Moscow to cap their own nuclear arms race, by the 1960s they were firmly united in limiting the proliferation of nuclear weapons among other states. Neither side wanted to see unstable countries lead by messianic and irrational leaders armed with nuclear weapons. Even worse than the fear that someone like Libya's President Muamar Kaddafi, Iraq's President Saddam Hussein, or North Korea's Kim Il Sung, to name a few, might get their hands on the nuclear trigger, was that terrorist groups could acquire them.[9]

Not everyone agrees that nuclear proliferation is necessarily bad. Some argue that "the spread of nuclear weapons is something that we have worried too much about and tried too hard to stop...the measured spread of nuclear weapons is more to be welcomed than feared."[10] If nuclear deterrence can work for the superpowers, why not for everyone else including the Third World, or so the argument goes. American conservatives, for instance, are adamantly opposed to all international arms control just as they attack regulations on gun ownership within the United States.

Washington and Moscow sponsored and guided the negotiations for the Nuclear Proliferation Treaty (NPT), which was signed in 1968 and came into force in 1970. NPT signatories pledged not to receive, make, or transfer nuclear weapons. The International Atomic Energy Agency (IAEA) is empowered to regulate the NPT by inspecting nuclear energy and other facilities to ensure they are not being used to create nuclear weapons. By 2010, 153 countries had signed the NPT. Unfortunately, some holdouts include those that already possess or others that could possess nuclear weapons including Argentina, Brazil, India, Israel, Pakistan, Chile, and South Africa. North Korea withdrew from the treaty in 2003.

In addition to the NPT, the 1959 Antarctic Treaty, 1967 Outer Space Treaty, 1967 Treaty for the Prohibition of Nuclear Weapons in Latin America, 1971 Seabed Arms Control Treaty, and 1985 South Pacific Nuclear Weapons Treaty limited nuclear weapons in those regions. Washington attempted to strengthen NPT by founding the Nuclear Suppliers' Group in 1975, which regulated the export of nuclear technology and materials. It followed this up in 1978 when Congress passed the Nuclear Non-Proliferation Act that authorizes the White House to retaliate against any nuclear transfers that violate the NPT or Nuclear Suppliers' Group.

Although the NPT has clearly slowed proliferation, it has not stopped it. As the nuclear weapons program of countries like Israel, North Korea, Pakistan, India, Iran, and Iraq prove, there are ways in which states determined to develop nuclear weapons can bypass the NPT. There are over 850 nuclear power plants in more than 60 countries. Running a nuclear plant and dealing with its plutonium by-product provides some of the essential expertise and raw materials necessary to build a nuclear bomb. The rest can be obtained from illegal imports of technicians, parts, and plans from advanced nuclear powers. With the Soviet Union's breakup and recent nuclear treaties reducing the Commonwealth of Independent State's nuclear weapons and facilities, it is feared that thousands of unemployed nuclear experts may sell their services abroad.

The NPT may not have prevented horizontal proliferation, but it did limit the number of new states that developed nuclear weapons. So far only two states—South Africa and Libya—dismantled their nuclear weapons programs. Other states like Taiwan, Argentina, South Korea, and Algeria appear to have shelved their efforts. Iraq's nuclear weapons program was partly destroyed during the 1991 Gulf War and then completely dismantled by the United Nations inspectors. Iran claims that its nuclear program is for energy only, although United Nations inspectors discovered an eighteen-year secret program to enrich uranium beyond levels needed to generate electricity; to date, there is a stalemate between Iran's refusal to yield to demands by the United

States and European Union that it give up its enriched uranium program and open all its facilities to inspection. The most successful effort to curb horizontal proliferation was after the Soviet Union broke up in 1991 when three other countries than Russia held nuclear weapons—Ukraine with 1,650, Kazakhstan with 1,400, and Belarus with 72. On May 23, 1992, those three countries signed a treaty with Moscow and Washington in which they agreed to either destroy or surrender their nuclear weapons to Russia.[11] Despite those successes, China, Britain, France, Israel, India, Pakistan, and North Korea hold varying degrees of nuclear weapons, in addition to the United States and Russia.

Throughout the Cold War and beyond, the American and Russian leaders clearly recognized the horrors of nuclear war. As President Kennedy put it in 1961,

> Today, every inhabitant of this planet must contemplate the day when this planet may no longer be habitable. Every man, women, and child lives under a nuclear sword of Damocles, hanging by the slenderest of threads, capable of being cut at any moment by accident or miscalculation or madness…The mere existence of modern weapons—ten million times more powerful than any that the world has ever seen, and only minutes away from any target on earth—is a source of horror, and discord and distrust…in a spiraling arms race, a nation's security may well be shrinking even as its arms increase.

A year later Soviet Premier Nikita Khrushchev put it even more starkly succinct when he declared that after a nuclear war "the survivors would envy the dead."

By the 1960s, the Cuban missile crisis, nuclear parity, and MAD gave Washington and Moscow powerful incentives to negotiate some limits to the nuclear arms race. The object was not to eliminate nuclear weapons but to achieve a stable nuclear balance. Ideally, nuclear deterrence would be based solely on each side enjoying a limited number of invulnerable second-strike weapons. The worst case would be if both sides had only first-strike weapons, the equivalent of each holding a revolver to the head of the other. In any crisis the impulse would be to either fire first or die. From the 1960s, Washington and Moscow negotiated and signed a series of treaties that either restricted nuclear testing or the numbers and types of nuclear weapons.

Each of four treaties imposed ever more restrictions on nuclear testing. The multilateral 1963 Nuclear Test Ban Treaty prohibited tests in the air, underwater, and outer space. The bilateral 1974 Threshold Nuclear Test Ban Treaty prohibited underground tests of bombs with explosive yields greater than 150 kilotons, while the 1976

Peaceful Nuclear Explosions Treaty outlawed explosions greater than 150 kilotons for peaceful purposes like mining or excavation. The 1990 Underground Testing Verification Treaty specified the means for verifying compliance with the 1974 and 1976 treaties. Finally President Bill Clinton initiated negotiations that culminated with a Comprehensive Test Ban Treaty (CTBT) in 1996, which has since been ratified by over 160 countries.

The United States is legally committed to all of those treaties except the last one. Clinton never submitted CTBT to the Senate for ratification. He knew well its fate. Conservatives had captured the Senate and declared war on that arms control treaty and all others. After taking power, President George W. Bush declared the CTBT dead and buried.

Though they could kill the treaty the conservatives could not kill the treaty's logic. The end of nuclear field tests cemented America's nuclear lead for a decade or so because only the United States then had the computer technology sophisticated enough to test weapons without actually exploding them. Testing is essential to ensure the safety, effectiveness, and thus deterrent value of nuclear weapons. So the United States can continue to upgrade its nuclear forces while those of other countries deteriorate. Indeed, computer technology has allowed the United States to forgo actually exploding nuclear weapons since 1992, thus saving billions of dollars. Exploding bombs is actually an inefficient way to detect possible defects in the 4,000 components of a nuclear bomb. From 1958 to 1993, less than 1 percent of 830 defects discovered were revealed by test explosions.

That was not the CTBT's only advantage for the United States. The treaty would be a boon for American intelligence gathering. To reinforce compliance, over 321 monitoring stations—including 170 to detect underground vibrations, 80 to sniff airborne radioactivity, 60 to reveal sounds, and 11 to sense underwater signs—would be constructed around the world. They could detect a blast of less than 1 kiloton, equal to 1,000 pounds of explosives. In contrast, the atomic bomb dropped on Hiroshima packed 15,000 kilotons of explosives. The United States would provide 25 percent of the detection system's cost.[12]

The 1972 Strategic Arms Limitation Treaty (SALT I) and Anti-Ballistic Missile (ABM) treaties were the first attempt to slow the nuclear arms race between the United States and Soviet Union. SALT I restricted the growth in the number of ICBM and SLBM launchers for five years though allowing their upgrade. The Soviets were allowed to have 1,408 ICBMs and 950 SLBMs and the Americans 1,000 ICBMs and 710 SLBMs. The negotiators reasoned that the

Soviet advantage in the numbers was offset by the American lead in bombers (450 US versus 150 USSR) and greater number of MIRVed ICBMs. The ABM Treaty restricted any ABM systems to one protecting their respective capitals and another elsewhere. The 1979 SALT II Treaty was more comprehensive. The superpowers agreed to limit the combined number of ICBM launchers, SLBM launchers, heavy bombers, and ASBMs (air-to-surface ballistic missiles with ranges over 600 kilometers) to 2,250 launchers and 1,320 MIRVs, of which no more than 820 could be land-based, on each side.

Although SALT I was ratified by both sides, Carter withdrew SALT II from the ratification process begun in the U.S. Senate following the Soviet invasion of Afghanistan in December 1979. Nonetheless, each side followed SALT II's tenets. In order to gain even initial Senate approval for SALT II, Carter had to promise to develop the MX ICBM, which further fueled the arms race. SALT II, however, did prevent the scheduled deployment of 7,600 additional weapons by 1985—2,500 more ICBMs for the Soviet Union and 5,100 for the United States.

There was no progress on arms control for nearly another decade. The Cold War worsened with the Soviet invasion of Afghanistan in 1979 and Carter's return to a global containment strategy. In 1981, the Reagan administration came to power ideologically opposed to arms control and committed to a massive conventional and military expansion. Soviet politics were in disarray with succession problems as their leaders kept dying—Leonid Brezhnev in 1982, Yuri Andropov in 1983, Nikolai Chernenko in 1985.

It was only after Mikhail Gorbachev took power in the Soviet Union in 1985 that the impasse was broken on nuclear weapons, conventional forces, and several other important issues. He stunned the White House by agreeing to the "zero-option" position on missiles in Europe, which conservatives had asserted in hopes the Soviets would never accept it. The 1987 Intermediate Range Nuclear Force Treaty (INF) was a turning point in arms control—for the first time, the superpowers were actually required to destroy certain weapons rather than just limit their expansion, thus reversing decades of nuclear buildup with the beginning of decades of builddown. Each side would eliminate all missiles in Europe with ranges between 300 and 3,400 miles, which required

the United States to destroy 859 missiles: 429 medium range Pershing 2S and ground launched cruise missiles deployed in Europe, 260 medium range missiles not employed, and 170 Pershing 1A shorter range missiles stockpiled in the United States. The Soviet Union was required to destroy 1,752 missiles: 470 medium range SS-20 and SS-4 missiles deployed, 356 medium range missiles not deployed, 387 deployed shorter range missiles and 539 of those weapons in storage.[13]

Also groundbreaking were the verification procedures that allowed each side to conduct on-site-inspections of the other.

The Strategic Arms Reduction Talks (START) began in 1982. The Reagan administration called for cutting the number of warheads from 7,500 to 5,000, of which no more than half could be on ICBMs. After nine years of sporadic negotiations, the START I treaty was finally signed on July 31, 1991. Each side agreed to reduce their land, sea, and air-based ICBMs to 1,600 and their warheads to 6,000. The treaty allowed for twelve types of on-site inspections of both missile sites and production facilities.

START was followed by a series of unilateral announcements in which both sides reduced their nuclear forces. In September 1991, President George H.W. Bush announced the cancellation of the twenty-four–hour alert for long-range bombers, the removal of nuclear weapons from many navy ships, and the halt of the planned deployment of MX ICBMs on railway cars, and called for even greater bilateral cuts in nuclear weapons. President Boris Yeltsin announced in January 1992 that Russia no longer considered the United States its enemy and would no longer target American cities. Four days later, Bush responded by announcing that the United States would cease production of the B-2 bomber, the Midgetman mobile nuclear missile, advanced cruise missiles, and Trident SLBM warheads. Hours later, Yeltsin countered by calling for cuts of up to 2,500 warheads for each superpower and the elimination of all strategic nuclear weapons by 2,000, and announced he would cut Russian military spending to one-seventh the previous year's budget and to halve the Russian army. At this point the momentum of arms cuts broke down as Bush refused to reduce SLBMs, in which the United States had an advantage, below one-third of the then current level and instead called for the elimination of ICBM MIRVs, in which the Russians were superior. But at the June 1992 Washington summit, Bush and Yeltsin agreed to reduce their combined warheads from 16,000 to 6,527 by 2003, of which they would be allowed roughly 3,250 each, and eventually eliminate all of their land-based MIRVs. This agreement eliminated "the most threatening Russian missiles while allowing the United States to retain its most advanced missiles."[14] Although the United States clearly got the best deal, by eliminating the most destabilizing weapons Russia and all of humanity benefit.

Although START I was to have lasted fifteen years, a START II agreement was signed in January 1993 that incorporated many of the unilateral announcements and additional bilateral agreements. Under START II, by 2003, the United States and Russia would cut their nuclear forces to 3,500 and 2,997, respectively. Moscow and Washington agreed to eliminate all MIRVed ICBMs. Each side would retain about 500 single-warhead ICBMs, while the United States would keep 1,728 SLBMs and 1,272 cruise missiles and Russia 1,744 SLBMs and 752 cruise missiles. While the previous nuclear treaties were balanced, START II overwhelmingly favored the United States. Russia had to eliminate the backbone of its ICBM forces while the United States retained its superior SLBM and cruise missile forces. Unfortunately, right-wing hardliners in both countries stalled the American Senate and Russian Duma from ratifying START II. In November 1998, the U.S. Defense Department tried to break the impasse by urging the Clinton White House and Republican controlled Congress unilaterally to cut America's nuclear arsenal to START II levels in hopes of both annually saving billions of dollars on unnecessary weapons and encouraging the Russians to reciprocate. The Republican Party split over the issue, with its realists supporting the Pentagon's initiative and its ideologues opposed. The unilateral cuts did not occur. Clinton and Yeltsin tried to negotiate a START III treaty that would have reduced their respective strategic forces to 2,000 each, but Senate conservatives scuttled that deal.

Like Ronald Reagan, George W. Bush came to office adamantly opposed to arms control before eventually succumbing to the overwhelming intellectual and political logic in its favor. In 2002, American and Russian negotiated Strategic Offensive Reduction Treaty (SORT), which required each side to reduce its strategic nuclear forces to below 2,200 by the year 2012. Unlike the START treaties, SORT did not include provisions to destroy weapons, but only to dismantle and warehouse them.

The most recent reduction occurred in 2010, when President Barack Obama and Russian President Dmitry Medvedev agreed to cut their respective number of ICMBs to 1,550 bombs and 700 launchers.

Lessons of the Nuclear Arms Race

Was the nuclear arms race necessary? Could deterrence, assuming that either side ever had any intention of attacking the other, have been purchased at a much lower cost in financial, technological, and human resources? Did the nuclear arms race make the superpowers and the world more or less secure? Was World War III prevented because of or despite the nuclear arms race?

The United States did use nuclear weapons to compel other states to change their behavior. By one account, America's nuclear strategy may have prevented at least ten crises from escalating into war. In his book *Nuclear Blackmail and Nuclear Balance*, Richard Betts carefully examined four crises when Washington's nuclear forces either probably prevented war or protected American interests—Cuba (1962), Berlin (1948), Korea (1953), and Taiwan (1955), and were of uncertain value in the another six crises—Berlin (1958–1961), Middle East (1973), Suez (1956), Lebanon (1958), Taiwan (1958), and the Persian Gulf (1980).[15] But Washington's power to compel others diminished steadily as Moscow achieved parity.

And what of nuclear deterrence? Although deterrence is supposed to prevent an attack, we can never truly know whether deterrence has actually worked. It could be that the other side never intended an attack in the first place regardless of how much or little military power its opponent held. Nuclear deterrence, like power, is more about psychology than weapons. It also involves paradoxes—Moscow and Washington safeguarded peace by preparing for nuclear annihilation, and expanded their number and type of weapons while negotiating arms control treaties.

If deterrence worked at all, it did so because both sides' forces were relatively invulnerable to an enemy first strike, and thus retained enough power to wipe out the other. The Americans and Russians protected their second-strike capabilities by several means. One is through sheer numbers—simply producing so many ICBMs, SLBMs, and bombers that enough would survive even the enemy's luckiest first strike. Dispersing those weapons as widely as possible increases their invulnerability, as does protecting ICBMs in hardened sites, keeping SLBMs underwater and bombers in the air, and both constantly on the move and hidden.

Nuclear weapons have become useless for actually fighting wars or even preventing a war with a nonnuclear country. When the United States dropped atomic bombs on Hiroshima and Nagasaki, no one understood the danger that radiation posed humanity. As an awareness of that danger grew, more governments and people became convinced that nuclear weapons should never be used. The nuclear standoff and international morality have deterred the other nuclear powers from using their weapons even against nonnuclear countries. The Americans in North Vietnam (1964–1972) and Iraq (1991, 2003), the Soviets in Afghanistan (1979–1989), the Chinese in Vietnam (1979), and the British against Argentina (1982) never considered even threatening to use, let alone use, nuclear weapons to fight those wars.

Barking Up the Wrong Tree?: America, Iraq, and North Korea and Weapons of Mass Destruction

President George W. Bush and his administration repeatedly claimed that Iraq possessed chemical and biological weapons, and was building nuclear weapons, all of which posed an imminent threat to the United States. The United Nations inspection teams, which operated in Iraq from 1991 to 1998, dismissed that claim. They explained that they had uncovered and disarmed nearly all those weapons and if a few escaped detection, they posed no threat. The United Nations Security Council rejected a Bush administration demand for permission to war against Iraq. In defiance of international law, President Bush ordered the invasion and conquest of Iraq in March 2003. It seems the experts were right after all. The Americans found no weapons of mass destruction in Iraq.

Meanwhile, the Bush administration merely protested helplessly as North Korean's dictator Kim Jong Il broke a 1994 deal that mothballed the Yongbyon nuclear complex, extracted 8,000 fuel rods backed with plutonium, used that to build perhaps half a dozen nuclear bombs, and tested one in 2006.

What psychological, ideological, political, and economic factors could explain why the Bush team went to war against Iraq that had no weapons of mass destruction, and avoided war with North Korea that has weapons of mass destruction? What are the results of those two policies?

Nuclear weapons may well diminish rather than enhance a nation's power. Clearly nuclear weapons provide the bearer with prestige. Yet the scientific, financial, and psychological costs of developing and deploying nuclear weapons are enormous. Those same resources invested properly elsewhere in a state's economy could produce far larger amounts of wealth and ultimately power. Nuclear weapons are largely very elaborate and costly ornaments. They can be brandished, but their use might well result in national suicide.

Given those realities, why did the nuclear arms race lasted nearly five decades? There were many obstacles to slowing let alone reversing the nuclear arms race.[16] Each side held a mirror image of the other as aggressive, deceitful, and dedicated to achieving superiority. Neither side trusted the other nor was it willing until recently to include the verification procedures in a nuclear agreement that could have strengthened that trust.

Some of that distrust was merited. Profound ideological differences and the aggressive actions and statements of both sides were the most important reasons for the arms race. Moscow's assertion that it was leading a global communist revolution; its subjection of East Europe; crushing of revolts in East Germany, Poland, Hungary, and Czechoslovakia; invasion of Afghanistan; and machinations in dozens of other countries were certainly aggressive by any measure and ultimately a threat to American security. Washington's assertion of a containment policy from 1947; its nuclear arms buildup; creation of NATO; military intervention in Korea, Vietnam, Grenada, and Panama; and indirect manipulation of politics in scores of other countries certainly seemed threatening to the Soviet Union.

But domestic politics were also important in fueling the nuclear arms race. As the budget, personnel, institutions, and duties of each side's military industrial complex expanded, they acquired increasing political power to demand and receive even more resources. All those involved in military policies and industries—bureaucrats, politicians, contractors, labor unions, scientists—had a vested interest in continually getting bigger budgets. Once a weapons program was begun, it proved almost impossible to kill it. Many weapons began as "bargaining chips" but, often for political rather than strategic reasons, soon became "vital" to national security. It often took decades to build a new weapons system from the first blueprints and models, through the testing, to the finished product. Canceling a project would put people out of work and threaten the reelection of the congressional representatives from those districts.

Politics often resulted in weapons systems being built even if they were obsolete or unworkable. For example, the Carter administration canceled the B-1 bomber, arguing that it was a waste of money that could be better spent elsewhere since existing B-52s armed with cruise missiles could do the job far more effectively. The Reagan administration revived the B-1 project that eventually cost American taxpayers $40 billion, and accelerated the B-2 Stealth bomber, which has cost about $50 billion so far. Although the first B-52s became operational in 1954, it remains a superior bomber to the newer B-1 and B-2 bombers that appeared during the 1980s and 1990s. There have been eight different B-52 versions, each a large improvement over the previous. Technical problems have repeatedly grounded both the B-1 and B-2 bomber fleets. The Reagan administration claimed that it would enhance American security by completing the B-1 and B-2 bombers. Critics argue that American security was actually undermined because those bombers consumed vast amounts of scarce financial, human, political, and scientific resources that could have been much more profitably employed elsewhere. Also, Moscow felt compelled to counter the B-1 and B-2 with its own new weapons systems, and the nuclear arms race accelerated.

The arms talks themselves often bogged down over several issues, of which verification was perhaps the biggest obstacle. Each side feared that the other would cheat, yet resisted opening up its own military industrial complex to a comprehensive inspection system that would minimize that chance. Even with verification agreements, the process becomes ever more difficult in an age of cruise missiles that are highly mobile, can fit in a trailer truck, are relatively inexpensive, can carry both nuclear and conventional warheads, and have a range of thousands of miles. The 1987 INF treaty was the first to allow on-site inspections, and subsequent treaties have included that provision.

Paradoxically, arms control talks seemed to quicken the arms race as each side tried to develop duplicate and sometimes triplicate weapons systems that it then used as bargaining chips at the negotiating table. As a result, each side scrambled to build ever more advanced systems that would either match or surpass the others'.

Would the world be better off without nuclear weapons? Ideally, yes, of course. But the nuclear genie is loose and increasing numbers of governments are able to use its powers. Whether nuclear power deters war and promotes stability or the opposite depends on who controls it. Complete nuclear disarmament would involve all states agreeing not only to give up all nuclear weapons technology but also to submit to extensive inspection of their facilities and budgets. Knowledge, however, cannot be dismantled. A nuclear disarmament treaty would put hundreds of thousands of scientists and technicians out of work. A global fear would be that even with a disarmament treaty and inspection regime, somehow, somewhere a terrorist group or government is feverishly attempting to put together a nuclear bomb. It seems humanity must exist under the nuclear shadow for the foreseeable future.

Ultimately, nothing guarantees that deterrence, controls, or reason will continue to work. Luck may well have been the most important factor in so far sparing the world from nuclear warfare. As long as there are nuclear weapons on earth, there is a chance they will be used either from cold rational choice, frenzied fear, or unforeseen accident.

BIOLOGICAL AND CHEMICAL WEAPONS

Alas, nuclear bombs are not the only weapons of mass destruction that threaten humanity. Biological and chemical weapons are also capable of killing large numbers of people. Developing those weapons is much less expensive and technological daunting than nuclear programs, and thus more common. It is unknown exactly how many states and terrorists groups have tried or succeeded in developing chemical and biological weapons. By one count, at least twenty-six states have produced chemical weapons and ten states have biological weapons programs. Many other states are seeking to obtain those weapons. In addition, as many as twenty more Third World states are considered "likely" or "possible" either to develop or already possess chemical weapons while an additional four are considered likely developers of biological weapons.

During the twentieth century both governments and terrorists unleashed chemical and biological weapons to murder countless numbers of people. Chemical weapons were widely used during World War I, resulting in over 100,000 deaths and 1 million casualties. Those horrors were not unleashed again until the 1980s when Saddam Hussein used them against Iran and Kurds within Iraq. In 1995, Japan's Aum Shinrikyo cult released sarin gas in Tokyo's subway system; twelve died and hundreds sickened.

Japan is the only country known to have conducted biowarfare. During World War II, Japan's notorious Unit 731 murdered several thousand people in medical experiments at its camp near Harbin, Manchuria, and sowed the plague and other diseases, which murdered perhaps millions of Chinese. Since then the only two clear cases of bioterrorism were inflicted by cults rather than countries. In 1984, followers of the Bhagwan Shree Rajneesh secretly sprayed salad bars with salmonella, sickening over 750 in Oregon. Then, in fall 2001, a right-wing terrorist sent anthrax-laced letters to Tom Brokaw, the NBC news anchor, and Tom Daschle, the Democratic Senate leader. Though those two men escaped harm, the anthrax killed a half dozen others.

To help curtail those horrors, the international community outlawed those weapons with treaties. The 1972 Biological and

Toxin Weapons Convention prohibits the development, production, and stockpiling of biological weapons, which followed up a 1925 Geneva Convention treaty banning the use but not possession of biological and chemical weapons. In 1990, Washington and Moscow signed the Chemical Weapons Destruction Agreement in which they pledged to stop the production and reduce the numbers of chemical weapons. The 1997 Chemical Weapons Treaty established the Organization for the Prohibition of Chemical Weapons; a forty-seven–country council oversees the organization. Of its 500 employees, 200 inspect suspected chemical weapons factories and storage facilities.

How dangerous is the threat that a hateful group will acquire and detonate a biological or chemical weapon of mass destruction against the United States or another country? Although not impossible, it is not as easy as potboiler spy novels and Hollywood action flicks insist. For terrorists each type of weapon poses serious challenges for secretly constructing and transporting it to a target.

Biowarfare is aided by the ease with which terrorists can get control of deadly germs. There are over 1,500 germ banks around the world that nurture diseases in laboratories in order to research medicines and methods of ultimately destroying them. Only 472 banks are members of the World Federation for Culture Collections that has fairly strict standards for the dissemination of research and the germs themselves to outsiders. Most other germ banks have minimal security and will provide pathogens to those who request them.[17] With those germs and the proper equipment, scientists can mass produce and store them in facilities the size of a small room or trailer truck.

The Russian threat in insecure stocks of weapons of mass destruction is not confined to nuclear bombs and materials. The Soviet biowarfare program peaked in the late 1980s with 60,000 scientists and technicians presiding over thousands of tons of 50 of the world's deadliest diseases, including anthrax, smallpox, and the plague. In 1992, President Yeltsin announced that Russia would dismantle that program by bioweapons those diseases and redeploying the personnel. But not all those diseases were eradicated nor were all the scientists gainfully employed elsewhere in Russia. How many vials of biotoxins or skilled minds fell into the hands of hostile governments or groups is unknown.

Chemical weapons are far more difficult to make, requiring large laboratory and production facilities. Nonetheless, Aum Shinrikyo was able secretly to make enough sarin gas to kill millions of people; they intended to do just that but bungled the delivery. Where did they get the weapons? The cult amassed nearly a billion dollars through various businesses and used some of that cash to buy the technology from Russia's underground arms bazaar.

Yet it is no easy task to disperse germs and chemicals that can kill large numbers of people. The vulnerability of targets varies greatly. Popular fears that their water supplies will be poisoned are exaggerated. Most germs or chemicals dumped into reservoirs would be diluted by the volume of water; chlorine would kill the germs. If crop dusters suddenly appeared over a sports stadium packed with 50,000 or more fans and began spraying, more people would die from the panicked stampede than inhalation; heat rises over cities and stadiums alike thus pushing and dispersing any poisons skyward. The most cataclysmic attacks could involve hijacking a truck hauling deadly chemicals and exploding it or dive-bombing a plane packed with explosives into a chemical plant in or near a dense population.

On a smaller scale, a germ or chemical attack could be quite easy. Food sources could be contaminated by surreptitious spraying in grocery stores. Crowded enclosed spaces like office buildings, stations, and subway cars would also be relatively easy targets.

Cyberwarfare and Energy Weapons of Mass Destruction

The ever thickening worldwide computer Web provides ever more benefits to its users, but those online are also vulnerable to a new type of threat. "Cyberwarfare" is a type of MWD, but more a "weapon of mass disruption" than a "weapon of mass destruction," that involves hacking into an enemy's vital defense, financial, manufacturing, corporate, utilities, transportation, and communications facilities, and firing electronic "viruses" or "worms" into their computers that destroy those systems. An effective cyberwarfare attack can potentially shut down an entire national economy. Bank records could disappear wiping out business and household accounts. Electricity could burn out leaving people in the dark with food rotting in refrigerators. The radar screens in airport control towers could blank out preventing planes from taking off and imperiling those trying to land. Life support equipment in hospitals could shut down killing patients. The possible destruction and even death is endless. The result would be economic, social, and political chaos.

The greater a nation's computer power, the greater its vulnerability to cyberwarfare. America's computer prowess is at once an enormous source of national power and an Achilles' Heel. A computer genius could launch a cyberwarfare assault from any terminal anywhere with little chance of being traced as he skips the weapon from one terminal to the next around the world. Cyberwarfare will increasingly be wielded by terrorists and aggressive governments alike.

To its credit the Pentagon recognizes the importance of cyberwarfare. In 1999, it set up a cyberwarfare center at the Air Force Space Command at Colorado Springs. The goals are to strengthen America's defenses against an attack while developing the ability to conduct cyberwarfare against an enemy. It tried to wage cyberwarfare against Yugoslavia during the 1999 war over Kosovo, apparently with limited success since that country was not heavily dependent on computers. During that war, the Pentagon blunted cyberwarfare attacks on its computers as hackers failed to penetrate the system. But those were just the first skirmishes in a new form of war that will become ever more common and sophisticated in the decades ahead. To defend themselves from that threat, America's governments, businesses, and individuals will have to invest hundreds of billions of dollars to protect their computer systems against cyberattacks. Yet how secure can we ever really be?

Two events in January 2010 revealed how vulnerable the United States and the rest of the world is to cyberwarfare. Google announced that it would withdraw from China after suffering a wave of attacks that were routed through servers in Taiwan but appeared to emanate from China; Beijing vociferously denied being behind the attack and refused to openly investigate its source. As that was happening, America's top military commanders were conducting a cyberwar game in which the United States was incapable either of thwarting the attack or determining definitively who launched it.

A concerted, highly sophisticated cyberattack can devastate such crucial infrastructure as electrical power grids, telecommunications, and the financial system. That might not immediately physically harm anyone but could inflict hundreds of billions or even trillions of dollars damage to the economy. As disturbing is the inability to pinpoint the perpetrator. The worst case scenario would be for a terrorist group to lead a "false flag" trail back to, say, China, just as China apparently tried to implicate Taiwan for its attack on Google.

How then would a president respond? If the United States openly launched an equally devastating cyberattack on China without definitive proof, that could provoke an escalation to an actual conventional or even nuclear war! But would most American politicians and people simply endure an attack without retaliating against a suspect?

Deterrence depends on a potential attacker believing that its enemy has both the capacity and will to retaliate with overwhelming force. If a government or group can launch an anonymous attack, then it will not be deterred from doing so. Likewise, preemption of such an attack cannot occur if the source is unknown.

In a few years, the United States will start deploying an array of DEWs that utilize laser, electromagnetic, microwave, and plasma fuel technologies to destroy the people and property of enemies. Those new weapons are so revolutionary that they may render obsolete killing with bullets and even missiles! As always, once one state has freed a deadly technological genie from the bottle of human creativity, others will do whatever they can to get their hands on those new weapons. It will only be a matter of time after the Pentagon deploys DEWs for the Chinese and Russians to unveil their own versions. And not far behind them will be the North Koreans, Iranians, and Al Qaeda. Battlefields of the not so distant future may resemble something out of Star Wars, with satellites, aircraft, and soldiers firing death rays at one another.

But, for now, the ultimate nightmare remains nuclear weapons in the hands of terrorists. How feasible is that? Making nuclear bombs is too technologically and financially exorbitant for any group to undertake alone; they would mostly need to do so under a government's patronage. The most likely nuclear scenario is a radiological or "dirty bomb" in which low grade radioactive material is packed around a conventional bomb and detonated. If such a bomb were exploded on, say, Wall Street, it would kill few people but devastate New York's population economically and psychologically.

And then there is the chance of stealing a nuclear bomb, apparently not impossible given Russia's chaotic military system. In 1998, Russian Defense Minister Alexander Lebed let slip the chilling word that as many as 100 mininuclear weapons were missing from its arsenal, their whereabouts unknown! Could one of that be ticking away near you?

CHAPTER 6

War, Peace, and the Global Community

The basic requirement for peace is that states have the wit to coop-
erate in pursuit of national interests that coincide with those of
others.

David Mitrany

As globalization deepens and broadens interdependence among all
countries, national and international interests merge. The theory
of functionalism explains that phenomenon and its consequences.
Common interests inevitably lead to common laws and organizations
to protect and enhance those interests. The success of those international laws and organizations in managing some challenges encour-
ages countries to undertake more ambitious common efforts to deal
with threats to common interests in other areas.

Until recently war has loomed above all other manmade scourges
of humanity as by far the most destructive. Although tentative steps
toward forging international laws and organizations dedicated to
limiting war were taken before the twentieth century, those of the
past hundred years were truly revolutionary. The body of international law of war has proliferated while two successive international
organizations, first the League of Nations and then the United
Nations, were established with global collective security their core
mission.

What explains that vast expansion of international organizations
and laws dedicated to reducing the destructiveness and frequency
of war? How much, if at all, have those forces contributed to a
sharp reduction of international wars in the late twentieth and early
twentieth centuries?

COLLECTIVE SECURITY

Collective security, or the notion of "one for all and all for one," is not a new idea nor did it originate with the fictional Three Musketeers. It is likely as old as humanity as a commonsense security nostrum, akin to "the enemy of my enemy is my friend" as a fundamental guiding principle. Depending on circumstances, it could potentially work just as well for a group of individuals, clans, bands, tribes, or states up the political sophistication ladder.

Throughout early modern European history, some thinkers such as Dante Alighieri, William Penn, Jean Jacques Rousseau, Benjamin Franklin, Immanuel Kant, and Jeremy Bentham, to name the more famous, called for the creation of an international organization dedicated to waging peace by uniting against any and all aggressors. During that time the European powers took several tentative steps in that direction.

The 1648 Peace of Westphalia, also known as the First European Congress, was the first attempt of European states to impose restrictions on warfare and reasons to go to war. The treaty took three years to negotiate as a series of agreements first forged among diplomats from the protestant states at Osnabruck and Catholics at Munster in the region of Westphalia, and only then with each other. The Treaty of Westphalia's major tenets were reconfirmed at the 1713 Treaty of Utrecht ending the War of the Spanish Succession. Even if no permanent collective organization emerged from either the Westphalian or Utrecht congresses, they were at least collective attempts to forge and keep a general peace.

It would take the Europeans another century before they first tried to create a collective security regime. The Congress of Vienna concluded a quarter century of almost constant warfare from shortly after the French Revolution's outbreak in 1789 to Napoleon's defeat at Waterloo in 1815. A glittering array of delegations from all the states of Europe were present from October 1814 until June 1815, including 5 monarchs, 216 princes, hundreds of nobles, and assorted party-crashers. Ironically, nearly all of them would do little more than dance, dine, and seduce for nine months. Austria, Prussia, Russia, and Britain would decide all questions behind firmly closed and guarded doors, with limited input from France, Sweden, Spain, and Portugal; together they were called the Preliminary Committee of Eight. The formal Congress of Vienna met only one day, on June 9, 1815, when nearly all the envoys gathered to ratify the 121 articles of the Final Act, also known as the Charter of Europe, which tried to undo the territorial, political, and above all ideological changes that had transformed the continent over the previous blood-soaked quarter century.

Europe's Great Powers—Britain, Prussia, Russia, Austria, and later France—followed up the Final Act by forming the Concert of Europe, a collective security community in which they mobilized diplomatically and at times militarily against any forces that threatened Europe's peace. Overlapping with the Concert of Europe was the Holy Alliance, the brainchild of Tsar Alexander I who envisioned a unified Christendom in which Orthodox, Protestant, and Catholic sovereigns would work together to keep the peace; only Austria and Prussia joined Russia in that Holy Alliance.

The primary threat both the Concert of Europe and Holy Alliance sought to thwart was internal rather than international. The French Revolution had unleashed the power of liberalism and nationalism against Europe's monarchies and empires, and those revolutionary forces continued to smolder and periodically flare even after Napoleon's defeat and a king once again reigned over France. For more than three decades after 1815, Europe's two overlapping collective security communities crushed a series of revolutionary movements dedicated to overthrowing aristocracies and foreign rule across the continent. They also peacefully resolved most disputes among themselves. Between 1815 and 1914, Europe was spared a general war while the Great Powers fought only three limited wars among themselves: the Crimean War (1853–1856) in which France and Britain along with Turkey fought Russia, the Prussian-Danish War (1864), the Prussian-Austria War (1866), and the Franco-Prussian War (1870–1871).

Meanwhile, the first genuine international organizations were created to deal with more prosaic shared interests—the Rhine River Commission (1815), the International Telegraphic Union (1856), the Danube River Commission (1857), the Universal Post Union (1874), the International Telecommunications Organization (1875), and the International Office of Weights and Measures (1875). Those international organizations in turn bolstered the interdependence among the members and, thus, weakened the logic for war. Of course, wars often break out when logic breaks down.

During the late nineteenth century, statesmen attempted to limit war's brutality. These efforts culminated with the twenty-six nations represented at the 1899 Hague Conference and the forty-four at the 1907 Hague Conference. The very fact that those meetings took place was notable. Never before had peace talks been held during peacetime, but only after a war. What the delegates accomplished was even more important. They negotiated and signed a score of treaties that outlawed types of weapons and tactics, and protected prisoners of war and civilians. Hopes were high that those states could take even more sweeping measures at the next session scheduled to convene in 1915. Those hopes died brutally when World War I erupted in August 1914.

That war's horrors, however, only stirred advocates of collective security to renew their efforts. In January 1918, to justify America's participation in World War I, President Woodrow Wilson presented before Congress his Fourteen Points, one of which was the creation of an international organization dedicated to collective security. Wilson was not the only advocate. Groups in all the major powers lobbied their governments for some international peace organization. That vision would be partially realized.

Sections of the Versailles Treaty that ended World War I created the League of Nations and Permanent Court of International Justice (PCIJ) in which participants would settle disputes according to international law. The League was organized into an Assembly that included representatives of all members and met for about a month once a year; a nine-member Council in which the four Great Powers (Britain, France, Italy, and Japan) were permanently represented while the other seats rotated, and met four times annually; and a Secretariat that administered the organization. Decisions only passed in both the Council and Assembly with unanimous approval. Forty-five countries were members at the first session in 1920 at its Geneva headquarters; at the League's peak it had fifty-nine members.

The League of Nation's core purpose was collective security. The Covenant or constitution creating the organization empowered it to keep the peace in several ways. Covenant Article 12(1) stated that

> if there should arise between [the members] any dispute likely to lead to a rupture, they will submit the matter either to arbitration or judicial settlement or to inquiry by the Council, and they agree in no case to resort to war until three months after the award by the arbitrators or the judicial decision, or the report by the Council.

Article 16 declared that

> Should any member of the League resort to war…it shall…be deemed to have committed an act of war against all other members of the League, which hereby undertake immediately to subject it to the severance of all trade or financial relations, the prohibition of all

intercourse between the nationals of the Covenant-breaking State and the State, and the prevention of all financial, commercial, or personal intercourse between the nationals of the Covenant-breaking and the nationals of any other State, whether a Member of the League or not.

If that failed to deter the aggressor, the League Council could recommend that member-states contribute troops to an alliance that would defeat the peace-breaker.

These seemingly powerful means of managing conflicts were reinforced by the Kellogg-Briand Pact, signed on August 27, 1928, by the great powers, including the United States, and many other countries. Signatories renounced

> the recourse to war for the solution of international controversies, and...as an instrument of national policy in their relations with one another...the settlement or solution of all disputes or conflicts of whatever nature or of whatever origin they may be...shall never be sought except by pacific means.

That principle was reaffirmed in the 1933 Rio de Janeiro Anti-War Treaty.

Contrary to popular belief, the League of Nations was actually quite successful—it addressed over sixty international problems and resolved about half. The IPCJ ruled on an additional sixty conflicts. Of those geopolitical disputes in which the League became directly involved, it failed to keep the peace in only four cases brought before it—Japan's invasion of Manchuria, Italy's invasion of Ethiopia, the Chaco War between Paraguay and Bolivia, and the Soviet Union's attack on Finland. Although the League identified aggression in some of these disputes, it never threatened to use military force to deter that aggression, and the economic sanctions it applied were disregarded by most states. Unfortunately, the League failed to get involved in the worst cases of aggression such as Japan's invasion of China in 1937, or across Southeast Asia and the Pacific starting in 1941, or the attack of Germany and the Soviet Union on Poland in 1939, or Germany's imperialism across ever more of Europe starting in 1940. Thus did the League stand impotently by as World War II exploded in its face.

Behind these failures were some important weaknesses. First, the United States refused to join. Although President Wilson was the most important force behind the League's creation, because of his conflict with key Senate leaders and America's traditional political isolationism, the Senate voted down the Versailles Treaty that would have made the United States a member. Without the world's largest industrial power lending its weight to decisions, the League was hobbled from the start. Second, members could decide for themselves when a breach of peace occurred and whether or not to impose sanctions against the aggressor. States almost always put their immediate economic needs before more abstract military threats and thus turned a blind eye to aggressors. By 1941, the League of Nations was thoroughly discredited. But visionaries refused to abandon the collective security dream.

During World War II, President Franklin Roosevelt became just as determined to create an international organization dedicated to keeping the peace as Wilson had during World War I.[1] When the United States and Britain signed the Atlantic Charter on August 14, 1941, they pledged themselves to, among other things, create a United Nations. At the Moscow Conference of Foreign Ministers in October 1943, the American and British envoys convinced their Soviet and Chinese counterparts to support a future collective security organization. At the Dumbarton Oaks Conference in August 1944 and the Yalta Conference in February 1945, the participants debated and began to forge a consensus on the United Nations' institutions and functions. Perhaps the most significant addition occurred at Yalta. Fearing the Soviet Union would continually be outvoted by the Western powers, Stalin insisted on veto power for the permanent members of the Security Council. Roosevelt and Churchill agreed.

The finishing touches to the UN Charter or constitution were negotiated by representatives of fifty-one countries at the San Francisco Conference from April through June 1945. The San Francisco Treaty was signed on June 26, 1945, and was rapidly ratified by its signatories. On July 28, the American Senate overwhelmingly voted 89 to 2 to ratified that treaty and thus commit the United States to the United Nations.

The Charter's preamble clearly states the United Nations' ideals— peace, human rights, international law, prosperity, and collective security, of which the last is the most important. Article 2(3) maintains that all "members shall settle their international disputes by peaceful means in such a manner that international peace and security, and justice, are not endangered." Article 2(4) prohibits "the threat or use of force against the territorial integrity or political independence of another state." Three articles of Chapter VII empower the Security Council to uphold the peace. Under Article 39, the Security Council is authorized to determine whether a breach of peace occurred; under Article 41 it can impose economic, transportation, and communications sanctions on the aggressors; and, if those fail, under Article 42 can "take such actions by air, sea, or land forces as may be necessary to maintain or restore international peace and security…" National sovereignty is upheld by Article 2(7), which states: "Nothing contained in the present Charter shall authorize the United Nations to intervene in matters which are essentially within the domestic jurisdiction of any state or shall require the members to submit such matters to settlement under the present Charter; but this principle shall not prejudice the application of enforcement under Chapter VII." In addition to these powers, Article 43 gives the United Nations international legal personality by empowering it to make treaties with sovereign states. This was reinforced by the favorable International Court of Justice ruling in the 1948 Reparations for Injury case in which the United Nations asked for an opinion as to whether it had the legal personality to take a sovereign state to court and receive compensation for damages.

There were 192 UN members in 2010. It is expected that the membership will slowly rise into the twenty-first century as more states win their independence. Who can join? Membership is "open to all other peace-loving states which accept the obligations contained in the present Charter, and, in the members' judgment, are able and willing to carry out these duties." Some nonsovereign states like the Palestinian Authority enjoy nonvoting observer status. The Security Council and General Assembly vote on the admission of candidates.

The United Nations can vote to suspend the membership of a state that violates the Charter. There are no provisions, however, for voluntary withdrawal from the United Nations, thus avoiding the League of Nations situation where aggressor states like Japan quit the organization rather than subscribe to its duties. In 1965, Indonesia announced its withdrawal in protest against Malaysia's (with which it had a territorial dispute) election as a nonpermanent member of the Security Council. Indonesia later quietly retook its seat.

For over two decades following the Chinese revolution in 1949, there was a dispute over which government should occupy the seat reserved for China. The contenders were the Communist Party, which controlled the mainland, and the Nationalist Party, which had retreated to the island of Taiwan after losing the civil war. Washington initially lined up enough members to recognize the Nationalists in China's seat, and for nearly a quarter century vetoed all Soviet-led attempts to unseat Taiwan. Then, in 1972, the UN General Assembly voted to expel the Nationalists and seat the Communists. Until that year Washington clung to the position that the Nationalist Party was

China's legitimate government and thus deserved that seat. President Richard Nixon changed American policy to the more realistic and legal position that accepted the Communist Party as China's actual government.

Member dues are based on a complicated "ability to pay" formula that takes into account GNP and population. In 2010, the United States was required to pay for 22.0 percent of the budget, Japan 16.6 percent, Germany 8.6 percent, Britain 6.1 percent, France 6.0 percent, China 2.6 percent, and Russia 1.2 percent, or altogether 63.1 percent of the budget while casting only 4 percent of the General Assembly votes. Seventy-nine countries pay the minimum of 0.01 percent, and nine countries 0.02 percent. Half of the General Assembly votes are cast by those countries that pay the minimum 0.01 percent assessment or contribute less than 1 percent of the United Nations' budget.

Power in the United Nations is concentrated in the Security Council that can make legally binding decisions for the entire organization. Of its fifteen members, five—the United States, Russia, China, Britain, and France—are permanent and have veto power on nonprocedural issues, and the other ten are elected for two-year terms by the General Assembly. In practice, there is a quota system for the nonpermanent members—five come from Africa and Asia, two from Latin America, one from Eastern Europe, and two from the advanced industrial countries. The post of president of the Security Council rotates each month to another country among the members.

A measure passes the Security Council with a nine or more vote majority, unless, of course, it is vetoed by a permanent member. The pattern of the 241 vetoes cast in the half century from 1946 to 2010 changed significantly. The United States did not cast a veto until 1970 and 82 since then. In contrast, the Soviet Union and its successor, Russia, cast 92 vetoes between 1945 and 1960, 13 in the 1960s, 9 in the 1970s, only 4 between 1980 and 1989, and 5 since then for a total of 123. Of the other members, Britain cast 32, France 18, and China 6.[2]

There are two vital reasons for that shift in the balance of vetoes. During the first decade, Moscow often used its veto to block the admission of states with pro-Western governments. In 1956, Washington and Moscow agreed not to block each other's allies from membership, so Soviet vetoes fell sharply after that time. The shift in vetoes also reflected changes in the General Assembly's composition. Up through the 1960s, most of the General Assembly members voted with the United States on most issues, and Moscow vetoed many Security Council resolutions that seemed to challenge its interests.

The proliferation of newly independent states during the 1960s and 1970s, many of them pro-Soviet, anti-Israel, and committed to a New International Economic Order (NEIO) involving a redistribution of global wealth, put the United States on the defensive, leading Washington, London, and Paris to increasingly use their veto power. Since the Cold War's end, vetoes have become rare.

Each member has one vote in the General Assembly, which has the power to study, debate, and issue statements on any issue, as well as approve the annual budget. Decisions, however, are binding only if they achieve a two-thirds majority and are confined to UN administrative issues. The General Assembly can issue "declarations" or broad statements of principle such as its 1948 Declaration on Human Rights, and "resolutions" or policy recommendations for specific issues. It can also convene "special sessions" that address a particular issue like disarmament, "conferences" that deal with broader issues like global warming, and "conventions" that are treaties among UN members or between the United Nations and other states. Although they are not legally binding, General Assembly resolutions often represent global opinion and thus carry heavy political pressure. They may also identity international customs or principles that eventually can be codified into law.

There has been a significant shift in the power balance within the General Assembly from 1945 through today. In 1945, of the 51 members, 44 percent were from the Western bloc, 12 percent from the Soviet bloc, 16 percent from Asia and the Pacific, 8 percent from Africa, and 20 percent from Latin America. Today only 14 percent of the UN membership is from the Western bloc, 32 percent from Asia and the Pacific, 33 percent from Africa, and 21 percent from Latin America, while the Soviet bloc is no more. Today the most important voting bloc is the 132-member Group of 77 composed of the poorer countries, which pressure the richer countries on various issues.

The voting records of the United States and Soviet Union in the General Assembly paralleled their veto record in the Security Council in which at first it was Washington that favored resolutions and Moscow that voted "no" until gradually they reversed themselves. In 1986, Washington and Moscow voted for 81 percent and 8 percent, respectively, of the resolutions. In 1989, the United States voted with the majority on only 16.9 percent of all resolutions, and even with the European Community only 59.5 percent and North Atlantic Treaty Organization (NATO) 57.3 percent of the time, in contrast to the period between 1945 and 1950 when it voted with the majority 71 percent of the time. Most American vetoes in the Security Council and negative votes in the General Assembly involved resolutions that condemn Israeli aggression or human rights abuses.[3] The Secretariat administers the United Nations. In 2010, the secretariat included about 10,000 personnel (down from over 12,000 in 1985) and supervised the dozens of UN agencies whose personnel number about 50,000. The United Nations' total yearly operating and peacekeeping budget is about $20 billion or about three dollars for each person on earth. The Secretariat is headed by a Secretary General who is nominated by the Security Council and elected by the General Assembly for a five-year renewable term. The secretary general's role is to administer rather than lead the United Nations, and has only the power to persuade. There have been seven UN general secretaries, all from neutral or nonaligned states: Trygve Lie of Norway (1946–1952), Dag Hammarskjold of Sweden (1953–1961), U Thant of Burma (1961–1971), Kurt Waldheim of Austria (1972–1982), Javier Perez de Cuellar of Peru (1983–1991), Boutros Boutros Ghali of Egypt (1992–1997), Kofi Annan of Ghana (1997–2007), and Ban Ki Moon (2007–present).

Although Kofi Annan was perhaps the most diplomatically active secretary general, that post's powers were established by Dag Hammarskjold who saw crisis management as his primary role. In 1960, he issued his policy of "preventive diplomacy" for those cases

> where the original conflict may be said either to be the result of, or to imply risks for, the creation of a power vacuum between the main blocs. Preventive action...must...aim at filling the vacuum so that it will not provoke action from any of the major parties...[t]he United Nations enters the picture on the basis of its noncommitment to any power bloc...to provide...a guarantee in relation to all parties against initiatives from others.[4]

After Hammarskjold died in a plane crash in 1961, his successors have largely concerned themselves with administration rather than policy. Kofi Annan broke that pattern by playing often decisive roles in defusing various crises, most notably that leading up to America's war with Iraq in 2003. Ban Ki Moon, the current secretary general, has been less assertive in tackling international problems.

There are three other less prominent core UN organizations. The fifty-four–member Economic and Social Council (ECOSOC) oversees sixteen affiliated organizations, consults with over two hundred and fifty NGOs, of which thirty-five are designated Category I, which can contribute issues to ECOSOC's agenda, organizes conferences, and dispenses funds; members serve for three-year terms.

The International Court of Justice (ICJ) includes fifteen judges who serve nine-year terms and hear cases referred to it from any state or UN organization. Although the ICJ's decisions are binding, its jurisdiction is not. The five-member Trusteeship Council oversaw those states that were given territories to manage for eventual independence; with all those territories now independent, the Trusteeship Council is in abeyance.

Thus do the core UN organizations and their affiliates address a range of issues including war, peace, poverty, health, nutrition, education, decolonization, human rights, the environment, law of the sea, natural disasters, women's equality, trade, investments, agriculture and food, and so on. One important UN contribution is simply gathering information on the socioeconomic conditions of every country, which helps identify problems and the means of alleviating those problems. These issues boil down to two core values—development and peace.

UN peacekeeping, peacemaking, and collective security actions differ. Governments volunteer to contribute personnel to peacekeeping and peacemaking missions; collective security requires all UN members to act against an aggressor. A peacekeeping mission is invited by the warring sides to help keep the peace after a ceasefire has occurred. A peacemaking mission is the use of force against an aggressive alliance, state, or group. Although the UN members have never collectively gone to war, they have collectively acted numerous times by imposing economic sanctions against rogue states.

Peacekeepers can be dispatched only after three conditions have been met: all parties in the conflict agree to accept UN forces, the Security Council and General Assembly agree to send them, and members agree to provide troops for the operation. The Charter does not explicitly empower the United Nations to dispatch peacekeeping forces. The practice was inspired by Secretary General Hammarskjold's concept of "preventive diplomacy." A mission involves sending military or police into a country or region to separate and cool down enemies to prevent more bloodshed. Other peacekeeping actions can include disarming opponents, clearing landmines, monitoring elections, training military and police, providing security for the distribution of humanitarian aid, demarcating boundaries, aiding and repatriating refugees, reconstructing a war shattered country, running a government, promoting human rights, and monitoring the withdrawal of foreign troops.

The United Nations has no troops of its own. Whenever the Security Council identifies a peacekeeping mission, it determines the mission's strength and timeframe, then calls for volunteers. Interested nations contribute whatever troops and equipment they wish. While the Security Council retains operational command, the troops remain in their own national units and uniforms. For a peacekeeping mission, the soldiers wear blue helmets or berets and UN patches, are lightly armed, and fire only in self-defense; UN observers and police are usually unarmed. The United Nations compensates each contributing government for $1,000 a month for each soldier. The government then pays its own troops. Since that salary often far exceeds what soldiers get in most countries, volunteers are not lacking. By contributing to missions, poorer countries receive compensation and combat experience that would otherwise elude them.

From 1948 through 2009, the United Nations dispatched 63 peace, observer, or humanitarian missions, which cost $61 billion; the 15 missions in 2009 alone included 82,843 troops, 12,684 police, 2,244 military observers, and 5,790 civilians from 115 countries; the operating costs were $7.75 billion.[5]

The United Nations has committed itself to peacekeeping only when the issue (1) did not directly involve the superpowers or the East-West conflict; (2) was not opposed by Washington, Moscow, and the Security Council; (3) involved fighting that was in danger of spreading beyond the states involved; (4) involved a decolonization issue and small and medium sized states; and (5) was identified as a threat to peace by the secretary general who actively lobbied the United Nations to overcome it.[6]

The biggest constraint on an expansion of UN peacekeeping missions is financial rather than political. Although most nations agree in principle to UN peacekeeping missions, few willingly pay their share. In 2009, UN members were $2.06 billion in arrears to the total peacekeeping budget.

Peacemaking can occur when peacekeeping fails. Under peacemaking or "enforcement" mission, the Security Council takes sides in a conflict, authorizes the coalition to use "all necessary means" to fulfill its resolutions, and to those ends deputizes a country either to form a "coalition of the willing" or tap an existing alliance that then musters the resources of its own members.

Peacemaking is as rare as peacekeeping has become common. To date, there have been only three official peacemaking missions, with Korea (1950–1953), Iraq (1990–1991), and Serbia (1999). When communist North Korea attacked South Korea, the Security Council was able to intervene only because the Soviet Union, which otherwise would have vetoed the resolution, was boycotting the

United Nations in protest that the nationalist government still held China's seat after the Communists won their civil war. The Iraq and Serbian interventions occurred after the Cold War ended and only after those who favored it engaged in extensive diplomacy to convince those who were reluctant to do so. As President George H.W. Bush said before the General Assembly in October 1990, "this is a new and different world. Not since 1945 have we seen the real possibility of using the United Nations as it was designed, as a center for international collective security."[7]

The United Nations often acts as an intermediary in negotiations.[8] The techniques UN diplomats use to help make peace include (1) Inquiry: investigating a conflict and publishing a neutral account; (2) Good Offices: providing a neutral setting in which opponents can negotiate; (3) Mediation: actively suggesting ways the opponents can resolve their conflict; (4) Arbitration: proposing a systematic solution to the conflict; and (5) Adjudication: having the International Court of Justice rule on the conflict.

Collective security depends on more than an international organization and ideals. The Security Council had to be united ideologically and politically before the United Nations could live up to its promise. From 1945 through 1991, the United States and Soviet Union manipulated or joined many international and internal conflicts, and thus would veto each other's attempts to secure UN intervention.[9] International cooperation and consensus has grown since the collapse of Communism and the Soviet empire.

A related reason for the Cold War deadlock was the existence of the NATO and Warsaw Pact alliances dedicated to defeating the other should war break out. Alliances and collective security are incompatible. Collective security can work only if states agree to resist aggression no matter who commits it. If a state's alliance commits aggression, that state would be more likely to fulfill its alliance rather than collective security duties. Those problems diminished with the dissolution of the Warsaw Pact in 1991 and NATO's need to justify its continued existence in the post–Cold War era.

And then there is the problem of defining aggression itself. Although UN Charter Article 2 clearly prohibits the use of force, there are some exceptions. Under Article 51, every sovereign state has "the inherit right of individual or collective self-defense if an armed attack occurs." States that attack other states try to justify their actions by citing "self-defense." For example, was the United States the aggressor when it invaded Grenada in 1983, Panama in 1990, or Iraq in 2003? While many argued that those invasions were clear examples of aggression, the White House attempted to legally justify them by claiming that the United States was simply responding defensively to aggressive threats by the Grenadian, Panamanian, and Iraqi governments. Critics scoffed at the notion that Grenada's several hundred troops or Panama's several thousand could pose any threat to anyone, let alone a superpower like the United States. They also pointed out that UN sanctions against Iraq successfully contained its military power and thus prevented it from threatening any of its neighbors let alone the United States 8,000 miles away.

The United States is certainly not alone in defying the United Nations. The global power imbalance allows the most powerful states to act with impunity. The Soviet Union was the aggressor in Hungary in 1956, Czechoslovakia in 1968, and Afghanistan in 1979. The United States and Soviet Union tolerated each other's aggression in their respective sphere of influence for a very good reason. To do otherwise might have led to World War III and a nuclear holocaust killing not only most Americans and Soviets, but millions of other people around the planet.

How effective has the United Nations been in keeping the peace? Was John Kennedy right when he once said the United Nations "is our last hope in an age where the instruments of war have far outpaced the instruments of peace"?

Any evaluation of the United Nations' effectiveness must first address its central role—that of keeping the peace. It was hoped that the United Nations would succeed where the League of Nations had failed. Since 1945, there has been no third world war nor use of nuclear weapons. What role, if any, the United Nations played in keeping the peace between the superpowers is impossible to say, although most would agree that it was peripheral at best. UN efforts, however, have been important and often decisive in hundreds of other conflicts, alleviating about half of all disputes brought before it and outright settling a quarter. Clearly, had the United Nations never existed, international conflicts would most likely have been much more frequent and bloody.

Although the United Nations was founded on the collective security ideal, it was structured to preserve sovereignty and national interests, particularly that of the great powers. By concentrating power in the Security Council, the architects hoped to avoid the inevitable indecision of a General Assembly of all members. Few if any states would consider threatening the peace if they faced the combined military forces of the Five, plus any other forces contributed by other UN members. It was not anticipated, however, that given the five great powers' conflicting interests and ideologies, there was just as much chance of stalemate in the Security Council as in the General Assembly. In fact, granting veto power to each of the five virtually ensured deadlock since it allowed them even more leeway to act as they wished in the global system. Although the Five were empowered to uphold international law, they themselves could follow or break it as they wished. Their behavior was constrained not by the United Nations, but by the global balance of power and spheres of influence.

Even when a consensus emerges, financial constraints hamper the United Nations. Virtually everyone favors peace; few willingly pay for it. In 2009, the United States still owed the United Nations over $1.7 billion. Many American politicians and citizens justify this debt by arguing that their country's share and the United Nations' inefficiencies are too great. Critics of Washington's refusal to pay charge it with "representation without taxation," a twist on America's revolutionary slogan.[10]

Many have criticized the United Nations. Presidents Ronald Reagan and George W. Bush were especially outspoken in demanding reforms for what they believed was the United Nations' inept, wasteful, corrupt, and anti-Western practices. In 1983, the United States and Britain withdrew their membership and funding from the UN Educational, Scientific, and Cultural Organization (UNESCO), charging it with a persistent anti-Western bias and mismanagement of funds. In 1985, Congress passed a law threatening to cut American contributions by 20 percent unless the United Nations undertook reforms and gave Washington a say in budget matters equal to its 25 percent contribution. In 1987, Washington began cutting back its membership dues. This pressure partially worked. The United Nations agreed to cut its staff by 15 percent, allowed all budgetary decisions to be approved unanimously, toned down some of the anti-Western rhetoric, and revamped UNESCO. The United States finally rejoined UNESCO in 2003.

Many criticize the United Nation's "one state-one vote" system that is based on the concept of the sovereign equality of states. There are some obvious flaws in this system. A two-thirds majority in the General Assembly can be assembled by states whose combined population is less than 8 percent of the world's total. Some states argue that it is ridiculous that tiny states like Nauru with 7,000 people should have the same voting weight as China with 1.3 billion, and advocate that voting power should be proportional to a state's population. The smaller states are naturally opposed to that proposal. Some

Americans argue that voting power in the United Nations should be based on one's financial contributions. The combined contributions of over eighty members make up less than 1 percent of the total budget. Since the United States contributes a fifth of the United Nations' budget, it should enjoy a fifth of the votes. Virtually all other UN members object to basing voting on budget contributions. The five permanent Security Council members are criticized for their monopoly of power. Some propose abolishing not just the veto power but the entire notion of "permanent members." All Security Council members would be elected by the General Assembly. Other proposals would make Japan, Germany, Nigeria, India, and Brazil permanent members with veto power, which critics point out would only make stalemates more likely. To these proposals, some counter that although the veto has created deadlock on hundreds of issues, it has also preserved the Security Council—without veto power, any of the permanent members, especially the superpowers, may well have walked out if a vote severely affected its national interests.

UN politics have always mirrored global politics. The East-West and North-South standoffs limited the United Nations' ability to deal decisively with international problems for much of its first forty-five years. The Cold War is now over and the emergence of newly industrializing countries has diluted the rancor between the world's rich and poor countries. Cooperation among the permanent Security Council members allows the United Nations to embark decisively on peacekeeping and humanitarian missions that formerly would have been unlikely.

The United Nations provides the world's poorest and least populated states with a forum in which to cite their grievances and proposals. The Third World has attempted to use the General Assembly as a law-making body. Although General Assembly resolutions are not binding, they can create new customs and principles that later become the basis of treaties. The Third World attempts during the 1970s to create a New International Economic Order (NIEO) and during the 1980s and 1990s to implement a New World Information Order (NWIO) respectively involved vastly different legal views of property and the mass media from the dominant Western one. Many Third World states believe there is a double standard in the application of international law, in which the more powerful states can literally get away with murder and other violations while the weaker states are forced to comply. Even if many governments believe their interests are not being met, the United Nations allows communication and debate of issues sometimes not possible elsewhere. For example, although the United States did not have diplomatic relations with the Palestinian Liberation Organization (PLO) before 1993, it could meet informally with its UN envoys.

The United Nations will continue to expand its duties and power. A consensus is building within the United Nations that sovereignty is no longer sacrosanct and can be set aside when a government violates human rights and self-determination. There is increasing support for reviving the old UN trusteeship system in which unstable countries are administered until they become capable of self-rule. Many Third World countries, however, object that United Nations calls for human rights, self-determination, and trusteeship are neocolonial attacks on their rights as sovereign states.

In all, the United Nations has aided the often related challenges of peacekeeping and development in many countries and regions around the world. The Cold War's end freed the United Nations from some of the shackles that held back its peacekeeping duties. Nonetheless, the United Nations continues to play largely a secondary role in international relations. Will the United Nations expand its duties and powers in the coming decades? Could it ever become the world government that inspires hope in some people and provokes dread in others? Time will tell.

INTERNATIONAL LAW OF WAR

While international organizations are a relatively recent phenomena in history, international laws are as old as international relations. By definition, every treaty between sovereign states constitutes an international law. The first recorded treaty dates to 1283 BC between the Egyptians and Hittites. The first international laws addressing war are nearly as old.

International law of war includes war's causes (*jus ad bellum*), conduct (*jus in bellum*), and consequences (*jus post bellum*). Those laws address three critical questions: Is a war just? Is a war fought justly? Is a war settled justly?

Those principles are well-established. Just what they mean and how they are applied is not. The debate over the international law of war is not new.[11] History records attempts by some states long ago to negotiate arms control or more humanitarian ways of warring against each other. Treaties among ancient civilizations in China, India, and the Middle East created often elaborate restrictions against certain means of killing and tactics. For example, the fourth-century BC Indian text *Manusmṛti* (The Laws of Manu), among other things, forbade using concealed, barbed, poisoned, or fire-tipped weapons, and killing those not bearing weapons. Although the debate over when going to war is justified can be traced to the ancient Greeks, it was St. Augustine (345–430) who most deeply explored the subject before the modern era. He argued that a just war was "usually defined as those which avenge injuries, when the nation or city against which war-like action is to be directed has neglected either to punish wrongs committed by its own citizens or to restore what has been unjustly taken by it. Further that kind of war is undoubtedly just which God himself ordains."[12] In other words, killing is not murder when it is done in self-defense or for God's glory.

To Mine or Not to Mine, That Is the Question...

Land mines are an efficient defensive weapon. They have the capacity to deter an attack by making it too costly for the attacker. Land mines kill or maim thousands of people each year. Most of those victims are civilians rather than soldiers. In 1997, a treaty banning land mines was signed by 122 countries. One person with vision and drive was responsible for that achievement. Jody Williams was appalled when she learned of the carnage reaped by landmines and in 1994 formed the Campaign to Ban Land Mines that lobbied governments to that end. After the treaty was signed, she and her organization won a Nobel Peace Prize for their efforts.

Is anyone for land mines? The United States was among a half dozen states that spurned the treaty, arguing that its military would be more vulnerable to attack if it could not use land mines. International law declares aggression legal and defense illegal. What weapons are appropriate for defense and which, if any, should be outlawed? Do the means always justify the ends?

During the sixteenth century, three Spanish legal scholars—Vitoria, Ayala, and Suarez—attempted to synthesize ancient and medieval writings on warfare, partly to justify Spain's conquest of the Western Hemisphere. Horrified by the slaughter of the Thirty Years War, Hugo Grotius, the Dutch legal scholar, built upon their efforts. Grotius accepted war's inevitability, but argued that there should be treaty and ethical constraints governing its conduct. He distinguished between the justice of a war in which a government must decide whether its decision to go to war is just, and justice in a war in which governments accept restraints on the tactics used in warfare. His arguments influenced the Peace of Westphalia of 1648, which initiated a period of restraint in warfare that lasted until the Napoleonic era.

Throughout the modern era, as war became more destructive, international attempts to restrict its destructiveness have increased. The earliest attempted to protect nonbelligerents. In 1815, Swiss neutrality was forever guaranteed by signatories of the Congress of Vienna's Final Act. In 1817, the United States and Britain signed a treaty demilitarizing the Great Lakes. In 1839, a treaty guaranteed Belgium's neutrality. In 1856, Britain, France, Austria, Prussia, Russia, Sardinia, and Turkey signed the Declaration of Paris, which protected neutral shipping during war. In 1864, a dozen European states signed the Geneva Red Cross Convention protecting hospitals and medical personnel.

During the late nineteenth century, there was a growing consensus that states should limit the weapons and practices of war itself. During the American Civil War, the Union army issued a manual instructing officers how to deal with such aspects of war as prisoners, civilians, private property, and so on. Many European countries subsequently issued their own manuals. The first international agreement restricting war occurred with the 1868 Declaration of St. Petersburg, signed by seventeen nations, which outlawed the use of certain types of explosives and weapons.

Many of today's restrictions on warfare derive from the 1899 and 1907 Hague Conventions, which produced a score of treaties. A third Hague Convention was scheduled for 1915, but no one showed up because most were fighting World War I. In January 1918, President Wilson announced his Fourteen Points or goals for a "just peace" that would settle World War I, and, which he hoped would be "the war to end all wars." Some of Wilson's ideas were incorporated into the 1919 Versailles Peace Treaty, the most important of which was the creation of a League of Nations dedicated to collective security in which members pledged to peacefully resolve conflicts and unite against aggressors. Signatories of the 1928 Kellogg-Briand Pact agreed to renounce aggressive war.

The League of Nations and Kellogg-Briand Pact were reinforced by some significant arms control agreements during the 1920s. The 1919 St. Germain Convention, 1925 Geneva Convention, and 1929 Geneva Convention all restricted certain types of weapons, arms exports, and war practices. The Washington (1921–1922) and London (1930) naval treaties among the great naval powers imposed a strict ratio of warship tonnage among them. There were no limits, however, on the amount of firepower that those ships could deploy, and the tonnage limitations helped stimulate a technology arms race.

All of these treaties were no more successful in preventing World War II than the two Hague conventions were in preventing World War I. Like President Wilson, President Franklin Roosevelt was determined to create a lasting peace. He helped found the United Nations in 1945 as a new and improved version of the League of Nations that shared the goal of achieving collective security. Since then there have been several important multilateral treaties that have attempted to further restrict war and weapons. The 1949 Geneva Convention, 1977 Geneva Conference, and 1980 UN Conference systematized existing laws governing the conduct of war.

To date, the legal restrictions on the waging of war include (1) no attacking of unarmed enemies; (2) no firing on undefended localities without military significance; (3) no use of forbidden arms or munitions; (4) no improper use of immune buildings (e.g., embassies) for military purposes; (5) no pillaging; (6) no killing or wounding those who have surrendered or are disabled; (7) no poisoning wells or streams; (8) no murder, torture, or humiliation of war prisoners; (9) no assassinations of leaders; (10) no compelling the inhabitants of an occupied territory to supply information about the enemy; (11) no air bombardments of civilian populations; (12) no assaults on enemy ships that have surrendered by striking their colors; and (13) no destroying civilian cultural objects or places of worship (table 6.1).

Today, according to Inis Claude, international relations are governed by

> the neo-just war doctrine...[which] no longer seriously purports to accept the view that peace is unconditionally a higher view than justice. We have returned to the medieval view that it is permissible...to fight to promote justice, broadly conceived. Evil ought to be overturned, and good ought to be achieved, by force if necessary.[13]

The "neo-just war theory" includes six key components: (1) war can be fought only after all other means of resolving the issue have been exhausted; (2) only legitimate governments can decide to go to war; (3) wars should be fought for self-defense and not revenge; (4) there should be a good chance of winning; (5) the war should be fought to achieve conditions that would have been better than

Table 6.1 Recent Conventional and Nuclear Restriction Treaties

Treaty	Provisions	Year Signed	Signatories
Anti-Ballistic Missile (ABM)	limits United States- USSR each to one ABM site on land. The United States abandoned the treaty in 2003.	1972	2
Antarctic	internationalizes and demilitarizes	1959	39
Biological Weapons	bans production and possession	1972	112
Chemical Weapons	bans production and possession	1993	14
Comprehensive Test Ban	bans nuclear weapons tests	1997	161
Conventional Forces in Europe (CFE)	reduces troop levels	1990/1992	20/27
Environmental Modification	bans as a form of warfare	1977	55
Geneva Protocol	bans gas or biological warfare	1925	125
Intermediate Range Forces (INF)	eliminates all nuclear missiles with ranges from 500 to 5,500 kms. from Europe by United States and USSR	1987	2
Latin America Nuclear Free Zone	bans nuclear weapons in region	1967	23
Limited Test Ban	bans nuclear tests in atmosphere, under water, or outer space	1963	119
Non-Proliferation	bans selling, giving, or receiving nuclear weapons technology	1968	17
Outer Space	internationalizes and demilitarizes	1967	93
Seabed Arms Control	bans nuclear weapons on or in seabed	1971	83
South Pacific Nuclear Free Zone	bans nuclear weapons in region	1985	11
Strategic Arms Limitation Treaty (SALT I)	limits numbers and types of strategic weapons by United States and USSR	1972	2
SALT II	limits numbers and types of strategic weapons by United States and USSR	1979	2

Continued

Table 6.1 Continued

Treaty	Provisions	Year Signed	Signatories
Strategic Arms Reduction forces Treaty (START I)	reduces United States and USSR strategic nuclear	1991	2
START II	reduces United States and USSR strategic nuclear forces	1993	2
Comprehensive Test Ban (CTBT)	bans all testing of nuclear weapons	1996	54
Land Mine	bans production and exports of landmines	1997	152
START III	reduces United States and USSR strategic nuclear forces	2002	2
NPT Review Conference	renews commitment	2005	123

Source: Charles Kegley, *World Politics: Trend and Transformation* (New York: Thomson/ Wadsworth, 2006), 514–15.

those that have occurred through nonresistance; and (6) war should be fought to resist aggression, not change the enemy's government or society.

These principles have been codified in a range of treaties throughout the twentieth century. Even self-defense is limited. Literally interpreted, the right to self-defense does not extend to launching an attack in response to the belligerent actions or words of another state unless an attack is imminent. International Court of Justice rulings clarify three other restrictions on self-defense. Attacks on one's nationals abroad does not justify retaliation. Self-defense does not allow reprisals against the enemy territory. Any force used in self-defense must be necessary and proportional to the armed attack.

While one state can sell arms to or station troops in another state, it is illegal for a state to do so without that other state's permission. In 1986, Nicaragua sued the United States for blockading its ports and aiding rebels fighting against the government. The White House argued that its actions were justified under the principle of collective self-defense—the Nicaraguans were sending arms to rebels fighting against the neighboring state of El Salvador. The International Court of Justice ruled that collective self-defense was valid only in the event of any actual attack, which never transpired. Thus it ruled against the United States and ordered it to compensate Nicaragua for its losses.

The Reagan administration dismissed the Court's rulings, claiming that it did not have jurisdiction. International law has been used to prosecute war criminals. Defendants at the Nuremburg and Tokyo war trials were charged with three crimes: (1) Crimes against Peace: namely, planning, preparation, initiation, or waging of a war of aggression, or a war in violation of international treaties, agreements, or assurances, or participation in a common plan or conspiracy for the accomplishment of any of the foregoing; (2) War Crimes: namely, violations of the laws or customs of war. Such violations shall include, but not be limited to, murder, ill-treatment or deportation of slave labor or any other purpose of civilian population of or in occupied territory, murder or ill-treatment of prisoners of war or persons on the seas, killing of hostages, plunder of public or private property, wanton destruction of cities, towns, or villages, or devastation not justified by military necessity; and (3) Crimes against Humanity: namely, murder, extermination, enslavement, deportation, and any other inhumane acts committed against any civilian population, before or during the war, or persecutions on political, racial, or religious grounds in execution of or in connection with any crime within the jurisdiction of the Tribunal, whether or not in violation of the domestic law of the country where perpetuated.

International Law of Human Rights

Few would dispute the international right of self-defense. Much more controversial is the growing body of international law establishing not just the right but duty of the international community to stop a government from systematically violating the human rights of its own citizens. If the UN Security Council identifies a grievous violation of human rights, it can legally employ the full spectrum of power, starting with pure persuasion and extending all the way to violent coercion if need be.

That relatively new legal concept of human rights is at odds with more traditional right, sovereignty. Political philosophers originally conceived sovereignty as the location of ultimate power within a state. Jean Bodin in his book *The Republic* (1576) defined sovereignty as the highest law-making and law-enforcing authority in a territory. Eventually, it came to mean the recognition and relationship of states with one other. According to the 1933 Montevideo Convention on the Rights and Duties of States, a

sovereign state has a clearly defined territory, permanent population, government with the highest authority over that territory
and people, and recognition of independence by the people and
other sovereign states.

Sovereign states are legal equals. Emmerich Vattel made the classic
natural law case for equality among sovereign states:

> Since men are naturally equal, and a perfect equality prevails in their
> rights and obligations, as equally proceeding from nature, nations
> composed of men, and considered as so many free persons living
> together in the state of nature, are naturally equal, and inherit from
> nature the same obligations and rights. Power or weakness does not
> in this respect produce any difference. A dwarf is as much a man as a
> giant; a small republic is no less a sovereign state than the most power-
> ful kingdom.[14]

A sovereign state is independent but is not above the law. A change
in government does not affect the state's sovereignty or that state's
obligations incurred by the previous governments. For example, the
Soviet government that came to power after the November 1917 revolution was still responsible for the foreign debts owed by the Russian
government that it overthrew, even though it repudiated those debts.
Likewise, the Russian government that broke from and dissolved the
Soviet Union in December 1991 is still beholden to its predecessor's
duties.

International law thus has a Janus face regarding whether or not
states are free from external interference in their internal affairs. On
one hand, states are legally considered sovereign powers accountable
to no higher authority; traditionally that meant that governments
were free to rule their inhabitants and war against their neighbors
as they saw fit. Yet states can also be condemned and sanctioned for
their human rights abuses, are prohibited from launching aggressive
wars, and have eroded their own sovereignty by signing countless
treaties and the UN Charter that expand their international duties
and limit their behavior.

Although the principle of sovereignty is as old as international relations, for a couple of centuries it has been steadily eroded by the
principle of human rights. That erosion began in 1814 when Britain
launched perhaps the first human rights effort by trying to forge an
international treaty suppressing the slave trade. The next big step were
the Hague Conferences of 1899 and 1907 whose treaties protected
civilians in warfare. At the 1919 Versailles Conference, deals were
struck protecting the rights of certain minorities in Eastern Europe

while the International Labor Organization was created to protect the rights of workers.

KEY HUMAN RIGHTS AGREEMENTS

- United Nations Charter (1945)
- United Nations Commission on Human Rights (1946)
- Genocide Convention (1948)
- Universal Declaration of Human Rights (1948)
- Geneva Conventions (four separate treaties) on war (1949)
- European Convention on Human Rights (1950)
- Convention Relating to Status of Refugees (July 1951)
- Convention on the Political Rights of Women (1952)
- Convention on Status of Stateless Persons (1954)
- Convention Abolishing Slavery (1956)
- Convention on Abolition of Forced Labor (1957)
- Convention on Consent to Marriage (1962)
- Convention on Elimination of Racial Discrimination (1965)
- Covenant on Economic, Social, and Cultural Rights (1966)
- Covenant on Civil and Political Rights (1966)
- Convention on the Suppression of Apartheid (1973)
- Protocols (two) to Geneva Conventions (1977)
- Convention on Elimination of Discrimination against Women (1979)
- Convention against Torture (1984)
- Convention on the Rights of the Child (1989)
- International Criminal Tribunal for Ex-Yugoslavia (1993)
- International Criminal Tribunal for Rwanda (1994)
- Treaty for the International Criminal Court (1998)
- Convention Prohibiting Trafficking of Women and Children for Prostitution (2000)
- Protocol to Convention against Torture (2002)

Yet, despite these efforts, no systematic attempts to address human rights occurred until the United Nations was formed in 1945. The Preamble of the UN Charter required signatories to "reaffirm faith in fundamental human rights, in the dignity and worth of the human person, in the equal rights of men and women and of nations large and small." Article 55 states that the United Nations will "promote . . . universal respect for, and observance of, human rights and fundamental freedoms for all without distinction as to race, sex, language or religion." Article 56 then requires that "all members pledge themselves to take joint and separate action in cooperation with the organization for the achievement of the purposes set forth in Article 55." Although the word "pledge" implies a legal duty, it leaves to states the freedom to decide in what ways and degrees to implement that duty. Thus only states that regress in their fulfillment of human rights would be liable to legal criticism.

A Religion and Nation without a State: The Tibetans

What should be done about Tibet?

Tibetan Buddhism and an independent Tibetan kingdom date back to the seventh century and developed in relative isolation until the 1300s when the Mongols, who had conquered China, asserted control. China's Ming dynasty granted Tibet autonomy and designated the Dali Lama as its leader in 1577. It was not until 1751 that China invaded Tibet and incorporated that remote theocracy into its empire. The Tibetans declared independence in 1911 when a revolution toppled China's imperial dynasty and the country dissolved into civil war. It was not until 1950, the year after the Communists took power, that the Chinese reinvaded Tibet and asserted control. Tensions between Tibetans and the Chinese colonizers grew. In 1959, the Chinese crushed a Tibetan revolt. The Dali Lama and eventually a million followers reached exile at Dharmasala in northern India and there formed a government and nation in exile.

In the five decades since then Beijing has engaged in a systematic policy of "ethnic cleansing," murdering 1.2 million Tibetans, razing 6,000 monasteries, destroying ancient writings and works of art, and flooding the country with millions of Chinese settlers who now outnumber the 2.4 million Tibetans. The Chinese deny having committed these atrocities and claim that they have modernized Tibet with schools and health clinics, replacing a repressive regime in which 90 percent of the people were illiterate. The current fourteenth Dali Lama, the equivalent of a pope, wants autonomy rather than independence for Tibet. He won the Nobel Peace Prize in 1989. But the Chinese government refuses to negotiate with him and continues to destroy Tibet's culture. In 2008, pent-up Tibetan rage exploded into protests and riots that lasted for a week until the Chinese army crushed them.

What international principle should prevail in this conflict, sovereignty or human rights? What will be the likely fate of Tibetan culture if the Chinese persist in their policies? If you believe that China should be forced to stop its policies, how would you do so?

Each UN member is required to uphold all the principles of the UN Charter, including those articulating human rights. To help fulfill that solemn commitment, the United Nations set up the

Commission on Human Rights in 1946. The Commission is empowered only to monitor countries and publicize cases of human rights abuses. The hope is that states will curtail their violations if they are spotlighted.

That principle and the institution to protect it were reinforced on December 10, 1948, when the General Assembly passed the Universal Declaration of Human Rights with 48 votes in favor, none against, and 10 abstentions—the 8 communist countries, South Africa, and Saudi Arabia. The Declaration proclaims itself "as a common standard of achievement for all peoples and all nations, to the end that every individual and every organ of society...shall strive by teaching and education to promote respect for these rights and freedoms and by progressive measures, national and international, to secure their universal and effective recognition and observance." More specifically, the Declaration listed dozens of civil, political, social, economic, and cultural rights.

While the Commission was able to get the General Assembly to debate and approve the Human Rights Declaration relatively swiftly, Cold War politics delayed for nearly two decades two supplementary treaties. In 1966, after twelve years of negotiations, the United Nations offered for signature the Covenant on Civil and Political Rights, and the Covenant on Economic, Social, and Cultural Rights. Although both treaties came into force in 1976, the United States has yet to sign either. Because human rights represents such a fundamental principle along with ever more prevalent customs, states are bound by those treaties whether or not they are signatories. The 1968 UN Conference on Human Rights asserted that "the Universal Declaration on Human rights...constitutes an obligation for the members of the international community."

Human rights extend to foreign nationals as well as citizens residing in a country. States cannot prosecute foreigners for crimes they have committed elsewhere although they can extradite them to the country where the crime was committed. States, however, do not have to extradite their own citizens unless required by treaty. Foreigners cannot be drafted into the army unless they are permanent residents in that country. When a state expels a foreign citizen back to his own country, that state must receive him unless he is willing to go to another state. International law allows each state to decide its own citizenship requirements.

Alongside the legal right to expel is the moral duty to admit. The 1951 Geneva Convention declared that refugee status depends on "a well-founded fear of persecution for reasons of race, religion, nationality, membership in a particular social group, or political opinion." Recently, there has been an attempt to broaden the definition to include those displaced because of environmental catastrophes.

States are not obligated to accept foreign nationals, although when they do those individuals deserve full human rights. If a violation occurs, the government of that individual may sue for compensation on his behalf. States may agree to settle the dispute by arbitration or court, and if it was found that an injury was inflicted, the compensation goes to the victim's government rather than the aggrieved. Of course, after winning compensation the government can and usually does pass on the reward to its affected citizens.

States are liable for those crimes that its officials commit only if they are following clear orders. States are never liable for the actions of private citizens. Yet states are liable when they encourage their citizens to attack foreigners; fail to provide enough protection for foreigners in case of an imminent attack; fail to punish crimes committed by their citizens against foreigners; fail to provide foreigners with the legal ability to gain compensation for losses; materially benefit from an attack; or express approval of the attack.

Western governments have consistently argued that states were liable for harm to foreign nationals if they did not meet minimum international standards of human rights. Third World countries counter that they are only required to treat foreign nationals as they do their own citizens. One possible solution to this impasse is that "if the minimum international standard appears to give aliens a privileged position, the answer is for states to treat their own nationals better, not for them to treat aliens worse; indeed the whole human rights movement may be seen as an attempt to extend the minimum international standard from aliens to nationals."[15]

Europe is the world's only region with institutions that protect human rights, the European Union's European Court of Justice (ECJ) at Luxembourg and the European Council's European Court of Human Rights (ECHR) at Strasbourg. Unlike the ICJ, the ECJ has compulsory jurisdiction over the European Union's member-states, which have broken the rules. The ECJ's thirteen judges hear cases brought by states, organizations, or private litigants, including firms, interest groups, and individuals, which involve a breach of EU law. The ECJ has the power to overturn decisions by the executive Commission and Council. The ECJ case load is far greater than that of the ICJ.

There is disagreement over whether or not the ECJ is a true international court. Some argue that EU law differs so significantly from international law that they are different species. Furthermore, the European Union is seem as increasingly a federal state and its laws thus municipal rather than international. Others argue that because members retain their sovereignty and can withdraw from the European Union, the laws uniting them are by definition international, and in most cases do not differ substantially from those international laws with a global dimension.

The ECHR is based on the 1953 European Convention on Human Rights, eventually signed by the forty members of the Council of Europe. All members accept its jurisdiction as their highest appeals court for individuals. States not only comply with its decisions, they sometimes adjust their laws accordingly. For example, after receiving adverse rulings, Britain and France revised their wiretapping laws; German courts have provided interpreters for nonnative speaking defendants; Ireland legalized homosexuality; and Austria dropped its state satellite and cable television cartel. The successful transition of Spain, Portugal, and Greece to democracy in the 1970s was in part guided by ECHR standards.

But the ECHR's reputation for fair, powerful decisions has a downside. It is so popular that supplicants must queue for a long five-year wait before their case is heard. Of course, the court's success is hardly surprising. After all, human rights are an integral part of liberal democracy, which all those European countries have embraced if not fully realized. Still the ECHR can be a beacon for regions of the world still darkened by governments that systematically violate the rights of the people under their rule.

Human rights in the Western Hemisphere are shaped by the 1948 Charter of the Organization of American States (OAS). In 1960, the OAS created the Inter-American Commission on Human Rights to investigate allegations of human rights violations. The 1967 Buenos Aires Protocol and 1969 American Convention on Human Rights strengthened the Inter-American Commission's powers and created the Inter-American Court, both modeled on Europe's human rights institutions. Only 18 of the 31 OAS members have ratified the Convention; the United States has refused to sign. Although the Commission and Court do render decisions, they have no means to enforce their decisions.

Just because laws and institutions exist does not mean that they will be followed. Politics also delayed until 1970 the Commission's authorization to investigate accusations of human rights abuses and have stymied its work ever since. The General Assembly, which votes on Commission proposals to condemn countries for human rights violations, tends to single out Israel for human rights abuses while turning a blind eye to the several score dictatorships that systematically violate those same principles.

As in other areas of international law, the upholding of human rights depends largely on the actions of sovereign states. John Rouke juxtaposed two speeches giving very different views of the importance of human rights in foreign policy.[16] In 1978, on the thirty-ninth anniversary of the Universal Declaration of Human Rights, President Jimmy Carter declared himself

> proud that our nation stands for more than military might or political might... Our pursuit of human rights is part of a broad effort to use our great power and our tremendous influence in the service of creating a better world in which human beings can live in peace, in freedom, and with their basic needs met. Human rights is the soul of our foreign policy.[17]

Former secretary of state to President Carter, Cyrus Vance, later argued that it was a "dangerous illusion" to belief that "pursuing values such as human rights... is incompatible with pursuing U.S. national interests... Our own freedom, and that of our allies, could never be secure in a world where freedom was threatened everywhere else."[18]

Secretary of State George Shultz gave a very different view in 1985 when he said that

> we Americans have had to accept that our passionate commitment to moral principles could not be a substitute for sound foreign policy in a world of hard realities and complex choices... our moral impulse, noble as it might be, could lead either to futile and perhaps dangerous global crusades, on the one hand, or to escapism and isolationism, equally dangerous, on the other.[19]

For five decades the United Nations restricted itself solely to encouraging human rights and condemning war crimes. Then, in the 1990s, the UN Security Council initiated three institutions that enforced international war and human rights laws, and tried to bring violators to justice. The first crucial steps came with the establishment of the International Criminal Tribunal for Yugoslavia in 1993 and another for Rwanda in 1994. The Yugoslavian tribunal has so far issued a hundred and sixty-one indictments against suspects from all three Bosnian factions, and found guilty forty-three of eighty-five of those caught, including Yugoslavia's former president Slobodan Milosevic, who died of a heart attack in prison in March 2006. The Rwandan tribunal has issued forty-five indictments, nabbed thirty-two of the suspects, and convicted twenty-eight of them. As with national courts, many criminals evaded being brought to trial in those tribunals either because they could not be apprehended or, more commonly, no formal charges have been filed. Nonetheless, the punishment of some war criminals is surely better than none, as was true throughout history before the International Criminal Court (ICC).

The international community took an even more essential step forward in the quest for upholding international law of war and human rights when, in July 1998, representatives of 120 countries gathered in Rome to debate a proposed treaty that would establish a permanent ICC. All but seven of the countries that attended the conference signed the treaty. Presumably the idea of an international court dedicated to prosecuting war criminals made those holdouts very nervous. Who were they and what did they have to hide? Those who resisted the court's creation were China, Libya, Iraq, Qatar, Yemen, Israel, and the United States.

Why would a nation like the United States, which prides itself on its own highly developed liberal democracy and protection of human rights, be opposed to an international court that promotes those very values? During the prolonged negotiations over the treaty, Washington insisted that its own soldiers and citizens be immune from prosecution on war crime charges from any but its own courts. Not surprisingly, the other countries rejected the notion of a double standard for Americans and all other nations. That was not the first human rights treaty that Washington has rejected for itself but insisted upon for others. Although Washington did ratify the 1949 Geneva Convention with its intricate laws for how wars are to be fought and civilians and prisoners treated, it has either not ratified or actively campaigned against the 1948 Declaration on Human Rights, the 1984 Torture Convention, and the 1997 Land Mine Treaty, among others.

Why has Washington opposed such treaties upholding human rights? Under heavy pressure from the Republican party's right wing, various administrations have taken the principle that sovereignty—or at least American sovereignty—should prevail over human rights and war crimes. The conservatives who champion that cause were especially afraid that Ronald Reagan, George H.W. Bush, and George W. Bush could be charged with violating international law for their respective invasions of Grenada, Panama, and Iraq.

We're For Human Rights!—To a Point: America and International Justice

"Ladies and Gentlemen, We've got him!" With those words Paul Bremer, who was in charge of occupied Iraq, made the electrifying announcement that American troops had captured Saddam Hussein. It had taken nine long bloody months after President George W. Bush ordered the invasion of Iraq on March 19, 2003, before the dictator was found alone, filthy, baffled, and cowering in his "spider hole" across the Tigris River from one of his palaces on December 14.

Saddam's capture was a jubilant highpoint for the Bush administration. One of the core goals for Bush and most of his advisors after taking the White House on January 20, 2001, had been to destroy Saddam Hussein's regime. The problem was how to do so.

Under international law, a state can legally attack another state in only three circumstances: when the UN Security Council approves that attack; to retaliate against an attack; and to preempt an imminent attack. When the Security Council rejected President Bush's demand that it authorize an American-led war against Iraq, he justified his invasion order with two claims: Iraq possessed weapons of mass destruction, which posed an imminent threat to the United States (preemption); and Iraq was linked to Al Qaeda, which had attacked the United States on September 11 (retaliation).

After the conquest, no evidence was found to support either claim. While most foreign governments and people had opposed Bush's war against Iraq from the beginning, majorities in both houses of Congress and nearly four of five Americans had initially backed the president's decision to invade Iraq. But the failure to find weapons of mass destruction or ties with Al Qaeda combined with the worsening guerrilla war and toll in American blood and treasury provoked ever more Americans to question whether the war was just.

Thus Saddam Hussein's capture was a great public relations coup for the Bush administration. There was no question that the dictator was a vicious tyrant who was responsible for the murders of at least 300,000 Iraqis since he took power in 1979, and aggressive wars against neighboring Iran (1980–1988) and Kuwait (1990–1991), which took the lives of another million people. So now Bush could quietly drop his first two excuses for war against Iraq—retaliation for September 11 and preemption against an imminent attack—and instead celebrate his war as a crusade to bring an evil man to justice and convert a dictatorship into a democracy that would be a model for democratic revolutions across the Middle East and beyond. The White House announced that the tyrant would eventually be put on trial for war crimes and crimes against humanity.

The invasion of Iraq was not the only serious war crime charge against the Bush administration. In 2004 came the revelations that

American soldiers had tortured or humiliated prisoners at the Abu Ghraib, Guantanamo Bay, and other prisons. Thousands of photos revealed stomach-turning images: a smiling female American soldier leading by a leash a naked man on his hands and knees; a hooded man with outstretched arms and electric wires attached to his body; a human pyramid of naked men. There were also reports that Americans had sexually abused prisoners or desecrated the Koran. Those images and stories outraged virtually everyone who saw them and became recruiting posters for America's enemies in Iraq and beyond.

As so often happens in international relations and life in general, irony permeated both the conservative crusade in Iraq. Critics accused the Bush administration of acting like a lynch mob of vigilantes. Supporters cheered Bush for doing just that.

Realists disputed that conservative position and instead argued that, rather than outright reject those treaties, Washington could simply attach reservations to each, which specially protect its interests. Indeed, most signatories to the ICC and other human rights treaties did just that with the principle of "complementarity" whereby the new court would complement and not supersede their national courts. That would allow those governments to choose whether to allow their own accused nationals to be tried at home or in the ICC.

That was a key argument President Bill Clinton made when, as one of his last presidential acts, he signed the ICC treaty. He explained that in doing so the United States would

> join more than 130 other countries that have signed the treaty by the December 31, 2000 deadline...We do so to reaffirm our strong support for international accountability and for bringing to justice perpetrators of genocide, war crimes, and crimes against humanity.

He tried to assure opponents that the treaty would "not supersede or interfere with functioning national judicial systems." Instead, America's "signature will enhance our ability to protect U.S. officials from unfounded charges and to achieve...human rights and accountability objectives." Clinton did not, however, submit the treaty to the Senate for ratification. The reason was simple. Claiming contrary to evidence that the treaty violated American sovereignty, Senator Jesse Helms, the Senate foreign relations committee chair, declared that it would be dead on arrival.

Upon taking office, George W. Bush took up the conservative crusade against the ICC treaty. Putting the treaty to a losing vote in the

Senate could not adequately convey the hatred that conservatives harbored for the proposed ICC. On May 5, 2002, Bush informed UN Secretary General Kofi Annan by letter that he would "unsign" the treaty (an act unprecedented in American history) and swore that the United States would not recognize the court's jurisdiction or render any cooperation, including giving information in the trials of any suspected war criminals. But the conservatives were not yet done. To add potential injury to the insult, congressional conservatives attached a rider to a military appropriations bill that authorized the president to use force to rescue any Americans brought before the court and to embargo arms exports to any country that ratified the treaty.

Would the ICC really undermine American sovereignty? President Clinton had insisted that the final treaty included safeguards to screen any frivolous or harassing suits. The UN Security Council would bring nearly all cases to the ICC; any initiative thus would be subject to an American veto. Those brought by governments or groups would be screened by a pretrial ICC review panel with the power to throw out any frivolous cases. The ICC would notify any country of any case brought against it. That country would then have six months to investigate those allegations. Only if a country refused to do so would a three-judge ICC panel investigate and possibly prosecute the accused. A guilty vote would need at least two of the three judges. As Kofi Annan tried to explain to the White House, "The court will prosecute in situations where the country concerned is either unwilling or unable to prosecute. Countries with good judicial systems who apply the rule of law and prosecute criminals and do it promptly and fairly need not fear."

For realists the question of whether the ICC would advance American interests was a no-brainer. The international criminal court could be an important tool in America's war against terrorism and rogue states. For the Senate to reject or, even more outrageously, for Bush to unsign the treaty, would dismay the nation's allies and delight its enemies by violating American values to uphold international cooperation, institutions, and law. The Bush administration's threats to cut off military aid to countries that ratified the treaty would materially damage American security. But the worst self-inflicted blow to national security would be for Bush or some other conservative president to try to rescue Americans on trial at the ICC. The United States would be forever condemned as an international outlaw in the eyes of the world.

The ICC officially came into force on July 2, 2002, when the required seventy-sixth signatory ratified the treaty. It would take another nine months before the ICC would begin operations. The court's jurisdiction would apply only to crimes committed after it was established.

The Bush administration's war against the ICC entered a new phase. First it tried to get the United Nations to exempt peacekeepers from the court. When that measure failed, the White House announced that the United States would no longer participate in international peacekeeping missions. They followed up that assertion by vetoing on June 29 a proposed extension of the peacekeeping mission to Bosnia by the Security Council. The Europeans led a nearly universal international chorus in condemning that act. Eventually, the Security Council had no choice but to surrender to the Bush team's threat to end its funding and participation in international peacekeeping missions. A compromise was worked out whereby the Security Council would grant American peacekeepers a one-year exemption from prosecution subject to renewal. The vote was unanimous.

Meanwhile, the White House pressured individual countries to grant the United States immunity from prosecution. Although they later denied it, the Bush team apparently traded membership in NATO to Estonia, Latvia, Lithuania, and Bulgaria for their exemptions. Israel, Romania, East Timor, and Tajikistan were among the early signers. On August 25, the White House actually warned that it would reconsider America's ties with NATO if they did not get their way. NATO went along. The European Union strongly protested such strong-armed tactics, but on September 30, 2002, grudgingly agreed to grant a one-year exemption to the United States. The White House eventually got thirty-seven countries to sign treaties granting American citizens immunity.

The ICC's first session took place on March 11, 2003, when eighteen judges, including eleven men and seven women, took their sets; Philippe Kirsch of Canada was named the court's first president. Located in a former military barracks in The Hague, the Netherlands, the ICC includes a prison, a law library, and a hospital. The judges and their assistants had their work cut out for them—over 200 petitions had piled up over the 9 months since the treaty was ratified.

If most people celebrated the ICC's inauguration, the Bush administration figuratively sported black arm bands. The White House exerted enormous pressure on the Security Council to renew its grant of immunity for American peacekeepers for another year. This time twelve states voted for the measure, with France, Germany, and Syria abstaining.

Critics deplored any measure that allowed Americans to be above the law. UN Secretary General Kofi Annan warned that if such renewals become "an annual routine they would undermine not only the authority of the ICC, but also the authority of the Council and the legitimacy of United Nations peacekeeping."

Gutting those programs, of course, was high on the conservative agenda. The Bush team announced on July 1, 2003, that it would suspend $47 million in military aid and $613,000 in education programs that would have been distributed among thirty-five countries that had refused to grant the United States immunity. The president waived from that list an additional twenty-two countries that had signed but not yet ratified immunity deals. But by putting ideological correctness before American interests, the Bush administration undermined national security. All of those countries received aid because they supported the United States in various ways. For instance, two countries essential for the war against illegal drugs—Columbia and Ecuador—were on the list.

CONSEQUENCES

There is no question that international wars have diminished sharply since 1945. However, just what role international laws and organizations have played in that decline is debatable.

The UN Charter clearly represents shared global community values, thus fulfilling the Roman precept that "where there is society, there is law (ubi societas, ibi jus)." States signing the Charter legally commit themselves to those values whether they live up to them or not. International law can be considered important, only when virtually all governments think it is important and usually adjust their behavior, or at least their rhetoric, accordingly. In the post–Cold War world, the UN Security Council has increasingly served as a world court, police, and prosecutor, albeit sporadically and selectively.

Meanwhile, the body of international law continues steadily to expand. One of the most remarkable milestones of the twentieth century is the outlawing of aggressive war. Most states are at peace most of the time, and international law of war has shaped and been shaped by that reality.

Yet nation-states themselves rather than international organizations are undoubtedly the most important force upholding international law. National prosperity and security depend on a government's ability to promote its country's interests in an ever more interdependent world. Reputation matters, if only for reasons of self-interest. Virtually all states obey the law all of the time, and the rest most of the time. Law-abiding states generally shun or retaliate against those that regularly and grossly violate international law, to the latter's detriment.

In a profound sense, all international laws and organizations, whether or not they are explicitly dedicated to doing so, curb war and promote peace by deepening and broadening globalization. The greater the interdependence among nation-states, the costs of war soar and any conceivable benefits vanish. International law, and the institutions for enforcing it, will continue to evolve into the twenty-first century.

CHAPTER 7

Consequences

The triumph of the West, of the Western idea, is evident... in the total exhaustion of viable systematic alternatives to Western liberalism.

Francis Fukuyama

In the post–Cold War world, the most important distinctions among peoples are not ideological, political, or economic. They are cultural.

Samuel Huntington

The twentieth century was the most blood-soaked in history: more than a hundred million people died, hundreds of millions more were maimed physically and emotionally, and trillions of dollars worth of property were destroyed.

Appalled by the carnage, far-sighted statesmen initiated the establishment of international organizations devoted to collective security. Those efforts failed as first the League of Nations, set up after World War I, and then the United Nations, set up after World War II did little to keep the peace.

Like World War I, World War II ended with the great promise that it would be the war to end all wars. By September 1945, the attempts by Japan, Germany, and Italy to conquer regions of the world were decisively crushed. Henceforth, it was hoped, all the world's nations would settle all conflicts peacefully and justly through the United Nations. Never again would the world's economy break down into trade wars and depression as it did in the 1930s. Instead, a global "free trade" system would be created and carefully managed by networks of international trade and financial organizations like the General Agreement on Tariffs and Trade (GATT, later WTO), International

Monetary Fund (IMF), and International Bank for Reconstruction and Development (IRBD, better known as the World Bank). People all over the world would realize their national and human rights to be free as promised by the Atlantic and UN Charters. However, those dreams proved to be short-lived. The wartime alliance between the United States and Soviet Union broke down into nearly five decades of geopolitical conflict known as the Cold War, fueled by diametrically opposed ideologies, security needs, and threat perceptions.

In many ways, the twentieth century's central struggle was between two diametrically opposed internationalist visions: "Wilsonism" and "Leninism." The ideals enthusiastically espoused by President Woodrow Wilson included political, economic, and national freedom, and international cooperation to resolve conflicts. Vladimir Lenin advocated a contrasting vision characterized by class struggle, revolution, war, and totalitarian state power that imposed a radical economic egalitarianism.

The global struggle between Wilsonism and Leninism was not a traditional war. During the four and a half decades in which they were mortal enemies, the United States and Soviet Union never directly fought each other. Deterrence, not conquest, was the Cold War's essence. Perhaps the most important reason for that "cold peace" was Mutually Assured Destruction (MAD) as each side stockpiled tens of thousands of nuclear weapons, overshadowing humanity with a potential nuclear holocaust.

The Cold War finally ended by December 1991, with the Soviet empire dismembered and communism renounced almost everywhere except in China, Cuba, Vietnam, Laos, and North Korea. The Cold War ended partly as a result of four decades of America's containment of the Soviet Union, and partly by communism's inability to satisfy even the most basic economic let alone political needs of the people under its grip.

Unlike a traditional victory, no American and allied troops swept triumphantly into the enemy capital. Instead the celebration was muted as more thoughtful leaders and followers pondered the Cold War's costs in blood, treasury, and lost opportunities, along with the crises that only luck and skilled diplomats kept from igniting a nuclear holocaust. Nonetheless, the Cold War victory was as decisive as those over the fascist powers after World War II. Since then Russia and the other former communist states are being revolutionized by international corporate and financial leaders, and integrated ever more profoundly into the global economy.

The Cold War's end and globalization's relentless pace renders military means irrelevant for resolving nearly all international conflicts. While power is still the currency of international relations, the nature of the conflicts and the means by which states assert their interests is rapidly changing. National security traditionally meant freedom from the threat of foreign attack. Today and into the future, an ever smaller fraction of international conflicts will be over territory and ideology. Wars like Iraq's invasion of Kuwait in 1990 or America's invasion of Iraq in 2003 appear to be ever more anachronistic. In an interdependent world, states can much more cheaply acquire through trade, diplomacy, and other means the security, wealth, and prestige that they formerly won through the assertion of violence. The world's greatest military powers, the United States and Russia, are rapidly reducing their vast nuclear forces, and other states are either capping or reducing their own bloated military budgets. Without the Cold War, militant states can no longer play off the two superpowers against each other to receive huge amounts of economic and military aid. Edward Luttwak is among those who see profound changes in the nature of international conflict in the post–Cold War era:

> Except in those unfortunate parts of the world where armed confrontations or civil strife persist for purely regional or internal reasons, the waning of the Cold War is steadily reducing the importance of military power in world affairs . . . Everyone, it appears, now agrees that the methods of commerce are displacing military methods—with disposable capital in lieu of firepower, civilian innovation in lieu of military-technical advancement, and market penetration in lieu of garrisons and bases.[1]

Political liberty may be as powerful a global force as economic interdependence in diluting geopolitics. One place war will not intrude is in relations among liberal democratic countries. Depending on how one defines the concept, some argue that liberal democracies have never fought each other. Thus the more countries that achieve liberal democracy, the less chance for war. Combining George Hegel's notion that history moves by the clash of ideas with Immanuel Kant's notion of perpetual peace, Francis Fukuyama writes: "the triumph of the West, of the Western idea, is evident . . . in the total exhaustion of viable systematic alternatives to Western liberalism."[2] According to Fukuyama, liberal democracy has emerged triumphant from 7,000 years of a dialectical struggle between different ideologies. History is ending in an Hegelian sense and bringing with it an unprecedented and unending era of peace among humanity.

From the 1989 fall of the Berlin Wall through today, outright liberal democracies or quasidemocracies have replaced ever more authoritarian governments around the world, not just in the former Soviet empire but from Taiwan to Nicaragua, and Chile to South Korea. By the year 2010, according to the human rights group Freedom House, around 60 percent of the world's countries had "liberal democratic" constitutions, up from 30 percent fifty years earlier. Yet that same year another human rights organization, Amnesty International, pointed out that nearly 60 percent of the governments of all countries systematically abused human rights. What explains the discrepancy of this distorted mirror image? Was the human rights glass 60 percent full or 60 percent empty? Freedom House emphasizes the progress toward human rights while Amnesty International points out the continuing abuses. Both, however, do note a steady improvement. Yearly, it seems, another country or two sheds the more outrageous forms of political oppression and adopts the institutional trappings and sometimes even the substance of liberal democracy.

What explains the democratic revolution? Is democracy for everyone? There is clearly a correlation between economic and political development. The demands for political rights and representation grow along with a middle class. Certainly there is a link between economic prosperity and political freedom. The more people have of one, the more they tend to demand the other. Although most cultures do not have democratic values of political equality and liberty, democracy has become a universal good. Virtually every regime, even the most despotic, claims to be democratic in some ways. And as Fukuyama and others have pointed out, there is no universal alternative to democracy.

Cutting-edge technologies enhance the power of any group struggling to assert its interests at any level—international, transnational, national, or subnational. For instance, mobilizing followers within a country and in other countries is an essential element of power for those trying to undermine dictatorships. During the Cold War, dissidents in the Soviet Union and other communist tyrannies in Eastern Europe eventually acquired mass followings and international support by using fax machines. The creation of the Internet in the early 1990s allowed groups around the world to mobilize themselves in "swarms" to protest a policy or international meeting of opponents. Cellphones allow people to exchange not only words but also photographs and written messages that can reveal the strength of mass protests in the streets or the authoritarian governments repressing that movement. In 2009, those technologies allowed the world to watch as Iranian dissidents organized mass demonstrations to protest a rigged election of their government, followed by the brutal oppression of those demonstrations.

Assuming that this general trend toward democratization will continue, we cannot but face this question: what impact will it have on global politics? War, many argue, is history's engine. If it is true that liberal democracies have never fought each other, then wars should steadily diminish as the number of liberal or quasiliberal countries increase. Without war, what will drive history?

Any victory celebration over liberal democracy's triumph may be premature. In a controversial and thought-provoking book, Samuel Huntington rejects Fukuyama's "everyone is becoming more like us" theory. Geopolitics did not end with the fall of the Berlin Wall in 1989. Indeed, the fall of the World Trade Center in 2001 symbolized the emergence of a form of global politics that is increasingly shaped by the clash among civilizations rather than nation-states:

> In the post–Cold War world, for the first time in history, global politics has become multi-polar and multi-civilizational...In the post–Cold War world, the most important distinctions among peoples are not ideological, political, or economic. They are cultural.

And those fundamental differences among civilizations will be as divisive and at times as deadly as any other conflicts among people.[3]

Although Huntington's notion that clashes among his rather vaguely defined civilizations will fuel geopolitics has been as heavily criticized as Fukuyama's notion of a pending perpetual peace, there is no question that for the foreseeable future, war will continue to plague humanity. Liberal democratic states will continue to fight authoritarian states, and authoritarian states will continue to fight one another and restless peoples within their borders who demand freedom. The number of international wars, however, will likely diminish as all countries become so bound by the ever growing matrix of global economic, cultural, and environmental ties that the use of force to settle international conflicts becomes not just exorbitant but unthinkable. Globalization and the slow spread of liberal democracy have reduced the relative number of geopolitical conflicts and increased the relative number of geoeconomic conflicts.

War will increasingly be within rather than between nation-states or will pit a transnational terrorist group like Al Qaeda versus sovereign states and their transnational allies. While the world unites in many ways, parts of it are rapidly disintegrating into civil war and anarchy as long suffering minorities, or in the case of Kosovo, majorities, revolt against the dominant nationality. Nationalism rather than internationalism is the driving force behind the independence struggles of scores of suppressed peoples around the world. Many of those conflicts are also fueled by religious extremism, especially among Muslims. Al Qaeda, for instance, is dedicated to purifying all Muslim lands of Western influences, which specifically includes driving the Americans out of the Middle East and destroying the state of Israel. Nationalist and/or religious strife will undoubtedly breed violence within and among states for the indefinite future.

During the 1990s new terms such as "failed state," "ethnic cleansing," and "uncivil war" appeared to express horrors as old as humanity. There was a time when word of such distant tragedies was just a whispered rumor or a survivor's heartbreaking tale. But satellite television can beam into our homes stomach-turning scenes of heaps of mutilated rotting corpses, sobbing raped women, people whose arms and legs were hacked off by sadists with machetes, and starving orphans with bloated bellies and stick legs. The outrage at such brutality provokes demands for "humanitarian intervention" by the United States, United Nations, or some other global power to rescue those victims.

Those pleas often go unheeded, however. The lack of will is usually excused by a lack of money, troops, transport, and national interest, along with a surfeit of other humanitarian duties, the genocide's remote location, and the ferocity of the armed gangs. "Peacekeeping" or being invited in by the warring groups to restore order is difficult enough. "Peacemaking," or defeating an armed group or groups is far tougher. But the most difficult challenge of all is "nation-building," or transforming a failed state into a functioning state that maintains essential order, justice, nutrition, health, and shelter for ravaged people while they restore their livelihoods.

As the attacks on the World Trade Center and Pentagon on September 11, 2001, revealed, terrorist groups rather than rogue states pose the worst threat to the United States and most other Western countries. September 11 was not the first atrocity committed by Islamists against the United States, only the deadliest. The first attack was the 1993 bombing of the World Trade Center. In response to September 11, the United States and its allies routed Al Qaeda and its host the Taliban from power in Afghanistan and eventually arrested over 4,000 terrorist suspects around the world. Those efforts have diminished but not eliminated the power of Al Qaeda and other terrorist groups to commit future attacks.

A nightmare scenario is for a terrorist group like Al Qaeda to get its hands on nuclear, chemical, biological, and/or radiological weapons of mass destruction. For decades Washington and Moscow have initiated attempts to limit the proliferation of such weapons among states and terrorist groups alike. The two military superpowers have signed a series of bilateral treaties, which will eventually dismantle all but 1,600 ICBMs. The United States, Russia, and nearly all other states have negotiated other treaties that restrict them not to possess or develop chemical and biological weapons. The trouble is that some countries have either broken that promise or not signed those treaties.

Fortunately, the number of countries that have professed either openly or secretly to having weapons of mass destruction is dwindling. Besides America and Russia, most other countries known to hold nuclear weapons appear to have frozen their production, including Britain, France, China, Israel, India, and Pakistan. Following the 1991 Persian Gulf War, UN inspections forced Iraq to dismantle its nuclear, biological, and chemical weapons programs. In 2004, Libya agreed to give up its nuclear weapons program, which had not yet created a bomb. North Korea, however, defiantly brandishes it nuclear weapons despite the collective attempts by the United States, China, South Korea, Russia, and Japan to get to give them up. Iran, meanwhile, claims that its nuclear program is confined to developing energy rather than weapons. In time we will learn whether the Iranian government is telling the truth.

Despite or more likely partly because of those lingering geopolitical threats, nation-states are cooperating as never before. The United Nations has taken the lead in mitigating violence and finding solutions for ever more conflicts. In 2010, the it fielded sixteen peacekeeping missions, with only budget constraints and donor fatigue preventing others from intervening.

Thomas Friedman explains geopolitics today and for the foreseeable future as a struggle that pits the "World of Order" against the "World of Discord," which he calls World War III: "The World of Disorder comprises failed states (such as Liberia), rogue states (Iraq and North Korea), messy states—states that are too big to fail but too messy to work (Pakistan, Columbia, Indonesia, many Arab and African states), and finally the terrorist and mafia networks that feed off the World of Disorder. There has always been a World of Disorder, but what makes it more dangerous today is that in a networked universe, with widely diffused technologies, open borders, and a highly integrated global financial and internet system, very small groups of people can amass huge amounts of power to disrupt the World of Order." For Friedman September 11 "marked the first full-scale battlefield between a superpower and a small band of super-empowered angry men from the World of Disorder."[4]

Geopolitics will not disappear from the earth any time soon. A hard look around the world reveals a number of powder-kegs that could explode into international war, with those between the United States and North Korea or Iran, China, and Taiwan, or India and Pakistan the most dangerous. Yet war is not inevitable in any of those and other deadlocks. Wise diplomacy and compromises can resolve a conflict before it becomes a crisis, or defuse a crisis before it erupts into war. Wisdom, however, is often the most lacking where it is most needed. And that alone will ensure that the dilemmas of war and peace will plague humanity throughout the twenty-first century and beyond.

Notes

Introduction

1. The literature on globalization can be split among relatively balanced studies and those that are either decidedly optimistic or pessimistic about its nature and consequences.

   For broad overviews, see J. Martin Rochester, *Between Two Epochs: What Is Ahead for America, the World, and Global Politics in the 21st Century* (Upper Saddle River, N.J.: Prentice Hall, 2002); David Held and Anthony McGrew, eds., *The Global Transformations Reader* (Cambridge: Polity Press/Blackwell, 2003); K.J. Holsti, *Taming the Sovereigns: International Change in International Politics* (New York: Cambridge University Press, 2004); Peter Singer, *One World: The Ethics of Globalization* (New Haven, Conn.: Yale University Press, 2004); Edward Cornish, *Futuring: The Exploration of the Future* (Bethesda, Md.: World Future Society, 2004); Marvin J. Cetron and Owen Davies, *53 Trends Now Shaping the Future* (Bethesda, Md.: World Future Society, 2005); Charles W. Kegley and Gregory A. Raymond, *The Global Future* (Belmont, Calif.: Wadsworth/Thomson Learning, 2006).

   For pessimists, see Yale H. Ferguson and Richard W. Mansbach, *Remapping Global Politics: History's Revenge and Future Shock* (New York: Columbia University Press, 2004); Jared Diamond, *Collapse: How Societies Choose to Fail or Succeed* (New York: Viking, 2005); Louise Amoore, ed., *The Global Resistance Reader: Concepts and Issues* (New York: Routledge, 2005); Jan Aart Scholte, *Globalization: A Critical Introduction* (London: Palgrave, 2005); Worldwatch Institute, *State of the World 2007* (New York: W.W. Norton, 2007).

   For optimists, see Jadish Bhagwati, *In Defense of Globalization* (New York: Oxford University Press, 2004); Thomas Friedman, *The Earth Is Flat: A Brief History of the Twenty-First Century* (New York: Farrar, Straus, and Giroux, 2005); John F. Stack and Luis Hebron, *Globalization: Debunking the Myths* (Upper Saddle River, N.J.: Prentice Hall, 2006).

2. Thomas Friedman, *The Lexus and the Olive Tree: Understanding Globalization* (New York: Anchor Books, 2000).

3. Parts of this book appeared in William Nester, *International Relations: Politics and Economics in the 21st Century* (Belmont, Calif.: Wadsworth, 2001).

1 THE NATURE, CREATION, AND ASSERTION OF POWER

1. Harold Lasswell, *Politics: Who Gets What, When, and How* (New York: Smith, 1936, 1950).
2. Karl Deutsch, *Analysis of International Relations* (Englewood Cliffs, N.J.: Prentice Hall, 1968), 21–39. For the best book to date on soft power, see Joseph Nye, *Soft Power: The Means to Success in World Politics* (New York: Public Affairs, 2004).
3. C.W. Maynes, "Logic, Bribes, and Threats," *Foreign Affairs*, Fall 1985, 60:111–29.
4. John Rothgeb, *Defining Power: Influence and Force in the Contemporary International System* (New York: St. Martin's Press, 1993), 141. See also Lawrence Freedman, *Deterrence* (Cambridge, Mass.: Polity Press, 2004).
5. Among others, see R.J. Rummel, "Indicators of Cross-National and International Patterns," *American Political Science Review*, March 1969, 62:127–47. James Lee Ray and J. David Singer, "Measuring the Concentration of Power in the International System," *Sociological Methods and Research*, May 1973, 403–36; Ray Cline, *World Power Trends and U.S. Foreign Policy for the 1980s* (Boulder, Colo.: Westview Press, 1980); Jacek Kugler and Richard Arbetman, "Choosing Among Measures of Power: A Review of the Empirical Record," and Richard Merritt and Dina Zinnes, "Alternative Indexes of National Power," in Richard Stoll and Michael Ward, eds., *Power in World Politics* (Boulder, Col.: Rienner, 1989); David Baldwin, *Paradoxes of Power* (New York: Basil Blackwell, 1991); Michael Sullivan, *Power in Contemporary International Politics* (Columbia: University of South Carolina Press, 1990); Ken Booth, ed., *New Thinking about Strategy and International Security* (London: Unwin Hyman Academic, 1991).
6. James Lee Ray, *Global Politics* (Boston: Houghton Mifflin, 1990).
7. Nye, *Soft Power*.
8. Wolfram Hanrieder, ed., *Comparative Foreign Policy: Theoretical Essay* (New York: McKay, 1971), 128.
9. Halford Mackinder, *Democratic Ideals and Realities* (New York: Holt, 1919), 150.
10. Alfred T. Mahan, *The Influence of Seapower Upon History, 1660–1783* (Boston: Little Brown, 1965), 29.
11. Nicholas Spykman, *America's Strategy in World Politics* (New York: Harcourt Brace, 1942), 472.
12. For a good introduction, see Loch Johnson and James Wirtz, eds., *Strategic Intelligence: Windows into a Secret World* (Los Angeles, Calif.: Roxberry, 2005).
13. C. Webster, *The Art and Practice of Diplomacy* (London: Chatto & Windus, 1961); Harold Nicolson, *Diplomacy* (New York: Oxford University Press, 1963); I.W. Zartman and M. Berman, *The Practical*

Negotiator (New Haven, Conn.: Yale University Press, 1982); A. Eban, *The New Diplomacy: International Affairs in the Modern Age* (London: Weidenfeld & Nicolson, 1983); Raymond Cohen, *The Theater of Power: The Art of Diplomatic Signaling* (London: Longman, 1987); H. Binnedijk, ed., *National Negotiating Styles* (Washington, D.C.: United States Department of State, 1987); J. Gross-Stein, ed., *Getting to the Table: The Process of International Pre-Negotiations* (Baltimore: Johns Hopkins University Press, 1989); R. Cohen, *Negotiating across Cultures* (Washington: United State Institute of Peace, 1997); R.P. Barston, *Modern Diplomacy* (London: Longman, 1997); Jan Melissen, ed., *Innovation in Diplomatic Practice* (Basingstoke, U.K.: Macmillan, 1999); G.R. Berridge, *Diplomacy: Theory and Practice* (New York: Palgrave, 2002).
14. Paul Smith, *On Political Warfare* (Washington, D.C.: National Defense University Press, 1988).
15. See various online comparative survey results of the Pew Institute.
16. Andrew Kohut and Bruce Stokes, *American against the World: How We Are Different and Why We Are Disliked* (New York: Times Books/Henry Holt, 2006); Julia Sweig, *Friendly Fire: Losing Friends and Making Enemies in the Anti-American Century* (New York: Council on Foreign Relations Book/Public Affairs, 2006).
17. Theodore Von Laue, *The Revolution of Westernization* (New York: Oxford University Press, 1987), 376.
18. Quoted in Van Laue, *The Revolution of Westernization*, 338.
19. Cynthia Cannizzo, "The Costs of Combat: Death, Duration, Defeat," in J. David Singer, ed., *The Correlates of World War II: Testing Some Realpolitik Models* (New York: Free Press, 1980). See also Zeev Moaz, "Resolve, Capabilities, and Interstate Disputes," in A.F.K. Organski and Jacek Kugler, eds., *The War Ledger* (Chicago: University of Chicago Press, 1980).
20. Andrew Mack, "Why Big Nations Lose Small Wars: The Politics of Asymmetrical Conflict," *World Politics*, January 1975, 27:197; Joseph Nye, *Understanding International Conflicts: An Introduction to Theory and History* (New York: Addison Wesley, 1999).
21. William Riker, *The Theory of Political Coalitions* (New Haven, Conn.: Yale University Press, 1962), 32–33; See also Stephen Watt, *The Origin of Alliances* (Ithaca, N.Y.: Cornell University Press, 1987).
22. Randolph Silverson and Michael Tennefoss, "Power, Alliances, and the Escalation of National Conflict, 1815–1965," *American Political Science Review*, 78, December 1984:1063.
23. Bruce Bueno de Mesquita, *The War Trap* (New Haven, Conn.: Yale University Press, 1981).
24. Quoted in Robert Tucker and David Hendrickson, "Thomas Jefferson and American Foreign Policy," *Foreign Affairs*, Spring 1990, 69/2:138.

25. Tucker and Henderson, "Jefferson and American Foreign Policy Policy," *Foreign Affairs*, 69/2:147.

26. George Kennan, *The Fateful Alliance: France, Russia, and the Coming of the First World War* (New York: Pantheon, 1984), 238.

27. Bruce Russet and Harvey Starr, *World Politics: The Menu for Choice* (New York: Freeman, 1992), 89.

28. Nicolo Machiavelli, *The Prince and the Discourses* (New York: Modern Library, 1950), 310; Some of the following discussions and statistics were culled from William Nester, *American Power, the New World Order and the Japanese Challenge* (New York: St. Martin's Press, 1993), and William Nester, *European Power and the Japanese Challenge* (New York: New York University Press, 1993). See also William Nester, *Japanese Industrial Targeting: The Neomercantilist Path to Economic Superpower* (New York: St. Martin's Press, 1992); William Nester, *Japan and the Third World: Patterns, Power, Prospects* (New York: St. Martin's Press, 1992); William Nester, *The Foundations of Japanese Power: Continuities, Changes, Challenges* (Armonk, N.Y.: Sharpe, 1991); William Nester, *Japan's Growing Power over East Asia and the World Economy: Ends and Means* (New York: St. Martin's Press, 1991); William Nester, *Power Across the Pacific: A Diplomatic History of American Relations with Japan* (New York: New York University Press, 1996).

29. Richard Rosecrance, *The Rise of the Trading State: Commerce and Conquest in the Modern World* (New York: Basic Books, 1986), 13. See also Aaron Friedberg, "The Changing Relationship Between Economics and National Security," *Political Science Quarterly*, Summer 1991, 106:265–76; Ethan Kapstein, *The Political Economy of National Security: A Global Perspective* (New York: McGraw-Hill, 1992); Clyde Prestowitz, Ronald Morse, and Alan Tonelson, eds., *Powernomics: Economics and Strategy After the Cold War* (Lanham, Md.: Madison Books, 1991).

2   Why Nations Go to War and Stay at Peace

1. Some material and ideas from this chapter were taken from William Nester, *American Power, the New World Order, and the Japanese Challenge* (New York: St. Martin's Press, 1993). For some prominent works on war and peace, see Raymond Aron, *Peace and War: A Theory of International Relations* (New York: Praeger, 1968); Robert Gilpin, *War and Change in World Politics* (Cambridge: Cambridge University Press, 1981); Michael Howard, *The Causes of War and Other Essays* (Cambridge, Mass.: Harvard University Press, 1983); Robert J. Art and Kenneth Waltz, eds., *The Use of Force: International Politics and Foreign Policy* (Lanham, Md.: University

Press of America, 1983); Melvin Small and J. David Singer, eds., *International War* (Homewood, Ill.: Dorsey Press, 1985); John Stoessinger, *Why Nations Go to War* (New York: St. Martin's Press, 1985); Kalevi Holsti, *The State, War, and the State of War* (Cambridge: Cambridge University Press, 1996); Glenn Synder, *Alliance Politics* (Ithaca, N.Y.: Cornell University Press, 1997); Paul Diehl and Gary Goertz, *War and Peace in International Rivalry* (Ann Arbor: University of Michigan Press, 2000); John Mearsheimer, *The Tragedy of Great Power Politics* (New York: W.W. Norton, 2001); Barbara Harff and Ted Robert Gurr, *Ethnic Conflict in World Politics* (Boulder, Colo.: Westview Press, 2003); Charles Tilly, *The Politics of Collective Violence* (Cambridge, U.K.: Cambridge University Press, 2003); Michael Walzer, *Arguing about War* (New Haven, Conn.: Yale University Press, 2003); John Vasquez and Colin Elman, *Realism and the Balancing of Power: A New Debate* (Upper Saddle River, N.J.: Prentice Hall, 2003); Patricia Weistman, *Dangerous Alliances: Proponents of Peace, Weapons of War* (Sanford, Calif.: Stanford University Press, 2004); Scott Bennett and Allan Stam, *The Behavioral Origins of War* (Ann Arbor: University of Michigan, 2004); Ann Hironaka, *Neverending Wars: The International Community, Weak States, and the Perpetuation of Civil War* (Cambridge, Mass.: Harvard University Press, 2005); Joseph Nye, *Understanding International Conflicts* (New York: Longman, 2005).

2. James E. Dougherty and Robert L. Pfaltzgraff, *Contending Theories of International Relations* (New York: Harper and Row, 1990), 337.

3. Quincy Wright, *A Study of War* (Chicago: University of Chicago Press, 1942), 17. For other important statistic analyzes, see J. David Singer, *The Wages of War, 1816–1965: A Statistical Handbook* (New York: John Wiley and Sons, 1972); David Wilkinson, *Deadly Quarrels: Lewis F. Richardson and the Statistical Study of War* (Berkeley: University of California Press, 1980).

4. Bruce Bueno de Mesquita and David Lalman, *War and Reason* (New Haven, Conn.: Yale University Press 1992).

5. Clyde Eagleton, *International Government* (New York: Ronald Press, 1948), 393.

6. Karl von Clausewitz, *On War* (New York: Random House, 1943), 5.

7. Kenneth Waltz, *Man the State, and War* (York: Columbia University Press, 1959).

8. Waltz, *Man, the State, and War*, 3.

9. James Strachey, ed., *The Standard Edition of the Complete Psychological Works of Sigmund Freud* (London: Hogarth, 1964), 22:199.

10. Konrad Lorenz, *On Aggression* (New York: Harcourt Brace Jovanovich, 1966); see also Robert Ardrey, *The Territorial Imperative* (New York: Atheneum, 1966).

11. Adolf Hitler, *Mein Kampf* (Boston: Houghton Mifflin, 1943), 134.

12. B.F. Skinner, *Beyond Freedom and Dignity* (New York: Knopf, 1971).
13. Margaret Mead, "War Is Only an Invention," in Leon Bramson and George W. Goethals, eds., *War Studies from Psychology, Sociology, and Anthropology* (New York: Basic Books, 1968), 269–74.
14. Jack Levy, "The Causes of War: A Review of Theories and Evidence," in Philip Tetlock, Robert Jervis, Jo Husbands, and Paul Stern, eds., Behavior, Society, and Nuclear War (New York: Oxford University Press, 1989), 271.
15. Clyde Kluckhohn, *Mirror for Man: A Survey of Human Behavior and Social Attitudes* (Greenwich, Conn.: Fawcett World Library, 1960).
16. For a study that indicates that chemical imbalances may be responsible for aggressive behavior, see Douglas Masden, "A Biochemical Property Relative to Human Power Seeking," *American Political Science Review*, June 1985:448–57. See also R.T. Green and G. Santori, "A Cross Cultural Study of Hostility and Aggression," *Journal of Peace Research*, 1, 1969, 23–44.
17. Otto Klineberg, *The Human Dimension in International Relations* (New York: Holt, Rinehart, and Winston, 1964); Albert Somit, "Humans, Chips, and Bonobos: The Biological Basis of Aggression, War, and Peacemaking," *Journal of Conflict Resolution*, September 1990, 34:553–83.
18. See Margaret G. Hermann and Thomas W. Milburn, *A Psychological Examination of Political Leaders* (New York: Free Press, 1977).
19. Theodore Abel, "The Element of Decision in the Pattern of War," *American Sociological Reviews*, June 1941, 6:855.
20. Sigmund Freud, *Civilization and Its Discontents* (New York: W.W. Norton, 1984).
21. For an indepth analysis of the role of misperception and war, see John Stoessinger, *Why Nations Go to War* (New York: St. Martin's Press, 1985); See also Jack S. Levy, "Misperception and the Causes of War," *World Politics*, October 1983; Herbert Kelman, ed., *International Political Behavior* (New York: Holt, Rinehart, and Winston, 1965); Herman Kahn, *On Escalation* (New York: Praeger, 1965).
22. Arthur Gladstone, "The Conception of the Enemy," *Journal of Conflict Resolution*, 1959, 3:132.
23. Samuel Huntington, *The Clash of Civilizations and the Remaking of World Order* (New York: Touchstone Books, 1997), 254–65, 111. See also Ali E. Hillal Dessouki, ed., *Islamic Resurgence in the Arab World* (New York: Praeger, 1982); James Piscatori, ed., *Islamic Fundamentalism and the Gulf Crisis* (Chicago: American Academy of Arts and Sciences, 1991); Karen Armstrong, *Holy War: The Crusades and Their Impact on Today's World* (New York: Doubleday-Anchor, 1991); John Esposito, *The Islamic Threat: Myth or Reality?* (New York: Oxford University Press, 1992); Martin Marty and R. Scott Appleby, eds., *Fundamentalism and the State: Remaking Politics,*

Economies, and Militance (Chicago: University of Chicago Press, 1993); Kanan Makiya, *Cruelty and Silence: War, Tyranny, Uprising, and the Arab World* (New York: W.W. Norton, 1993).

24. R. Paul Shaw and Yuma Wong, "Ethnic Mobilization and the Seeds of Warfare: An Evolutionary Perspective," *International Studies Quarterly*, March 1987:5–32.

25. Georg Simmel, *Conflict and the Web of Group-Affiliations* (New York: Free Press, 1964), 93.

26. Geoffrey Blainy, *The Causes of War* (New York: Free Press, 1988), 71–86.

27. Randolph Rummel, "Dimensions of Conflict Behavior Within and Between Nations," *General Systems Yearbook*, VIII, 1963; Raymond Tanter, "International War and Domestic Turmoil: Some Contemporary Evidence," in *Violence In American: Historical and Comparative Perspectives: A Report to the National Commission on the Causes and Prevention of Violence*, June 1969 (New York: New American Library, 1969); Jonathan Wilkensfield, "Domestic and Foreign Conflict Behavior of Nations," in William D. Coplin and Charles W. Kegley, eds., *Analyzing International Relations: A Multimethod Introduction* (New York: Praeger, 1973), 96–112; Jonathan Wilkenfield, "Domestic and Foreign Conflict Behavior of Nations," *Journal of Peace Research*, 1968, 1:55–59.

28. Project Ploughshares, www.ploughshares.com.

29. Michael Doyle, "Kant, Liberal Legacies, and Foreign Affairs," *Philosophy and Foreign Affairs*, Summer 1987, 12:227–31.

30. Zeev Maoz and Nasrin Abdolali, "Regime Types and International Conflict, 1816–1976," *Journal of Conflict Resolution*, March 1989, 33:35.

31. Jack Levy, "Domestic Politics and War," *Journal of Interdisciplinary History*, Spring 1988, 18/1:661–62.

32. Melvin Small and J. David Singer, "The War-Proneness of Democratic Regimes, 1816–1965," *Jerusalem Journal of International Relations*, Summer 1976, 1:50–69. See also Steve Chan and Erich Weede, "Mirror, Mirror on the Wall...Are the Freer Countries More Pacific," *Journal of Conflict Resolution*, 28, December 1984:617–48; William Domke, *War and the Changing Global System* (New Haven, Conn.: Yale University Press, 1988).

33. R.J. Rummel, "Libertarianism and International Violence," *Journal of Conflict Resolution*, March 1983, 27:27–71; R.J. Rummel, "A Test of Libertarian Propositions on Violence," *Journal of Conflict Resolution*, September 1985, 27:419–55.

34. Levy, "Domestic Politics and War," 18/1:661.

35. Michael Doyle, "Kant, Liberal Legacies, and Foreign Affairs," *Philosophy and Public Affairs*, Summer 1987, 12/2:325.

36. Jack Synder and Edward Mansfield, "Democratization and the Danger of War," *International Security*, 20/1 (Summer 1995) 5–38.

37. The classic studies were Quincy Wright, *A Study of War* (Chicago: University of Chicago Press, 1942); Ruth Sivard, *World Military and Social Expenditures* (Leesburg, Va.: World Priorities, 1979), 3; Melvin Small and J. David Singer, *Resort to Arms: International and Civil Wars, 1816–1990* (Beverly Hills, Calif.: Sage, 1991); Project Ploughshares, *Armed Forces Report*, www.ploughshares.com, 5–6.

38. Wright, *Study of War*; Small and Singer, *Resort to Arms*, 58.

39. Thomas Friedman, *The Lexus and the Olive Tree: Understanding Globalization* (New York: Anchor Books, 2000), 248–49.

40. Lewis Richardson, *Statistics of Deadly Quarrels* (Pittsburgh: Boxwood, 1960).

41. Ernst Haas, "The Balance of Power: Prescription, Concept, and Propaganda," *World Politics*, July 1953, 5:442–77. For good discussions of the balance of power in history, see Quincy Wright, *A Study of International Relations* (New York: Appleton, 1955); Claude Inis, *Power and International Relations* (New York: Random House, 1962).

42. A.F.K. Organski, *World Politics* (New York: Knopf, 1968); Hans Morgenthau, *Politics Among Nations* (New York: Knopf, 1967); See also Richard Rosecrance, "Bipolarity, Multipolarity, and the Future," *Journal of Conflict Resolution*, 10, 1966:314–27.

43. See Michael Wallace, *War and Rank Among Nations* (Lexington, Mass.: D.C. Heath, 1973); Edward L. Morse, *Modernization and the Transformation of International Relations* (New York: Free Press, 1976); A.F.K. Organski and Jacek Kugler, *The War Ledger* (Chicago: University of Chicago Press, 1980); Jack Levy, "Declining Power and the Preventive Motive for War," *World Politics*, October 1987:82–107.

44. Organski and Kugler, *War Ledger*, 61.

45. J. David Singer, Stuart Bremer, and John Stuckey, "Capability Distribution, Uncertainty, and Major Power War," in Bruce Russet, ed., *Peace, War, and Numbers* (Beverly Hills: Sage, 1972).
   For other attempts to measure the frequency of war, see Melvin Small and J. David Singer, *Resort to Arms: International and Civil Wars* (Beverly Hill, Calif.: Sage, 1983); Richard Stoll, "Bloc Concentration and Dispute Escalation Among the Major Powers, 1830–1965," *Social Science Quarterly*, March 1984, 65:48–59.

46. John A. Vasquez, "Capability, Types of War and Peace," *Western Political Quarterly*, 39, June 1986:313–27.

47. Karl Deutsch and David Singer, "Multipolar Power Systems and International Stability," in James Rosenau, ed., *International Politics and Foreign Policy* (New York: Free Press, 1969).
   See also Kenneth Waltz, "International Structure, National Force, and the Balance of World Power," in James Rosenau, ed., *International Politics and Foreign Policy* (New York: Free Press, 1969).

48. Jack Levy, "The Polarity of the System and International Stability: An Empirical Analysis," in Sabrosky, ed., *Polarity and War*, 59; See also Jack

Levy, *War and the Modern Great Power System, 1495–1975* (Lexington: University of Kentucky Press, 1983); Alan Ned Sabrosky, ed., *Polarity and War: The Changing Structure of International Relations* (Boulder, Co.: Westview, 1985); Michael Haas, "International Subsystems: Stability and Polarity," *American Political Science Review*, 64, March 1970:98–123; Bruce Bueno de Mesquita, "Systematic Polarization and the Occurrence of War," *Journal of Conflict Resolution*, 22, June 1978:241–67; William Thompson, "Cycles, Capabilities, and War: An Ecumenical View," in William Thompson, ed., *World System Analysis: Competing Perspective* (Beverly Hills: Sage, 1983).

49. Karl Deutch, "Quincy Wright's Contribution to the Study of War: A Preface to the Second Addition," *Journal of Conflict Resolution*, December 1970, 14:474–75.

50. Organski and Kugler, *War Ledger*.

51. See J.F.C. Fuller, *Armament and History: A Study of the Influence of Armament on History From the Dawn of Classical Warfare to the Second World War* (London: Eyre & Spottiswoode, 1945); William F. Ogburn, ed., *Technology and International Relations* (Chicago: University of Chicago Press, 1949); John U. Nef, *War and Human Progress* (Cambridge, Mass.: Harvard University Press, 1950); Bernard Brodie and Fawn Brodie, *From the Cross Bow to the H-Bomb* (New York: Dell, 1962).

52. Some leading explorations of hegemonic stability theory include George Modelski, *Exploring Long-Cycles* (Boulder, Co.: Reinner, 1987); William Thompson, *On Global War: Historical-Structural Approaches to World Politics* (Columbia, S.C.: University of South Carolina Press, 1988); David Rapkin, ed., *World Leadership and Hegemony* (Boulder, Co.: Reinner, 1990).
   For theories of wars occurring in generations, in which peace lasts only so long as the memory of the last war's horrors remain vivid, and a new leadership seeks to glorify itself through success in war, see Frank Denton and Warren Philips, "Some Patterns in the History of Violence," *Journal of Conflict Resolution*, 1.2, June 1968:182–95; See also Oswald Spengler, *The Decline of the West* (New York: Knopf, 1926); J.E. Moval, "The Distribution of Wars in Time," *Journal of the Royal Statistical Society*, 1949, 112:446–58.

53. Jack Levy, "Long Cycles, Hegemonic Transitions, and the Long Peace," in Charles Kegley, ed., *The Long Postwar Peace* (New York: Harper Collins, 1991), 154–55.

54. Joshua Goldstein, *Long Cycles: Prosperity and War in the Modern Age* (New Haven, C.T.: Yale University Press, 1988), 436–37.

55. Jack S. Levy and T. Clifton Morgan, "The War-Weariness Hypothesis: An Empirical Test," *American Journal of Political Science*, February 1986, 26–49.

56. The term "security dilemma" was introduced in John Herz, *Political Realism and Political Idealism* (Chicago: University of Chicago

Press, 1951); The term "spiral model" in Robert Jervis, *Perception and Misperception in World Politics* (Princeton: Princeton University Press, 1976).

57. The psychology of the prisoner's dilemma is explored through game theory. See Thomas Schelling, *The Strategy of Conflict* (Cambridge, Mass.: Harvard University Press, 1960); Muzafer Sherif et al., *Intergroup Conflict and Cooperation: The Robber's Cave Experiment* (Norman: University of Oklahoma Press, 1961); Robert Jervis, "Cooperation Under the Security Dilemma," *World Politics*, January 1978, 30/2:167–214.

58. Nazli Choucri and Robert North, *Nations in Conflict* (San Francisco: Freeman, 1975), 218; See also Bruce Russett, "International Interactions and Processes: The Internal Versus External Debate Revisited," in Ada Finifter, ed., *Political Science: The State of the Discipline* (Washington, D.C.: American Political Science Association, 1983).

59. Lewis Richardson, *Arms and Insecurity* (Pittsburg: Boxwood, 1960); Samuel Huntington, "Arms Races: Prerequisites and Results," in Robert J. Art and Kenneth Waltz, eds., *The Use of Force* (Boston: Little, Brown, 1971), 365–401; Bruce Bueno de Mesquita, *The War Trap* (New Haven, Conn.: Yale University Press, 1981); Stephen Majeski, "Expectations and Arms Races," *American Journal of Political Science*, May 1985, 217–45; Paul Diehl, "Arms Races and Escalation: A Closer Look," *Journal of Peace Research*, 1983, 20/3:205–12; Paul Diehl, "Arms Races to War: Testing Some Empirical Linkages," *Sociological Quarterly*, 1985, 26/3:331–49; Paul Diehl, "Armaments Without War," *Journal of Peace Research*, 22/3:249–59.

60. Michael Wallace, "Arms Races and Escalation: Some New Evidence," *Journal of Conflict Resolution*, March 1979, 23/1:3–16.

61. Samuel Huntington, "Arms Races: Prerequisites and Results," in Robert Art and Kenneth Waltz, eds., *The Use of Force* (Boston: Little, Brown, 1971), 367.

62. Paul Diehl, "Races to War: Testing Some Empirical Linkages," *Sociological Quarterly*, September 1985, 26:342.

63. Paul Diehl, "Arms Races and Escalation: A Closer Look," *Journal of Peace Research*, 1983, 30/3:205–12.

64. David Ziegler, *War, Peace, and International Politics* (Boston: Little, Brown, 1987), 206.

65. Hans Morgenthau, *Politics among Nations: The Struggle for Power and Peace* (New York: Knopf, 1967), 392.

66. Charles Kegley and Gregory Raymond, "Alliances and the Preservation of the Postwar Peace," in Charles Kegley, ed., *The Long Postwar Peace* (New York: Harper Collins, 1991), 275.

67. Randolph Siverson and Michael Tennefoss, "Power, Alliance, and the Escalation of International Conflict, 1815–1965," *American Political Science Review*, December 1984, 78:1062.

68. Jack Levy, "Alliance Formation and War Behavior," *Journal of Conflict Resolution*, December 1981, 25:581.
69. J. David Singer and Melvin Small, "Alliance Aggregation and the Onset of War, 1815–1945," in J. David Singer, ed., *Quantitative International Politics* (New York: Free Press, 1968), 247–86.
70. Levy, "Alliance Formation."
71. Karl Deutsch et al., *Political Community and the North Atlantic Area* (Princeton: Princeton University Press, 1957), 5.
72. See Jack Levy, "The Causes of War: A Review of Theories and Evidence," in Philip Tetlock et al., eds., *Behavior, Society, and Nuclear War* (New York: Oxford University Press), 209–333.
73. Gilpin, *War and Change*, x; See also John Mueller, *Retreat from Doomsday: The Obsolescence of Major Power War* (New York: Basic Books, 1989).
74. Rosecrance, *Rise of the Trading State*, 160.
75. J. David Singer, "Peace in the Global System: Displacement, Interregnum, or Transformation," in Charles Kegley, ed., *The Long Postwar Peace* (New York: Harper Collins, 1991), 57.
76. Mark Townsend and Paul Harris, "Now the Pentagon Tells Bush: Climate Change Will Destroy Us," *Guardian Unlimited*, February 22, 2004.

3 Warfare in the Twenty-First Century

1. Quoted in Geoffry Blainey, *The Causes of War* (New York: Free Press, 1973), 108. For good overview of changes in the technology, tactics, strategy, and the distribution of global power, see MacGregor Knox and William Murray, *The Dynamics of Military Revolution, 1300–2050* (Cambridge: Cambridge University Press, 2001); John Mearsheimer, *The Tragedy of Great Power Politics* (New York: W.W. Norton, 2001); Gerald Schneider, ed., *Globalization and Armed Conflict* (Lanham, Md.: Rowman & Littlefield, 2003); Thomas Burnett, *The Pentagon's New Map: War and Peace in the Twenty-First Century* (New York: G.P. Putnam's Sons, 2004); William Lehneman, ed., *Military Intervention: Cases in Context for the 21st Century* (Lanthan, Md.: Rowman & Littlefield, 2004); Robert Lieber, *The American Era: Power and Strategy for the 21st Century* (New York: Cambridge University Press, 2005); Joshua Gilpin, *The Real Price of War* (New York: New York University Press, 2005); Stephen Walt, *Taming American Power: The Global Response to U.S. Primacy* (New York: W.W. Norton, 2005); Carl Hodge, *Atlanticism for a New Century: The Rise, Triumph, and Decline of NATO* (Upper Saddle River, N.J.: Prentice Hall, 2005); Lawrence Freedman, *Guns and Butter: The Political Economy of International Security* (Boulder, Colo.: Lynne Rienner, 2005); Michael Mandelbaum, *The Case for Goliath: How America Acts as the World's Government in*

the *Twenty-first Century* (New York: Public Affairs, 2006); Dan Caldwell and Robert Williams, *Seeking Security in an Insecure World* (Lanham, Md.: Rowman & Littlefield, 2006); Thomas Hammes, *The Sling and the Stone: On War in the 21st Century* (London: Zenith Press, 2006); Rob Thornton, *Asymmetric Warfare: Threat and Response in the 21st Century* (New York: Polity, 2007); Eric Haney and Brian Thompson, *Beyond Shock and Awe: Warfare in the 21st Century* (New York: Berkeley Trade, 2007); Bernard Loo, *Military Transformation and Strategy: Revolutions in Military Affairs and Small States* (London: Routledge, 2008); Christopher Croker and Caroline Holmquist-Jonsater, eds., *The Character of War in the 21st Century* (London: Routledge, 2010).

2. Hans Morgenthau, *Politics among Nations* (New York: Knopf, 1967), 392.
3. Correlates of War Study, www.correlatesofwar.org.
4. Herbert Tillema, *International Armed Conflict Since 1945: A Bibliographic Handbook of Wars and Military Interventions* (Boulder, Colo.: Westview Press, 1991).
5. Ruth Leger Sivard, *World Military and Social Expenditures* (Washington, D.C.: World Priorities, 1991), 20.
6. John Rouke, *International Relations on the World Stage* (Guildford, Conn.: Dushkin, 1991) 264; Francis Beer, *Peace against War: The Ecology of International Violence* (San Francisco: W.H. Freeman, 1988).
7. Bruce Russett and Richard Starr, *World Politics: A Menu for Choice* (New York: W.H. Freeman, 1990), 171.
8. Philip Zelikow, "The United States and the Use of Force: A Historical Summary," in George K. Osburn, ed. Democracy, Strategy, and Vietnam (Lexington, Mass.: Lexington Book, 1987), 31–84. For studies of evaluating the United States use of force, see Alexander George, David Hall, and William Simons, *The Limits of Coercive Diplomacy* (Boston: Little, Brown, 1971); Barry Blechman and Stephen Kaplan, "U.S. Military Forces as a Political Instrument," *Political Science Quarterly*, 94, 193–210.
9. Richard Rosecrance, *The Rise of the Trading State: Commerce and Conquest in the Modern World* (New York: Basic Books, 1986), 157; Center for Arms Control and Non-Proliferation, 2008, www.ArmsControlCenter.org.
10. Thom Shanker, "Global Arms Sales Rise Again, and the U.S. Leads the Pack," *New York Times*, August 19, 2001.
11. Stockholm Peace Research Institute, 2008, www.sipri.org.
12. Dwight Eisenhower, speech before the American Society for Newspaper Editors, April 16, 1953; Arthur Burns, "The Defense Sector and the American Economy," in Seymour Melman, ed. *The War Economy of the United States* (New York: St. Martin's Press, 1971), 115.

13. Steve Chan, "The Impact of Defense Spending on Economic Performance," *Orbis*, 29, Summer 1985:407–412. See also Paul Craig and John Jungerman, *Nuclear Arms Race: Technology and Society* (New York: McGraw-Hill, 1986); David Gold, *Misguided Expenditure: An Analysis of the Proposed MX Missile System* (New York: Council on Economic Priorities, 1981); Rouke, *International Politics*, 500.

14. Michael Klare, "The Arms Trade: Changing Patterns in the 1980's," *Third World Quarterly*, 9, October 1987:1279–1280; Sivard, *World Military and Social Expenditures*, 11.

15. Sun Tzu, *The Art of War* (New York: Basic Books, 1994).

16. Mao Tse-Tung, *The Art of War* (New York: El Paso Norte Press, 2005).

17. David Petraeus, James Amos, Sarah Sweall, and John Nagl, *The U.S. Army Marine Corps Counterinsurgency Manuel* (Chicago: University of Chicago Press, 2007), 47–51.

18. John Cushman and Thom Shanker, "A War Like No Other Uses New 21st Century Methods to Disable Enemy Forces," *New York Times*, April 10, 2003.

19. This information was drawn from UNEP 2006 Annual Report ; UN Report 2008: "Fact Sheet on Water and Sanitation"; For an in-depth analysis, see Michael Klare, *Resource Wars: The New Landscape of Global Conflict* (New York: Holtzbrinck Academic, 2002).

4 TERRORISM AND COUNTERTERRORISM

1. Bruce Hoffman, *Inside Terrorism* (New York: Columbia University Press, 2006), 26. For other good recent books on terrorism, see Charles Kegley, ed., *The New Global Terrorism: Characteristics, Causes, Controls* (Upper Saddle River, N.J.: Prentice Hall, 2003); James Lutz, *Global Terrorism* (New York: Routledge, 2004); George Meggle, *The Ethics of Terrorism and Counter-Terrorism* (New York: Transaction Books, 2005); Thomas Badey, ed., *Violence and Terrorism* (Dubuque, Iowa: McGraw-Hill/Dushkin, 2006); Walter Enders and Todd Sandler, *The Political Economy of Terrorism* (New York: Cambridge University Press, 2006).

2. Hoffman, *Inside Terrorism*, 90–93.

3. Walter Reich, ed., *The Origins of Terrorism: Psychologies, Ideologies, Theologies, States of Mind* (Cambridge: Cambridge University Press, 1990); Marc Sageman, *Understanding Terror Networks* (Philadelphia: University of Pennsylvania Press, 2004); Louise Richardson, *What Terrorists Want* (New York: Random House, 2006).

4. Martha Crenshaw, "The Causes of Terrorism Past and Present," in Charles Kegley, ed., *The New Global Terrorism, Characteristics, Causes, Controls* (Upper Saddle River, N.J.: Prentice Hall, 2003), 100.

5. Robert Pape, *Dying to Win: The Strategic Logic of Suicide Terrorism* (New York: Random House, 2005).
6. Robert Pipe, "Blowing Up an Assumption," *New York Times*, May 18, 2005.
7. Peter Lilley, *Dirty Dealing: The Untold Truth about Global Money Laundering, International Crime, and Terrorism* (London: Kogan Page, 2006).
8. Norman Abrams, *Anti-Terrorism and Criminal Enforcement* (St. Paul, Minn.: Thomson/West, 2005); William C. Banks, *Renee de Nevers, and Mitchel B. Wallerstein, Combating Terrorism: Strategies and Approaches* (Washington, D.C.: Congressional Quarterly, 2008).
9. James Boulden and Thomas G. Weiss, eds., *Terrorism and the UN: Before and After September 11* (Bloomington: Indiana University Press, 2004); Meghan O'Sullivan, *Shrewd Sanctions: Statecraft and State Sponsors of Terrorism* (Washington, D.C.: Brookings Institute, 2003).
10. Michael Stohl, "The Mystery of the New Global Terrorism: Old Myths, New Realities?" in Kegley, *New Global Terrorism*, 86.
11. Ted Gurr, "Terrorism in Democracies: When It Occurs, Why It Fails?" in Kegley, *New Global Terrorism*, 206; Hoffman, *Inside Terrorism*, 170.

5   Weapons of Mass Destruction

1. Ruth Leger Sivard, *World Military and Social Expenditures* (Washington, D.C.: World Priorities, 1991), 16. For some good books on weapons of mass destruction, see Graham Allison, *Nuclear Terrorism: The Ultimate Preventable Catastrophe* (New York: Henry Holt, 2004); R. Everett Langford, *Introduction to Weapons of Mass Destruction* (New York: John Wiley and Sons, 2004); Michael Levi and Michael O'Hanlon, *The Future of Arms Control* (Washington, D.C.: Brookings Institute, 2005); Jacques Hymans, *The Psychology of Nuclear Proliferation* (New York: Cambridge University Press, 2006).
2. John Spanier, *Games Nations Play* (New York: Holt, Rinehart and Winston, 1984), 157.
3. Sivard, *Wold Military*, 13.
4. Spanier, *Games Nations Play*, 157–59.
5. For such classic studies, see Robert Jervis, Richard Lebow, and Janice Gross, *Psychology and Deterrence* (Baltimore: John Hopkins Press, 1985); Graham Allison, Albert Carnesale, and Joseph Nye, *Hawks, Doves, and Owls: An Agenda for Avoiding Nuclear War* (New York: W.W. Norton, 1985); Richard Betts, *Nuclear Blackmail and Nuclear Balance* (Washington, D.C.: Brookings Institute, 1987); Richard Smoke, *National Security and the Nuclear Dilemma: An Introduction to the American Experience* (New York: Random House,

1987); Regina Karp, ed., *Security with Nuclear Weapons? Different Perceptions of National Security* (New York: Oxford University Press, 1991); Charles Kegley and Eugene Wittkopf, eds., *The Nuclear Reader: Strategy, Weapons, War* (New York: St. Martin's Press, 1991); David Tarr, *Nuclear Deterrence and International Security: Alternative Nuclear Regimes* (New York: Longman, 1991).

6. James Simpson, *Simpson's Contemporary Quotations* (Boston: Houghton Mifflin, 1988), 2. For an interesting argument that nuclear deterrence has not been the reason for peace between the superpowers, see John Vasquez, "The Deterrence Myth: Nuclear Weapons and the Prevention of Nuclear War," in Charles Kegley, ed., *The Long Postwar Peace* (New York: Harper Collins, 1991), 205–23.

7. Henry Kissinger, *White House Years* (Boston: Little, Brown, 1979), 238.

8. See James Schesinger, "Rhetoric and Fantasies in the Star Wars Debate," *International Security*, 1985, 10/1:3–12; Harold Brown, "Is SDI Technically Feasible?" *Foreign Affairs*, 64/3: 435–54; Sanford Lakoff and Herbert York, *A Shield in Space: Technology, Politics, and the Strategic Defense Initiative* (Berkeley: University of California Press, 1989).

9. Alva Myrdal, *The Game of Dismantlement: How the United States and Russia Run the Arms Race* (New York: Pantheon, 1976).

10. Kenneth Waltz, "The Spread of Nuclear Weapons: More May be Better," Adelphi Paper, 71 (London: International Institute of Strategic Studies, 1982), 29–30.

11. Eric Schmitt, "Despite Euphoria on Arms Control, Deterrence Remains a Potent Force," *New York Times*, July 30, 1991; David Sanger, "West Knew of North Korean Nuclear Development," *New York Times*, March 13, 1993. See also Stephen Meyer, *Nuclear Proliferation: Models of Behavior, Choice, and Decision* (Chicago: University of Chicago Press, 1984); Leonard Spector, *Nuclear Ambitions: The Spread of Nuclear Weapons 1989–90* (Boulder, Colo.: Westview Press, 1990).

12. Eric Schmitt, "50's Riddle Return in Treaty Debates," William Broad, "Undetected Indian Blasts, Cited as Monitoring Failures, May Themselves Have Failed," *New York Times*, October 10, 1999.

13. Marshall Shulman, "The Superpowers: Dance of the Dinosaurs," *Foreign Affairs*, Winter 1987–1988, 66/3:512.

14. Thomas Friedman, "Reducing the Russian Arms Threat," *New York Times*, June 17, 1999, A7.

15. See Robert Alexrod, *The Evolution of Cooperation* (New York: Basic Book, 1984); S. Plous, "Perceptual Illusions and Military Realities: The Nuclear Arms Race," *Journal of Conflict Resolution*, September 1985, 29/3:363–88; Joshua Goldstein and John Freeman, *Three Way Street: Strategic Reciprocity in World Politics* (Chicago: University of Chicago Press, 1990).

16. Jonathan White, *Terrorism: An Introduction* (Belmont, Calif.: Wadsworth Thomson, 2002), 251.

17. William Broad, Stephen Engleberg, and James Glanz, "Assessing Risks, Chemical, Biological, and Even Nuclear," *New York Times*, November 1, 2001; Jonathan Tucker, "How to Regulate the Trade in Toxins," *New York Times*, October 26, 2001.

6 War, Peace, and the Global Community

1. For an excellent recent overview, see Paul Kennedy, *The Parliament of Man: The Past, Present, and Future of the United Nations* (New York: Random House, 2006). For an older but still strong neofunctionalist perspective, see Ernst Haas, *Why We Still Need the United Nations: The Collective Management of International Conflict, 1945–1984* (Berkeley: Institute of International Studies, 1986).

2. Sally Morphet, "The Significance and Relevance of the Security Council and Its Resolutions and Vetoes," Paper presented to the International Studies Association, London, March 1989; Miguel Marin-Bosch, "How Nations Vote in the General Assembly of the United Nations," *International organization*, Autumn 1987, 41:713–18.

3. Theodore Coulombis and James Wolfe, *Introduction to International Relations: Power and Justice* (Englewood Cliffs, N.J.: Prentice Hall, 1990), 271.

4. See Francis W. Hinsley, *Power in the Pursuit of Peace: Theory and Practice in the History of Relations between States* (Cambridge: Cambridge University Press, 1963).

5. Center for International Cooperation, *Annual Review of Global Peace Operations, 2006* (Boulder, Colo.: Lynne Rienner, 2006); "Security Council Vetoes," Wikipedia; United Nations *Peacekeeping Missions* (New York: United Nations, November 29, 2009).

6. For an excellent evaluation of collective security, see Inis Claude, *Sword into Plowshares: The Problems and Progress of International Organizations* (New York: Random House, 1984).

7. George H.W. Bush Speech to UN General Assembly, *New York Times*, October 25, 1990.

8. Walter Jones, *The Logic of International Relations* (New York: Harper Collins, 1991), 569.

9. John Rouke, *International Politics on the World Stage* (Boston: McGraw Hill, 1999), 444.

10. For conflicting views see the pro-U.N. Better World Campaign and Global Policy Forum versus the anti–United Nations views in Eric Shawn, *The U.N. Exposed: How the United Nations Sabotages American Security and Fails the World* (New York: Sentinel Books, 2006).

11. Jean Bethke Elshtain, *Just War against Terror: The Burden of American Power in a Violent World* (New York: Basic Books, 2003); Anthony Lang et al., eds., *Ethics and the Future of Conflict* (Upper Saddle River, N.J.: Pearson/Prentice Hall, 2004); Eric Patterson, "Just War in the 21st Century: Reconstructing Just War Theory after September 11," *International Politics*, 42, March 2005:116–34; Michael Walzer, *Arguing about War* (New Haven, Conn.: Yale University Press, 2005).

12. Janis, *International Law*, 130.

13. Inis Claude, *Swords into Plowshares: The Problems and Progress of International Organizations* (New York: Random House, 1984).

14. Mark Janis, *An Introduction to International Law* (New York: Aspen, 2003), 51.

15. Michael Akehurst, *A Modern Introduction to International Law* (London: Routledge, 1993), 91.

16. John Rouke, *International Politics* (Guilford, C.T.: Dushkin, 1991), 27.

17. Jimmy Carter, "December 6, 1978 Speech," Department of State Bulletin, January 1979, 2.

18. Cyrus Vance, "The Human Rights Imperative," *Foreign Policy*, 1986, 63/11.

19. George Shultz, "Morality and Realism in American Foreign Policy," Department of State Bulletin, December 1985, 247.

7   CONSEQUENCES

1. Edward Luttwak, "From Geopolitics to Geoeconomics," *National Interest*, Summer 1990, 20:17.

2. Francis Fukuyama, "The End of History?" *National Interest*, Summer 1989, 16:3. See also Francis Fukuyama, *The End of History and the Last Man* (New York: Free Press, 1992).

3. Samuel Huntington, *The Clash of Civilizations and the Remaking of World Order* (New York: Touchstone Books, 1997), 21.

4. Thomas Friedman, "A New Global Power Structure," *IHT*, March 31, 2003.

INDEX

196 ✥ INDEX